The History of
CLYDEBANK

Coat of Arms
Clydebank District Council

The History of CLYDEBANK

Compiled by John Hood

with the assistance of:

Dr Callum Brown
Dr Alistair Clark
Dr Derek Dow
Andrew Gibb
Gordon Kennedy
Professor William Lever
Dr Catriona Levy
Dr Michael McDermott
Pat Malcolm
Dr Nicholas Morgan
Michael Moss
Iain Russell
Professor Anthony Slaven
Dr Carrick Watson

Parthenon Publishing

THE PARTHENON PUBLISHING GROUP LIMITED

Published by
The Parthenon Publishing Group Ltd.
Casterton Hall
Carnforth, Lancs LA6 2LA
U.K.

© Copyright Clydebank District Council 1988

First published 1988

ISBN 1–85070–147–4

Table of Contents

PART FOUR:
THE NEW CLYDEBANK

List of Figures

List of Tables

Notes on Contributors

DR CALLUM G. BROWN is a lecturer in History at the University of Strathclyde, and is the son of a 'Bankie'. His book *The Social History of Religion in Scotland since 1730* has been published recently, and he has contributed articles on religious and urban history to various academic journals and books.

DR ALISTAIR A. CLARK became a GP in Clydebank in 1946 where he practised until his retiral in 1981. Active in medical politics, he became a Fellow and Vice-President of the British Medical Association. Dr Clark played a key role in the setting up of a Health Centre in Clydebank, serving as Chair of both its Planning and Management Committees.

DR DEREK DOW graduated in history from the University of Edinburgh in 1973. In 1979 he became archivist to the Greater Glasgow Health Board, and has written extensively on the history of health care in the West of Scotland. Since 1983 he has acted as Joint Honorary Secretary to the Scottish Society of the History of Medicine.

ANDREW GIBB is a lecturer in Geography and a member of the Centre for Housing Research at the University of Glasgow. His principal interests lie in the fields of population dynamics and urban renewal. He has produced a variety of papers on these themes including his book, *Glasgow: The Making of a City*.

JOHN HOOD has been District Chief Librarian of Clydebank District Council since 1979. He has written various local publications including *The 1st Old Kilpatrick Boys' Brigade Company 1932-82, Clydebank in old Picture Postcards, Duntocher Trinity Parish Church 1836-1986, Clydebank 100 Years*, and *Gavinburn Primary School 1887-1987*.

GORDON KENNEDY is a graduate of Glasgow and Strathclyde Universities. Between 1982 and 1985 he worked as a planner with Clydebank District Council. He is now a Senior Economic Assistant in the Planning and Projects Directorate of the Scottish Development Agency.

BILL LEVER is Professor in Urban Studies at Glasgow University. Trained in Oxford, he came to the West of Scotland in 1967. His research has focussed on urban and industrial change, particularly in Britain but also in Europe and America, and he is the author of two recent books on industrial change and the urban problems of Clydeside.

DR CATRIONA LEVY is a graduate of Dundee University. Based in Glasgow since 1978, she has worked on a number of business history projects for Michael Moss, Glasgow University Archivist, and has produced several local history publications for the West of Scotland Workers Educational Association.

DR MICHAEL McDERMOTT is a graduate of Glasgow University. He is currently lecturing in International Business and International Marketing at the University of Strathclyde and is a consultant to the United Nations on international takeovers.

PAT MALCOLM has been Information Services Librarian with Clydebank District Council since 1976. She is responsible for Reference and Local Studies work within the Libraries Department and has contributed to various in-house publications.

DR NICHOLAS MORGAN is a lecturer in Scottish History at the University of Glasgow with responsibility for developing computer applications in teaching and research. He has been involved in a number of research projects on Scottish nineteenth and twentieth-century business, urban and social history and has recently completed *A History of the National Housebuilding Council, Fifty Years of Consumer Protection.*

MICHAEL MOSS has been Glasgow University Archivist since 1974. He is the author of several books on the history of the West of Scotland including the *Workshop of the British Empire — Engineering and Shipbuilding in the West of Scotland* and *Beardmore: the history of a Scottish industrial giant*, both written with John Hume. Together they helped to rescue the records of the Clydebank shipyard of John Brown & Co. at the time of the closure of UCS in 1971. These are now deposited in the University Archives.

IAIN RUSSELL is a graduate of Glasgow and McMaster Universities, and is currently working as a researcher at Glasgow University Archives. He has recently completed a history of the civil engineering contractors Sir Robert McAlpine & Sons Ltd and is currently writing, with Michael Moss, the history of Barr and Stroud Ltd.

ANTHONY SLAVEN is Professor of Business History and Head of Department of Economic History, University of Glasgow. Author of many papers and reports on Scottish shipbuilding, he has written extensively on the development of John Brown. Other works include *The Development of the West of Scotland 1760-1950*, and as co-editor, *The Dictionary of Scottish Business Biography* (2 vols).

DR CARRICK WATSON is Principal Teacher of History at Clydebank High School. A graduate of Glasgow University, he has done extensive research on the history of Clydebank in the inter-war years.

Acknowledgements

On behalf of Clydebank District Council, I would like to thank each of the contributors for their hard work and effort on this project. I would like especially to thank Michael Moss, Archivist, University of Glasgow, and Pat Malcolm, Information Services Librarian, Clydebank District Libraries, for their constant assistance, encouragement and advice. Thanks are also due to Prof. Anthony Slaven for his assistance in drawing up the initial structure for the *History;* to Glasgow University Archives personnel for their valuable comments on the draft sections; to Norman Macleod for examining and commenting on various draft sections; to Ian Baillie and Margaret Morrison of Clydebank District Libraries for assistance with proof-reading and the compilation of the Select Bibliography respectively; to Alex Gilchrist, Planning Department, Clydebank District Council, for assistance with graphical work on some of the illustrative material; to Cuthbert Douse for information on the Dalmuir Former Pupils; to John Billings for photographs and information relating to the Clydebank Male Voice Choir; to John Campbell for photographs and information relating to the Clydebank Camera Club; to Brian McAusland for photographs and information relating to the Clydesdale Harriers; to Margaret E. Bell for photographs and information relating both to her father, Sir Thomas Bell, and to the Clydebank nursing services; to James Cuthbertson for information on the development of the Community Education service within Clydebank; to Tom Connelly for information on Clydebank College; to Alan Urquhart for information on football in Clydebank, and to Hugh Doran for photographs relating to the Lomond Roads Cycling Club.

While many of the illustrations utilised within the *History* have been reproduced from the Clydebank District Libraries' excellent collection of photographs, I would like to thank the SDA; Alex Holmes, of Holmes of Clydebank; Fotoscene; and Nick Peacock, the *Glasgow Herald and Evening Times* for permission to reproduce photographs. I would especially like to acknowledge the kindness and consideration afforded to me by William Doig, Picture Librarian, *Glasgow Herald and Evening Times*, whilst searching his photographic archives for suitable illustrations. Finally, I would like to thank Paul and Sean Fennon of Image Machine of Clydebank for their assistance in the preparation of copy prints.

John Hood

Introduction

'A little over a score of years ago, the now thriving and populous burgh of Clydebank was totally unknown to fame, in fact it did not then exist.'[1]

So the local *Directory* for 1893-4 commented on the rapid emergence of Clydebank as an industrial town. The initial catalyst in the development of Clydebank came in 1871 when the Thomsons constructed their shipyard on the green fields of Barns o'Clyde. From this yard (later that of John Brown & Co. Ltd) would come, in time, a succession of the biggest, fastest and finest vessels the world has ever seen – none more so than the legendary Cunarder *RMS Queen Mary*, launched from Brown's yard into the waiting Clyde on a wet September day in 1934 by HRH Queen Mary. Some 11 years later a second major development occurred when the Singer Manufacturing Company began the construction of Europe's largest sewing machine factory at Kilbowie. From these foundations the population of Clydebank expanded from 3,000 in 1881 to over 43,000 by 1913. By 1904 Singer employed 9,000 people, and John Brown 5,000, while by 1910 Beardmore's nearby shipyard employed 6,000.[2]

It has often been commented that Clydebank was a 'new town' of the late nineteenth century. Its industries emerged from the expansion of established outside industries not from the area's existing pattern of industry. There was relatively little industry although, outwith farming, coal was worked at various sites and paper-making and print-working was carried out at Dalmuir. A major exception to this pattern was William Dunn's cotton mill 'empire' undertaken at four mills situated on the upper reaches of the Duntocher Burn. However, while mainly rural, Clydebank has been settled since ancient times — it can literally be said that 'early man left his mark'. The truth of this statement is to be found on the foothills of the Kilpatricks to the north of Faifley, for here can be seen stone outcrops carved with cup-and-ring symbols once thought to be associated with druid ritual. In the 1930s a neolithic burial site was discovered at Knappers, while there have been numerous discoveries of burial cairns, crannogs and dug-out canoes. In the later Roman period, the remnants of the turf-built Antonine Wall running 37 miles between Bo'ness in the east and Old Kilpatrick in the west, bear testimony to Roman occupation locally. In medieval times the district formed part of the important earldom of Lennox, the village of Old Kilpatrick being the centre of worship in this area. For many centuries, reputedly, the birthplace of St. Patrick, Old Kilpatrick Parish once held the title of Burgh of Regality. In the thirteenth century the parish church lands, along with neighbouring lands, were gifted to the emerging Paisley Abbey, in whose hands they remained for several

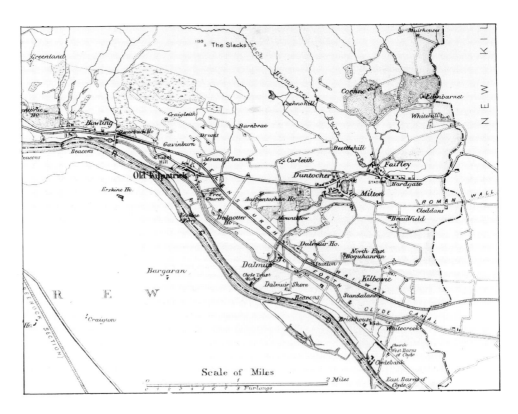

Figure I:1 *Early map of the district.*

centuries. In time the several lands fell into the hands of Claud Hamilton and his heirs.[3]

Clydebank officially came into existence when a Police Burgh was set up at noon on Thursday 18 November 1886. This history was commissioned in 1986 to mark the first eventful Centenary of the Burgh of Clydebank and a team of 14 contributors were invited to write on a variety of aspects of the town's history. The history of Clydebank falls into four distinct phases and these are mirrored in the structure of this book.

Part One, The Boom Town, covers the period 1886-1914 during which Clydebank rapidly emerged as an industrial town. Its pace of expansion was such that it gained the nickname of 'the risingest burgh'. It also became known as 'Tamson's Toon', reflecting the key role played by James R. Thomson of the shipyard in the early days. Part Two, The Town in War and Peace, charts the impact of two World Wars and the inter-war depression on the town and its industries. The period was a difficult one for Clydebank during which the town suffered high unemployment, the closure of Beardmore's shipyard, social unrest and problems symptomised in the Rent Strike, and finally the devastation of the Clydebank Blitz of 1941. Part Three, The Town in Transition, charts the town's post-war experience through the reconstruction of the town after the Blitz to the collapse of Clydebank's original economic foundations with the closure of the Singer factory in 1979 and the drastic contraction of the shipbuilding industry. Part Four, The New Clydebank, outlines the rigorous efforts made since 1979 to regenerate the economic life of Clydebank.

It has not been possible to cover every aspect of life in Clydebank and apologies are made for many omissions. However, it is hoped that this history will contribute to the body of works on the fate of some industrial communities in modern times and, in particular, that it will enable people in Clydebank to understand something of their own background. As the following chapters show, the remarkable striving for survival and the pursuit of excellence which so often featured in Clydebank's history comprise a heritage to be proud of.

Part One

The Boom Town, 1886-1914

CHAPTER ONE

The Shipbuilders

The Arrival of J. & G. Thomson

The former County of Dunbarton had a long history of shipbuilding, the early industry concentrating on the county town of Dumbarton. There, at the mouth of the River Leven, the McMillans and the Dennys came to dominate the industry on the north bank of the lower reaches of the Clyde. Apart from the town of Dumbarton itself, there was no settlement of any significance in the county for much of the nineteenth century. In the parish of Old Kilpatrick there was only a close network of small villages, notably Old Kilpatrick, Bowling, Little Mill, Milton, Dumbuck, Dalmuir, Dalmuir Shore, Yoker, Duntocher, Faifley and Hardgate. These housed a concentration of small-scale industry based on textiles, bleaching, dyeing, distilling and, to some extent, boat and shipbuilding. There was little in this pattern of activity to indicate the future rise of Clydebank, and the town did not grow out of this early network of industry. Clydebank was a green-field development, a transplant of the thriving company of J. & G. Thomson from the overcrowded upper reaches of the Clyde at Govan.

The Thomsons hailed from Partick where three brothers, Robert, James and George, were apprenticed to Graham Wellington & Co., Millwrights and Engineers, by their father, John Thomson, who was in business as a grocer. Robert then went to sea as an engineer with G. & J. Burns on the Glasgow-Liverpool route before joining the Cunard company as its superintendent engineer on the formation of the company in 1839. James went to Manchester but was persuaded to return to Glasgow by Robert Napier to be his leading smith, finisher and turner at the Vulcan Foundry. The remaining brother, George, became Napier's foreman at the Lancefield Works. From this background, James and George Thomson set up business on their own in April 1847 as marine engine builders. They named their works Clyde Bank Foundry, comprising both engine and boiler works at Finnieston Street. The name was to go with them as they expanded business. In 1851 a second establishment was opened at Cessnock Bank, Govan, to undertake building hulls as well as engines and boilers; the Clyde Bank Iron Shipyard was inaugurated on 30 September 1851 for an outlay of £75,000. These two sites comprised the establishment of J. & G. Thomson for the next 20 years. The next move was to a site that was to be the nucleus of the new town of Clydebank.[1]

By the 1860s the burgeoning of industry and trade around Glasgow had exhausted the available quayage in the upper harbour. The Clyde Navigation Trustees proposed to extend the facilities, and under the terms of the enabling Act the Trustees compulsorily acquired the site of the Thomsons' yard at Govan in 1872. The Thomsons' search for a new site further downstream took them first to Greenock, but the attraction of a flatter site, closer to their engine and boiler works, won the day. The site was the river frontage on part of the farmland of West Barns o' Clyde, on the estate of Miss Hamilton of Cochno. The site was purely agricultural, but lay opposite the mouth of the White Cart, a feature that was later to be of great importance for the launching of the largest vessels built on the Clyde.

The Clyde Navigation Trustees paid £90,660 for the Govan site, and this provided funds for the transfer and establishment of the new yard. By this time the original partners had passed out of the business, James by retiral in 1864, and George who died in 1866. The business was then conducted by the Trustees and managed by George Thomson's eldest son, James R. Thomson. They acquired the new site in 1871, and the first ground was broken to begin building their new yard on 1 May 1871, the ceremony being conducted by Miss Hamilton of Cochno. The workers were brought daily by river from Govan, no other form of transport being available. The Thomsons used a small paddle steamer, the *Vulcan*, for this work, replacing it with a larger vessel, the *Vesta*, in 1879. The *Vesta* continued to ferry workmen till 1882 when the Glasgow, Yoker and Clydebank railway was opened, providing a speedier form of transport for those men who still lived in Govan.[2]

Establishing the yard was a complex business since everything had to be brought in by river or by cart. The berths and ships were begun simultaneously, and, about as quickly, work was begun on blocks of four storey tenements to house 700 persons; these formed Clydebank Terrace (or Thomson's Buildings) and

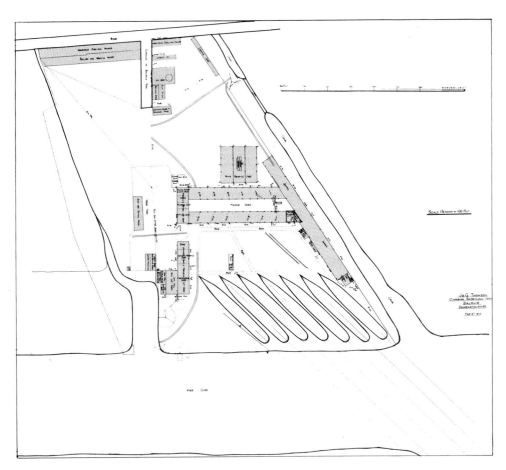

Figure 1:1 *Plan of Clydebank Shipyard, 6 February 1873*

became the core of the works village. By 1873 a large shed had been provided to act as a rudimentary canteen for workers coming each day from Govan; at other times it served as a focus for meetings, community activity and, on Sundays, as a church. The 'Tarry Kirk' as it was called, functioned in this capacity till the first real churches were established close by, St James' Parish Church in 1876 and the Union Church in 1877. In the midst of the activity, James Thomson and his younger brother George purchased the property from their father's Trustees and took over the business in the original name of James & George Thomson early in 1874. By then the first two vessels had been launched in 1873, both single screw steamers for Thomas Skinner & Co., the *Braemar Castle* and the *Cawdor Castle*. The Cunard vessel, *Bothnia*, had been the first keel laid at the new site, but it was not completed till 1874.

From this beginning the town of Clydebank was to grow. The Thomsons established the fabric of the new town around the works. A penny savings bank was opened in 1872 under the care of the yard cashier, Robert Carswell. In 1874 the first school opened with 64 pupils, this developing from the yard school operating from 1872. In 1875 the Thomsons introduced a horsedrawn omnibus service from the yard to the Glasgow Tramway terminus at Whiteinch to ease communications. They built further blocks of houses for the men, and more housing was provided with aid from the Glasgow Building Society. By 1880 about 2,000 men were employed and other employers had been attracted to the locality. In 1877 Napier, Shanks & Bell opened a small shipyard at East Barns o' Clyde, and between 1882 and 1884 the Singer Manufacturing Co. transferred its Scottish operations from Bridgeton to Kilbowie. By 1886 the settlement became a Police Burgh and the new Commissioners adopted the yard name as the name of the new burgh. Clydebank had officially arrived and in its first municipal elections James R. Thomson and his manager Samuel Crawford were elected as representatives. James Thomson was to become the first Provost of Clydebank.[3]

Shipbuilding: Production and Customers

The Thomson family involvement with Clydebank spanned some 25 years from 1871 to 1896. In that time the yard launched 100 merchant vessels totalling 223,095 gross tons. This gives an average of about four vessels each year, an output of just under 10,000 tons per year, and an average vessel size of just over 2,200 gross tons. In contrast to the later reputation of the yard, the Thomsons built mainly small craft

Figure 1:2 *View of the* Servia *built in 1881 and the first of a long line of superb passenger liners to be launched from the Clydebank Shipyard.*

with an emphasis on quality and features for special services. Their order book stretched over 44 different shipping lines with considerable emphasis on building for small passenger and cargo services.[4] Clyde steamers like the *Columbus* for David Hutcheson & Co., or the *Claymore* for Macbrayne's West Highland service; channel passenger ferries like the *Walrus* for G. & J. Burns, or fast cross channel vessels like the *Lydia* and the *Stella* for the London and South Western Railway Co. Most of the yard's output was of this smaller class of vessel, yet orders were dominated by the smaller number of very large vessels which J. & G. Thomson built for the transatlantic passenger services. For 30 years, from 1852 to 1882 the Cunard Company placed a regular stream of orders with J. & G. Thomson, first at Govan, and from 1872 at Clydebank. The initial connection came from Robert Thomson, brother to the founding partners of the company, who was Cunard's superintendent engineer. The quality of Thomson's work secured the most famous of their customers till 1882, when, with the exception of a small tender, the *Skirmisher* of 1884, the link with Cunard was broken for the seventeen years between 1882 and 1899. Between 1872 and 1884, Cunard placed ten vessels with Clydebank, an order book of 43,479 gross tons, nearly 20 per cent of the entire merchant output of the yard between 1872 and 1896. In fact, although Clydebank built for 44 customers, half its entire output of merchant tonnage came from six companies and 30 vessels in the period. Cunard was the most important, followed by Inman and International, both for the transatlantic passenger service. Next in importance of tonnage was the Union Steamship Co. plying the Cape route, Thomas Skinner & Co. in the China trade, the Brazilian Steam Navigation Co. in the South American trade, and the Canadian Steam Navigation Co., again in the fast transatlantic service.

It was the great liner business that kept the Clydebank yard in the forefront of technical change in shipbuilding in these years. In 1874, A. C. Kirk introduced the triple expansion engine to improve on the efficiency of the simple compound expansion marine steam engine. This coincided with the experimental use of steel plates instead of wrought iron for use both in boilers and in hulls. Utilizing steel plates in the cylindrical tank boiler, or Scotch boiler devised by David Howden, enabled high pressures of up to 150 lbs. per square inch to be sustained and, when linked to the triple expansion engine, this delivered great economies in fuel and enabled the steamship to conquer the longest routes from sail.[5] The application of steel to ships' hulls also made for savings in weight and improvements in strength. J. & G. Thomson did not innovate these developments, but were quick to exploit them. The Clydebank yard produced a steel paddle steamer in 1878, and, by 1881, had translated the new skill to the great transatlantic liners. In 1881 they produced the *Servia* for Cunard. It was the first Cunarder built of steel, and the first all-steel vessel built for the North Atlantic express service. It came with the advanced design of cellular double bottoms, electric light in the saloon, and it captured the Blue Riband for the Atlantic crossing, being the first vessel to make the westbound voyage to New York in under seven days. At 515 feet in length, and 7,392 gross tons, it was the largest merchant vessel in the world with the exception of the *Great Eastern*.

Naval Building

Until the 1880s, Clydebank was exclusively a merchant shipyard. Two small composite gunboats, each of 455 displacement tons and 400 HP, had been built for the Admiralty in 1877, and a similar craft had been produced at the Govan yard in 1868; but apart from that only merchant tonnage had been laid down. However, several circumstances brought J. & G. Thomson into naval building from 1885. First, Thomson's experience with the highest class of liners equipped them with the knowledge and staff necessary to contemplate taking on complex naval construction. Second, between 1871 and 1881, J. & G. Thomson still relied on their engine and boiler works at Finnieston in Glasgow to supply their vessels constructed at Clydebank. This separation of activity was time-consuming and costly. Consequently, preparations were made to integrate all the functions at Clydebank. The new boiler work opened in the yard in 1881 and the new engine work was inaugurated on 22 February 1884. The improved and extended facilities made it possible for J. & G. Thomson to tackle much larger and more powerful vessels. The extension of capacity also made it necessary for the Thomsons to find extra work to occupy their new equipment. The naval market was an obvious target. The third factor which pushed J. & G. Thomson in this direction was that in the 1880s the yard lost its hold on the Cunard business to Elder's yard at Govan. Since merchant shipbuilding experienced severe depression between 1884 and 1889, Clydebank had to find new business elsewhere.

Up until 1889 it was always difficult for private shipbuilders to acquire naval orders.[6] The Royal Dockyards built for the Admiralty and private yards were used mainly in a time of emergency, or to contribute as sub-contractors by supplying engines. Such an occasion came in 1884 when there appeared to be some prospect of war with Russia. Public concern at the state of the British navy and of the Royal Dockyards pushed the Government to authorise an emergency building programme — the Northbrook Programme — which provided for the building of a range of vessels in private yards. Given this opportunity, and their need for work, J. & G. Thomson tendered and between 1884 and 1889 received orders from the Admiralty for seven third class torpedo cruisers, all but one of 1,630 displacement tons and each of 3,500 HP. A further two large cruisers were built for the Australian navy. The Northbrook Programme, taking its name from the First Lord of the Admiralty, gave Clydebank the chance to demonstrate its abilities as a naval builder. The yard acquitted itself well, and by 1889, when the Navy Defence Act committed Britain to an extended naval building programme, the Clydebank yard was well placed to take a significant share of the naval orders that came to the Clyde. The pioneer naval builder had been Robert Napier; in the 1880s, John Elder and J. & G. Thomson also established themselves in this market, to be joined in the 1890s by Scott's Engineering and Shipbuilding Co., and the London and Glasgow Engineering and Iron Shipbuilding Co.

Yet such initiative was insufficient to keep J. & G. Thomson out of financial difficulty; while technically capable, the managerial expertise of the Thomsons was less sound and the extended programme of investment in the 1880s brought the yard to insolvency and liquidation. Between 1885 and 1890 J. & G. Thomson recorded trading losses of nearly £85,000, over half of this arising from the prestigious liners the *City of New York* and the *City of Paris*, constructed for the Inman and International Line. The two partners were also overdrawn on their capital account by more than £78,000, and deeply indebted to the bank. The result was a winding up of the company and a capital reconstruction. This was accomplished by converting the partnership to a public company; the bank advanced £250,000 to allow the partners to purchase the ordinary shares, and an issue of £150,000 in 5% debentures was also necessary to put the business on its feet. Even then the personal fortunes of the Thomsons were in disarray and by March 1891 their capital account deficiency was in excess of £112,000.[1]

The new company, Messrs James & George Thomson Ltd., came into being on 1 April 1890. The Chairman was W. A. Donaldson of Cochno, and James R. Thomson remained as Managing Director; his brother George P. Thomson was on the board together with J. G. Dunlop and J. Grant. In effect, the Thomsons lost control of the business in the reconstruction and were only able to continue as employees through the support of the bank which put up the money to refinance the business. In its new form, the Clydebank yard captured a large share of the new naval orders following the 1889 Defence Act. Orders for three cruisers and the battleship *Ramilles* provided work to a value of over £1 million. Six torpedo boat destroyers, two cruisers and a battleship followed up to 1896. The life of the yard had come to depend very heavily on naval construction, and the profitability of the yard had been transformed from the heavy losses of the late 1880s, to a trading profit of nearly £230,000 between 1890 and 1896.

This new profitability enabled the company to embark on a major extension and re-equipment of the works. However, since the Thomsons' personal fortunes had not improved, this was combined with a second reconstruction of the company which marked the passing of the Thomsons from a position of influence. On 1 February 1897 the company was renamed as the Clydebank Engineering and Shipbuilding Co., but this lasted barely two and a half years before the business was acquired in September 1899 by John Brown & Co. of Sheffield. The yard had by then had a profitable decade of naval orders. When it was acquired by John Brown its order book was worth £4.5 million, £1.4 million in merchant and £3.1 million in naval contracts; that was the lure that attracted John Brown & Co. to Clydeside.

John Brown Shipbuilding & Engineering Co. Ltd.

The plentiful naval work of the 1890s encouraged the creation of a small number of large scale vertically integrated steel and armament manufacturers in Britain. John Brown of the Atlas Works, Sheffield, was one of the group which included Vickers Son & Co., Sir W. G. Armstrong, Sir Joseph Whitworth & Co. and W. Beardmore & Co. In the 1890s Vickers took over the Barrow Shipyard and the Ordnance Factories of the Maxim Nordenfeldt Gun and Ammunition Co. At the same time Armstrong & Co. merged with Whitworth & Co. In this climate of merger John Brown believed that if it did not protect its own outlet for armour plate by acquiring an appropriate shipyard it would be squeezed out of a very lucrative market. John Brown's search for a shipyard revealed that the Clydebank Shipbuilding & Engineering Co., a major Admiralty contractor, was looking for an opportunity to expand, either by going public and issuing shares, or by negotiating a sale to a combine capable of expanding investment at Clydebank. Since Beardmore was also in the market and was showing an interest in Clydebank the deal was quickly concluded. John Brown of Sheffield, an integrated coal, iron, steel, engineering and armament manufacturer acquired the Clydebank yard on 1 September 1899 for £923,235. This was some £192,000 more than book value of the company, but it was quickly apparent that it represented a fair assessment of the value of the real assets. The Clydebank yard then became the shipbuilding division of the John Brown steel and armament empire. Its management retained considerable independence, but its future was then to be tightly bound to naval construction, and to building great ocean liners.[8]

John Brown, the parent company, was primarily interested in acquiring naval orders to provide a market for its own ordnance and armour plate. It pursued these orders with vigour and was extraordinarily successful in the first few years at Clydebank. Between 1899 and 1906 Clydebank built one battleship, four cruisers and four destroyers for the Admiralty and made a net profit of more than £576,000 on the work. The flood of orders arose from a backlog of naval repair and construction and a government policy decision to concentrate new construction in the private warship building yards. More was to follow, for Admiral Fisher, First Sea Lord from 1904, introduced the dreadnought, an entirely new class of battleship, the class named after the *Dreadnought* laid down at Portsmouth in October 1905. This class was faster and more mobile than earlier types and designed to attain 21 knots. In order to minimise engine weight this meant that the Admiralty was committed to installing the new steam turbines instead of the triple expansion engine. Clydebank was the only major warship yard in Britain with experience of building large turbine powered vessels, having installed these in Cunard's *Carmania* in 1905 and *Lusitania* in 1906. Not surprisingly the Clydebank yard then received an order for one of three new battle cruisers, the *Inflexible* of 17,290 tons and 41,000 HP.

The new management quickly set about extending the facilities, constructing new slipways at the west end of the yard, enlarging and modernising the engineering shops, and introducing the test tank facility in 1903. By 1905 over half a million pounds had been poured into new capital equipment; by the outbreak of the First World War over £855,000 had been expended on extensions, new equipment and modernisation, turning the yard into one of the most modern and well equipped in Britain, the premises covering over 80 acres and employing 8,500 men.[9] Although the new management at John Brown sought naval orders, they did not neglect the opportunity to support the order book with merchant tonnage. Under John Brown the old link with Cunard was revived. The Clydebank Shipbuilding & Engineering Co. had indeed gained the order for the *Saxonia* in 1899, but John Brown gained a further four Cunard contracts between 1902 and 1906; the *Panonia* in 1902, the *Caronia* in 1904, and the *Carmania* in 1905. These last two marked a transition for Cunard and John Brown. The *Caronia* was the last triple expansion engine liner built for Cunard at Clydebank while the *Carmania* was the first to have turbines installed. The *Lusitania* followed in 1906 and captured the Blue Riband in 1907, making the first westbound passage to New York in under five days.

Clydebank's reputation now rested squarely on great liners and on naval construction, both types demanding skill, quality and speed. The success of the yard rested heavily on the engineering developments in turbines. The man who bore the responsibility was Thomas Bell.[10] Bell had joined J. & G. Thomson in 1884 when they opened their new engine works at Clydebank. He had trained at the Royal Naval College at Devonport. When John Brown took over he was assistant to the engineering director, and became engineering manager in 1902. Under his guidance John Brown took out a Parsons licence in 1903 to build sets of

Figure 1:3 *Fitting-out basin in the Clydebank yard at the turn of the century with, left to right, the* Carmania, Antrim *and* Hindustan. *The* Carmania *and her sister ship* Caronia *marked a transition in ship design, the former being the first turbine engine passenger liner and the latter, the last triple expansion engine passenger liner built for Cunard at Clydebank.*

Parsons reaction turbines. Charles Parsons had patented this in 1894, and two years later the American, Charles Curtis, had patented his impulse turbine. Bell negotiated the UK licence for the Curtis turbine in 1908 and this was the beginning of the development of the Brown-Curtis turbine especially suited to heavy-duty naval service. The first warship to be fitted with this type at Clydebank was the *Bristol* in 1909; this type was soon taken up by sub-licences by nearly all naval builders in Britain.

The accession of the Liberals to power on the resignation of the Unionists in December 1905 introduced four years of curtailed expenditure on naval building, which coincided with a dearth of merchant orders. The pace picked up again from 1909, and from then to the outbreak of the First World War Clydebank gained Admiralty orders for sixteen vessels of over 90,000 tons, and engines delivering 855,000 HP. Merchant orders also revived and, between 1910 and 1913, Clydebank's output soared from 11,340 merchant tons to 55,933 tons, and naval launchings climbed from 6,840 displacement tons to 29,310 tons in 1913.

Between the end of 1899, when John Brown took over Clydebank, and the end of 1913, the Clydebank yard launched 51 merchant vessels to a total of 365,153 gross tons; at the same time, 28 naval craft of 157,639 displacement tons went down the slipways. Although the merchant tonnage seems much larger, the work content of the naval craft makes the tonnage equivalent to around 390,000 gross tons. This more nearly reflects the dependency of the Clydebank yard on naval orders. Merchant work was, in fact, not very profitable. The *Saxonia*, costing £2.9 million, made a net loss of £9,478; the *Lusitania* recorded only £50,972 net profit on a contract price of £1.6 million, while the *Aquitania*, Cunard's great liner of 45,647 tons, the largest vessel built as yet when launched in 1913, made only £19,489 net profit on a price of £1.4 million. Over the period the yard was heavily dependent on naval work for its profitability. The *Leviathan* made £144,937 net profit on a price of £705,000, while the *Inflexible* returned £124,809 on a contract of £1,249,782. During the period 1899 – 1913, the yard had sales valued at £11.8 million, of which £6.5 million were naval and £5.3 million merchant work. The total gross profit on this

Figure 1:4 Aquitania *in Brown's fitting-out basin prior to leaving the Clyde for Liverpool and her maiden voyage to New York. Built to partner Cunard's* Lusitania *and* Mauretania, *the* Aquitania *was launched on 21 April 1913 by Lady Inverclyde and served as a troopship in both World Wars.*

work was £3.3 million, this returning £782,000 net profit after allowances for depreciation and overheads. Although naval work contributed only 55 per cent of total sales, these contracts delivered 68 per cent of the gross profit, and 88 per cent of the net profit earned at Clydebank. In spite of the glamour of the great liners, merchant work barely paid for itself in these years before the First World War. It was this profitability of naval construction that made John Brown purchase Clydebank, and it was the desire to share in this market that drew Beardmore to Dalmuir to construct his great new yard there.

Beardmore

By 1899 William Beardmore junior had, in just 20 years since his father's death, converted the family's forge at Parkhead in the east end of Glasgow into one of the largest steelworks in Britain.[11] He had started manufacturing open hearth Siemens steel in 1879 and had installed a cogging mill capable of rolling armour plate ten years later. The market for the firm's products was the fast expanding local shipbuilding and engineering companies, particularly those undertaking Admiralty work. As the turn of the century approached, the business was robbed of one of its most important customers by the takeover of the Clydebank Shipbuilding and Engineering Works by John Brown & Co., the Sheffield steelmakers. Even before negotiations were complete, William Beardmore had responded to this threat by exploring the possibility of opening his own naval shipbuilding yard to provide a secure outlet for the products of the Parkhead Forge. He decided during 1899 to acquire the land in Dalmuir to the west of John Brown's yard where James Shearer & Sons, the owners of a shipyard and graving dock further up the Clyde at Scotstoun, were already planning to build a yard. The site had a river frontage of nearly a mile, interrupted to the west by the maintenance workshop of the Clyde Navigation Trust. These were in process of being transferred to a new complex at Renfrew to make way for a large graving dock to compete with an equivalent facility being built in Belfast.[12]

Simultaneously, one of the oldest marine engineering and shipbuilding concerns on the river, Robert Napier & Sons, foundered. This firm had a special relationship with Parkhead Forge and the Beardmore family. It was Robert Napier who had put the forge onto a sound footing after he purchased it in 1848, and he had brought William Beardmore senior to Glasgow from London in 1861 to help solve the problem of rolling armour plates.[13] Although the Napiers had played no part in the firm since Robert Napier's death in 1876, William Beardmore was, naturally, interested in its fate, particularly as the workforce was experienced in Admiralty work. In the expectation that he could transfer this pool of skilled labour to his new naval yard, he acquired the business for some £200,000 in the closing months of the century. He agreed to lease the Robert Napier yard at Govan and the Lancefield Engine Works on the other side of the river in Finnieston for two years while the Dalmuir plant was under construction.[14]

This was not the only major investment with which William Beardmore became involved at the turn of the century. During 1901 he rescued his brother-in-law, Duncan Stewart's heavy engineering business based in London Road in the east end of Glasgow and participated in a syndicate to acquire the Thames warship builders and general engineering firm, J. I. Thornycroft & Co.[15] All these ventures strained William Beardmore's financial resources and in the summer of 1901 he was forced to seek an amalgamation with Vickers & Son and Maxim Ltd., one of his leading competitors. In December Vickers purchased a 50 per cent stake in the company. Although Vickers already possessed a well-equipped naval construction works at Barrow on the Cumbrian coast, they encouraged William Beardmore to press on with his new Dalmuir works.[16]

Figure 1:5 *William Beardmore (1856-1936), dubbed a 'Field Marshall of Industry' for his role in creating the Beardmore empire centred on the Parkhead Forge and the Dalmuir Naval Construction Works. Created Lord Invernairn in 1921.*

In designing the shipyard and engine works, William Beardmore was determined that 'every well-tried system of modern manufacture should be adopted, with a view, not only of dealing with the heaviest class of work in the most efficient manner, but also of insuring that the highest degree of economy should be realized'. The work on the site, which had been delayed while the merger with Vickers was negotiated, went ahead rapidly during 1901. The wet dock, planned as the largest in the world, was excavated and 80,000 cubic feet of wood sunk into the foreshore to form the six berths. The following year a start was made on the vast engine and boiler works and an enormous gantry that was to cover the two longest slips. The whole ambitious complex took much longer to construct than William Beardmore had anticipated and was not nearing completion until 1906. The Govan yard and engine works had been closed the year before and all the serviceable plant shifted to Dalmuir. The first vessel to be built in the new yard was the *Zaza*, a steam yacht ordered by William Beardmore himself to test its facilities and the skill of the workforce. At the same time the Admiralty placed a contract for the Lord Nelson class battleship *Agamemnon*, exactly the type of naval vessel which William Beardmore hoped to construct.[17]

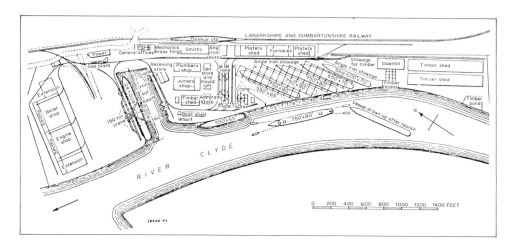

Figure 1:6 *Plan of Dalmuir Naval Construction Works in 1904 (From* Engineering, *1904, Vol 78, p.455).*

The Dalmuir Naval Construction Works were inaugurated on 22 June 1906 by the launch of the *Agamemnon*, 'the largest battleship yet built on the Clyde'. The magazine *Engineering* described the works as containing 'probably the finest collection of modern machine tools' of any comparable works in the United Kingdom.[18] The plant was not finally completed until 1908. The year before, William Beardmore had acquired the workshops and land adjoining the fitting-out basin from the Clyde Navigation Trust for £50,000, taking over the plan to build a large graving dock. The Dalmuir Dry Dock Co. was formed for this purpose, but nothing came of the scheme.[19] The move to a green field site forced William Beardmore & Co., like J. & G. Thomson 20 years before, to provide housing for their employees. Between 1905 and 1910 William Beardmore himself constructed or purchased from local builders large numbers of houses and tenements in Dalmuir to accommodate every class of employee.[20]

Despite the scale and the quality of the equipment in the new yard, William Beardmore found it difficult to win custom in the depressed years at the beginning of the century. Unlike his principal competitors he lacked a proven track record in building capital ships and an established link with liner companies. He was bitterly disappointed that the Admiralty excluded the company from its list of those invited to tender for the Bellerophon class of the new generation of dreadnought battleships. After protest, the Government relented, but the yard won no further contracts for heavy naval vessels until 1909-10 when the order for the battleship

Figure 1:7 *William Beardmore's steam yacht* Zaza, *completed in 1905 and the first vessel built in his Naval Construction Works at Dalmuir.*

Conqueror was placed.[21] In the expectation that the naval shipbuilding programme would be expanded to meet the German threat, machinery to make gun mountings was installed at Dalmuir in 1910.[22]

With the general boom in shipbuilding on the Clyde between 1910 and 1913, the Dalmuir yard flourished with a steady flow of orders for passenger vessels and naval units. Contracts included three 7,000 gross ton vessels for the Adelaide Steamship Co., two dreadnoughts, *Benbow* and *Ramilles*, two destroyers, and three light cruisers. Despite this apparent success, the yard was not profitable, almost certainly because the costs of production at Dalmuir were greater than in other yards. Between 1912 and 1914 the yard notched up a total loss of £357,043.

Figure 1:8 *The launch of the dreadnought* Conqueror *in 1911, the first heavy naval warship built by the Works since the* Agamemnon. *Orders were later secured for two further dreadnoughts, the* Benbow *and the* Ramilles.

Figure 1:9 *The 900 foot long fitting-out basin at Dalmuir in 1911 with the Russian cruiser* Rurik *to the left of the battleship* Agamemnon. *The Dalmuir Naval Construction Works was inaugurated on 22 June 1906 with the launch of the* Agamemnon, *then the largest battleship built on the Clyde.*

Nevertheless, the demand for steel and special forgings for the yard kept the Parkhead Forge in profit during these years. As war approached, William Beardmore planned to expand the Dalmuir works to build airships and aeroplanes. These initiatives were overtaken by the outbreak of hostilities in August 1914.[23] However, despite sharp fluctuations in fortune for its shipyards, by 1913, with the yards of John Brown and Beardmore, Clydebank had become the largest centre of naval and liner construction in Scotland, and had emerged as a world leader in scale and reputation in shipbuilding.

Table 1:1   *Clydebank shipyard annual launchings, 1873-1913*

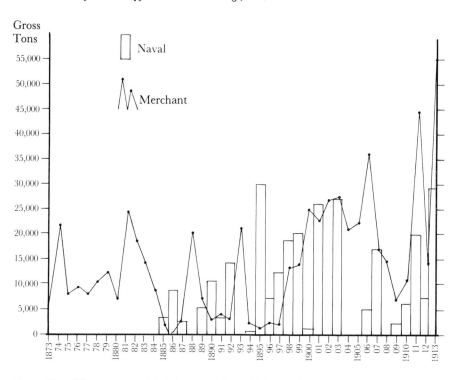

Source: List of Ships built at Clydebank, GUBA, UCS 1/93/40.

CHAPTER TWO

The Sewing Machine —
The Singer Factory

The American manufacturers I. M. Singer & Co. opened a branch office in Glasgow in 1856, as they strove to win a share of the European markets for their sewing machines. The company's agents in Britain and on the Continent employed aggressive sales techniques with great success and Singer became world market leaders. The Singer Manufacturing Co. (as it became in 1863) decided in 1867 that the level of demand in Britain justified the opening of a small assembly plant there.[1] Glasgow, which lay at the heart of a region famous for its iron and thread-making industries, and was the home of a thriving maritime trade, contained a vast pool of highly-skilled and relatively low-paid artisan labour, and it was chosen by Singer's Scottish-born general manager, George Ross McKenzie, as the most suitable location for the new venture. He obtained a lease for the premises at Love Loan in High John Street, near Queen Street Station, and had tools and machinery sent over to the works from the USA. A few men started work in October, and by the end of the year they were assembling 30 machines per week at Love Loan.[2]

The Love Loan factory obtained castings from George Ure & Co.'s foundry at Bonnybridge in Stirlingshire, and Scottish firms supplied some other materials, but most of the important sewing machine components were imported in a partly-finished state from Singer's factories in New York.[3] When serious delays arose in the supply of components, as the American plants struggled to meet an upturn in domestic orders for Singer sewing machines, and in order to eliminate expensive shipping costs, the company decided in 1869 to make the Scottish operation self-sufficient.[4] The construction of a new factory in James Street, near Bridgeton Cross in Glasgow's east end, began in August 1872, and the building was completed the following autumn.[5] As the volume of British and European sales continued to rise, a new japanning works was set up at Bonnybridge, in premises leased from the firm which continued to supply castings to Singer and George Ure & Co. In 1878, a new cabinet works was opened in Govan Street (now Ballater Street), just across the Clyde from the James Street factory.[6]

By 1881, Singer employed 2,000 people in Scotland and manufactured an average of 5,151 machines each week, but demand continued to outstrip the company's production capacity, even after extensions were made to the works in

Figure 2:1 *On 18 May 1882, 100 guests assembled at Kilbowie to witness the ceremonial cutting of the first sod for the new sewing machine factory performed by George R. McKenzie, Vice-President of the Singer Manufacturing Company. After the ceremony the company were taken by train, to Glasgow to attend a dinner in the George Hotel.*

the east end of Glasgow.[7] The company decided it was time to build a massive new factory, where the whole process of manufacturing sewing machines could be carried out on one site, and where Singer could provide the space and machinery required to meet future surges in the demand for their products.

Singer's attempts to acquire a site near Stirling in 1881 were unsuccessful, but the company was able to purchase just over 46 acres of farmland at Kilbowie instead.[8] The new site was bounded to the north by the North British Railway's Glasgow, Dumbarton and Helensburgh line, to the south by the Forth and Clyde canal, and it lay only a few hundred yards from the Glasgow Road, so it was ideally situated for a factory to which large quantities of raw materials had to be transported, and from which thousands of machines had to be sent to domestic markets and to ports for export overseas. George McKenzie, by now Vice-President of Singer, performed the ceremony of turning the first sod at Kilbowie on 18 May 1882, shortly before he became President of the company and shortly after the building contractors, McAlpine & Richmond, began work on clearing the ground for the new factory.[9] Reporting the ceremonial cutting of the first sod in 1882 the *Glasgow News* described the site as 'one of the most desirable in the kingdom'.[10]

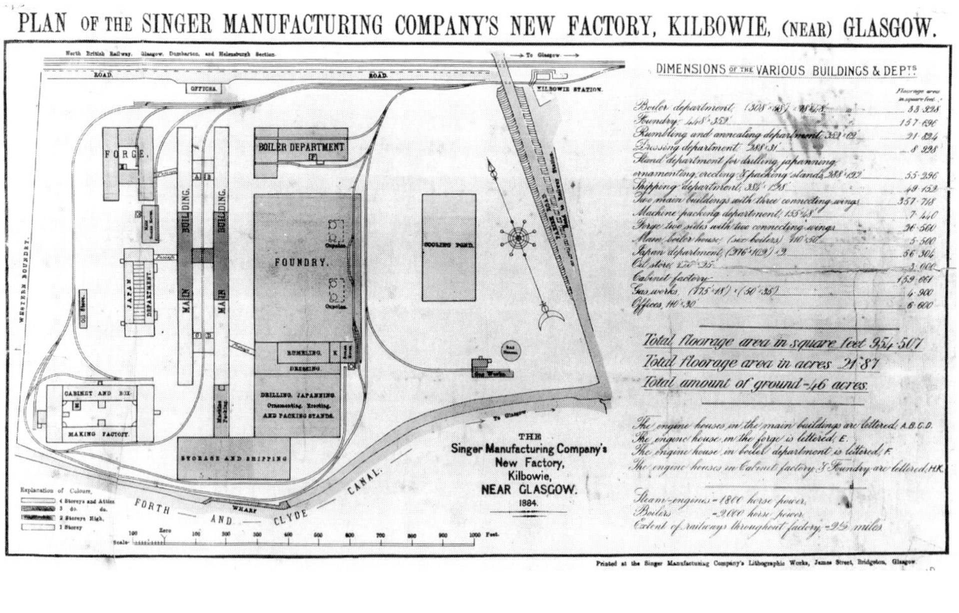

Figure 2:2 *Plan of the Kilbowie factory which, when completed in 1885, was the largest such factory in Europe.*

The contractor, McAlpine & Richmond was a small firm, little-known in the Glasgow area, and it had had a chequered history in housebuilding and general contracting in Lanarkshire and the western Highlands.[11] It is reputed that the contractors worked on extensions to one of Singer's Glasgow factories shortly before winning the small contract to clear the ground at Kilbowie,[12] but they had never worked on a contract worth more than £20,000. It must have come as a surprise to many of Glasgow's leading builders, therefore, when McAlpine & Richmond were awarded the contract for the brickwork of the new factory.[13] It was estimated that it would cost at least £300,000 to build the new works, and McAlpine & Richmond's contract would have been worth at least two-thirds of that sum.[14]

Singer engaged an architect from Glasgow, Robert Ewan, to design the new buildings. William Ewan, another Scot, who had supervised the construction of Singer's first factories in the USA as well as the recently-completed sister-plant of the Kilbowie works at Elizabethport, New Jersey, returned to Scotland to supervise the work of McAlpine & Richmond and the plumbers, glaziers, slaters and other sub-contractors in Clydebank.[15] McAlpine & Richmond set to work immediately. They put up two main buildings, each 800 feet long, 50 feet wide, and three storeys in height, with an additional floor on the central section to house the machinery shops. These two buildings were connected by three wings, and the contractors built a huge square clock tower, nearly 200 feet high, above the central wing. The cabinet and box works were also three storeys in height, and single storey buildings were erected to house the foundry, the foundry store and annealing departments, the stand manufacturing, japanning and annealing department, the storage and shipping department, the machine japanning and ornamenting department, the forge, a gasworks, and the boiler shop in which Singer planned to manufacture Babcock & Wilcox's patent water tube boilers under licence. Two and a half miles of railway were laid to the factory site, connected to the Glasgow, Dumbarton and Helensburgh line and connecting the various departments, and a small jetty was built on the canal, near the shipping and storage department.[16]

Figure 2:3 *View of factory and workforce, taken in the 1890s from the Kilbowie Road gate. Alongside the assembled workforce is the old railway line which was moved northwards in 1906 to permit expansion. On completion, the factory comprised two main buildings connected by three wings, the central of which included the imposing clock tower. In this view the original clock face can be seen.*

William Richmond quit the partnership with Robert McAlpine in January 1883, leaving the latter to carry on the business 'in his own name and on his own behoof'.[17] Robert McAlpine & Co. used 500 tons of cement and 20 million bricks (many of them manufactured in the contractor's own brickworks at Stonefield in Lanarkshire) in the construction of the building at Kilbowie.[18] Each building was designed to be fireproof, with iron doors and iron roof beams and columns supplied from Alexander Findlay's Parkneuk Foundry, and sprinkler systems were installed throughout the works.[19] The factory was considered to be the most modern and extensive in Europe; McAlpine himself told a newspaper reporter that 'no workshop of such magnitude has ever been erected at once in the world'.[20]

Singer began to transfer their workers to the new factory as each building was completed, 500 men and women starting at Kilbowie in the summer of 1884, and a further 2,500 by the end of January 1885. Two thousand more workers were recruited before the end of the year.[21] The factory was completed during the

Figure 2:4 *Close up of the Singer clock in its second phase. With the removal of the lettering 'THE SINGER MANU. COY.' from its outer rim, the clock face diameter was increased to 26 feet, making the clock the second largest in the world. In 1928 the clock was again altered and the mechanical movement replaced by an electrically driven movement.*

summer of 1885, six months ahead of schedule,[22] but the famous Singer clock, later featuring the largest clock-face in Britain, was not installed until the following year.[23] The completion of the plant was of prime importance to Clydebank. When Clydebank became a burgh in 1886, significantly, its coat of arms included a sewing machine.

Singer's decision to invest heavily in the construction of the Kilbowie factory was soon justified by the improved performance of their Scottish operation. With cheaper iron and labour prices than in the USA, the new works could produce up to 10,000 sewing machines each week, at 80 per cent of the cost of manufacturing them at the equally modern and almost equally large Elizabethport factory.[24] By 1900, weekly production was 13,000.[25] Back in America, management was delighted with these results, and in 1905 a British Corporation, the Singer Manufacturing Company Ltd. was founded to operate the factory. It was a wholly owned subsidiary of the Singer Company.[26]

Figure 2:5 *Although the area immediately north of the Singer factory was devastated in the 1941 Blitz, the factory itself suffered only minor damage, quickly resuming full production.*

In the meantime business continued to flourish and by 1906 demand was exceeding the production capacity of the world's largest factory, Singer's, Clydebank. To overcome this, additional storeys were constructed on all the buildings to make them a uniform height of five storeys, and a huge six-storey block was erected. Building upwards had not fully resolved the problem and so the northern perimeter of the 46 acre site was extended by 220 yards, after successful negotiations with the North British Railway Company. Not only did the Railway

Table **2:1**   *Annual Production Figures, 1867-1918 of Singer's Scottish Factories*

Year	Site	Domestic	Industrial	Total
1867	Love Loan	185	—	185
1868	,,	7,699	—	7,699
1869	James Street	11,638	—	11,638
1870	,,	14,549	2,374	16,923
1871	,,	35,739	5,470	41,209
1872	,,	49,665	7,134	56,799
1873	,,	54,024	5,024	59,048
1874	,,	76,493	6,837	83,330
1875	,,	93,376	6,748	100,124
1876	,,	104,251	6,938	111,189
1877	,,	124,277	8,331	132,688
1878	,,	155,925	7,852	163,777
1879	,,	172,367	5,622	178,089
1880	,,	211,807	6,530	218,337
1881	,,	247,336	4,952	252,288
1882	,,	248,022	9,322	257,344
1883	,,	221,870	11,422	233,292
1884	Clydebank (Kilbowie)	200,730	9,677	210,407
1885	,,	224,206	7,735	231,941
1886	,,	190,756	9,085	199,841
1890*	,,	335,851	37,930	373,781
1891	,,	349,969	51,035	401,004
1892	,,	352,005	49,286	401,291
1893	,,	331,805	56,178	387,893
1894	,,	391,465	59,654	451,119
1895	,,	372,302	65,334	437,636
1896	,,	369,672	70,889	440,561
1897	,,	380,195	71,153	451,946
1898	,,	402,651	71,153	473,804
1899	,,	461,738	85,106	546,844
1900	,,	504,348	96,186	600,534
1901	,,	529,275	97,547	626,822
1902	,,	529,256	104,141	633,397
1903	,,	626,591	108,683	735,274
1904	,,	681,652	117,225	798,877
1905	,,	766,525	121,077	887,602
1906	,,	896,615	143,835	1,040,450
1907	,,	956,840	143,246	1,100,086
1908	,,	700,275	129,917	830,192
1909	,,	801,988	161,548	963,536
1911	,,	754,201	177,180	931,381
1912	,,	962,362	195,665	1,158,027
1913	,,	1,097,391	204,460	1,301,851
1914	,,	889,337	203,891	1,093,228
1915	,,	556,638	196,626	753,264
1916	,,	653,742	84,999	738,741
1917	,,	516,644	67,730	584,374
1918	,,	509,616	86,580	596,196

Source: Dorman, A., *'A History of the Singer Company (UK) Ltd Clydebank Factory',* (unpublished, 1972).

* No records available 1887-89.

Company agree to construct a new stretch of line but it also built a new station to replace Kilbowie, which was now within the Factory's grounds, and called it 'Singer'.[27]

The factory's all-time production peak came in 1913 when 1,301,851 machines were produced (i.e. 25,000 per week) and employment rose to 14,000 as Table 2:1 shows.[28] Almost half of its output was exported to Russia which was Singer's largest market, accounting for 30 per cent of the Company's entire production.[29] Such was the potential of the Russian market that Singer opened a factory there, sometime between 1890 and 1914.[30] After the revolution of 1917, Singer found itself in the red — barred from the Russian market and its property in that country confiscated.[31] During the Great War, part of Clydebank's productive capacity had been channelled into the manufacture of munitions, but the dictum of the day was 'Business as Usual' and the factory continued to produce sewing machines. However, by 1917, with the loss of the Russian market and increasing demands for munitions, output was down to 584,374 machines, compared to 1,301,851 in 1913.[32]

Despite the fact that after the Russian Revolution it had suddenly lost the market for half its output, the Clydebank factory, by the late 1920s, had an output level approaching the 1913 figure. It is significant, however, that the factory's output was never again so consistently high as it was in the early years of the twentieth century when the factory catered for the Russian market. As Table 2:2 shows, output and numbers employed fluctuated in accordance with the national economic trends during the inter-war years and it also shows that the factory was a

Table 2:2   *Output and Numbers employed at Singer's Clydebank, 1919-43*

Year	Domestic Machines	Industrial Machines	Total Output	Size of Labour force (as during last week of December)
1919	573,543	118,777	692,320	
1920	670,499	85,369	755,868	
1921	354,563	37,621	392,184	
1922	665,113	62,732	727,845	9,026
1923	623,239	72,093	695,332	9,191
1924	701,780	95,904	797,684	10,777
1925	803,824	91,208	895,032	12,174
1926	790,645	65,948	856,593	11,037
1927	841,772	88,968	930,740	11,258
1928	910,550	107,247	1,017,797	12,507
1929	997,601	109,299	1,106,900	12,440
1930	634,956	72,687	707,643	9,463
1931	512,523	49,875	562,398	7,991
1932	247,366	35,462	282,828	6,798
1933	448,214	44,789	493,003	7,559
1934	433,326	47,376	480,702	7,614
1935	475,454	44,265	519,719	8,103
1936	534,103	51,538	585,641	8,405
1937	546,958	58,444	605,402	9,104
1938	394,141	40,814	434,955	7,375
1939	511,767	78,867	590,634	8,809
1940	321,661	68,776	390,437	
1941	190,576	55,515	246,091	
1942	50,066	12,210	62,276	
1943	26,687	14,216	40,903	

Source: Dorman, A., '*A History of the Singer Company (UK) Ltd Clydebank Factory*', (unpublished, 1972).

victim of the depression of the 1930s. Yet Singer apparently suffered less than the other major employer in Clydebank at the time, John Brown and Co. In 1932 Singer employed 6,798 people compared to 12,507 in 1928, whereas Brown employed only 422 people compared to 7,626 in 1928.[33] In Europe the depression provoked countries into erecting tariff barriers to protect indigenous firms. It has been suggested that Singer retaliated by establishing plants in France and Italy during the 1930s in order to evade the tariffs. If that is true then it had increased its manufacturing capacity in Europe merely to offset temporary conditions. It seems more likely that Singer expected an upsurge in world demand, and it hoped to continue unchallenged as the world's leading sewing machine manufacturer. It was logical, therefore, to build these two factories which would also compensate for the one lost in the USSR.

Apart from 1926, the year of the General Strike, 1911 was the only year of significant industrial conflict in any of Singer's Scottish factories between 1867 and 1945. The 1911 strike arose in one department against a management attempt to cut piecework rates by speeding-up. The strike spread throughout the factory and, by April 1911, 37 of the 41 departments were out, and a total of 11,000 men and women were on strike. However, the management sent postcards to all 'former employees' asking them to resume work. The strike was abandoned after 6,527 workers returned their cards to the management and only 4,025 to the strike committee.[34] Many of the strike leaders were dismissed and on 12 May 1911 the *Clydebank Press* reported that 500 sackings had followed the end of the unsuccessful strike. The Company found being multi-national had its advantages during a strike; it could 'manoeuvre to keep production low' at Clydebank, and 'it deliberately increased its imports' from its American and other European factories 'and put workers at Elizabeth, New Jersey, on overtime'.[35] After the General Strike and until closure, Singer's reputedly paid above average wages, in a conspicuous attempt to foster good labour relations. However, it still refused to 'totally recognise' trade unions until after the 1957 National Engineering Strike.[36]

Between 1939-1945 almost all of the factory's productive capacity was devoted to the war effort. The factory produced 60 million rifle components, 1,293,600 bayonets, 300 sten guns, 125 million bullets, 1.75 million fuses and 15,000 tank tracks.[37] Sewing machine output in 1943 was only 7 per cent of the 1939 level, and industrial machines accounted for 35 per cent compared to 13 per cent in 1939. Between 1867 and 1943 over 38 million Singer machines were produced in Scotland, 36 million produced in the Clydebank factory since it opened in 1884. By 1945 the name Singer had been synonymous with sewing machines for almost a century, and the company was selling more machines than all its competitors combined. With market conditions of high demand, and Singer's virtual monopoly of supply, there was a tremendous boom, in which the company could sell machines as fast as it could produce them. However, after 1945 Singer was to face a changing market, in particular, ferocious competition from low-cost producers of domestic sewing machines. Meanwhile Singer's international structure had altered considerably since 1884 when Clydebank alone produced for the entire European market. By 1945 Singer had plants in France, Italy and Germany. Clydebank was not to escape the consequences of Singer's post-war struggle to hold its markets.

CHAPTER THREE

The Town and its Politics

The Formation of the Burgh

The Burgh of Clydebank came officially into existence at noon on Thursday 18 November 1886. At that time Dunbartonshire's Sheriff-Substitute Gebbie announced the final result of the recent poll of ratepayers on the question of forming a Police Burgh. The announcement marked the formal transition of Clydebank from village to town. The transition had been rapid, as the local directory for 1893-4 noted:

> 'A little over a score of years ago, the now thriving and populous burgh of Clydebank was totally unknown to fame, in fact it did not then exist. . . . . Its rapid conversion from an ordinary rural district to a populous suburb, a great shipbuilding centre, and the home of an important manufacturer, has possibly no precedent in this country, though in the land of Stars and Stripes the making of a town in a night is of such frequent occurrence as almost to pass unheeded.'[1]

The burgh was formed under the General Police and Improvement (Scotland) Act 1862, also known as the Lindsay Act. Under this Act a burgh could be formed in an area with a population of 700 or more which wished to adopt a police system dealing with policing, lighting, paving, cleansing, water supply and drainage. In such a police burgh administrative authority lay in the hands of elected magistrates and commissioners of police.[2] Under the Lindsay Act the procedure to establish a burgh began with the presentation of a petition of seven or more householders to the local Sheriff asking him to fix the boundaries of the proposed burgh. The scheme was then put before a public meeting of householders to decide, by a show of hands, whether to adopt the Act. Any seven individuals present could demand a poll and only the agreement of a majority of those voting at such a poll could ensure the final adoption of burgh status. Male and female occupiers of land or premises worth £4 a year or more were entitled to vote on the question.[3]

Several factors led to the establishment of a burgh at Clydebank. One of these was the alleged inability of the existing local authority, the Parochial Board of Old Kilpatrick, to function satisfactorily in the increasingly urban area, especially in the sphere of public health. With the growing population of the area, especially after the completion of the Singer factory in 1884, the provision of adequate local drainage and sewage disposal was an important matter. Parochial Board Minutes of 2 March 1886 reported that nothing effective had been done to improve

Figure 3:1 *Throughout the early history of the burgh, drainage and sewage matters, proved to be contentious issues. On 29 November 1906 peace was restored between the burgh and Dunbarton County with the establishment of the Clydebank & District Water Trust. In this view, taken in 1926, members and officials rest between inspections of the several Water Trust premises and reservoirs before concluding their visit with dinner at the Half Way House.*

Figure 3:2 *James Rodger Thomson, first Provost of Clydebank (1886-88) and senior partner of J. & G. Thomson. Of the two brothers, James played a more active role in the community, generously assisting local organisations, and under his direction 'Tamson's Toon' quickly gained the nickname of 'the Risingest Burgh'. In addition to his chairmanship of the School Board, James was a Colonel in the Dunbartonshire Rifle Volunteers, deputy chairman of the Clydebank, Yoker and Partick Railway Company and a member of the Council of the Institute of Naval Architects.*

'dangerous' nuisances at Boquhanran Burn and the ditch at Skypes Road, Dalmuir, first reported to the Board in July 1885.[4] This failure led some important local proprietors, including William and P. P. MacIndoe, to ask the Parochial Board to form a special Drainage District in Dalmuir. Hitherto, sewage and drainage had been the individual financial responsibility of local proprietors. A Drainage District would allow for the development of a more effective sanitation system via a charge on every householder. The prospect of such a charge whipped up considerable opposition to the scheme amongst local ratepayers. A petition opposing the plan, signed by 253 ratepayers of Dalmuir and district, was presented to the Parochial Board at its meeting of 30 March 1886. The meeting voted against setting up a Special Drainage District by an overwhelming 51 to 7.[5]

The failure to set up a Special Drainage district apparently encouraged the emergence of a campaign to establish a burgh which would have powers to deal with sanitary problems. The *Dumbarton Observer* of 3 April 1886 reported that 'a movement is on foot to constitute Clydebank, Yoker and Dalmuir into a burgh.' The impetus behind the move to set up a burgh was very much associated with James R. Thomson of J. & G. Thomson's Shipyard. Samuel Crawford, the yard manager, was one of the scheme's strongest backers, and other shipyard employees featured prominently in petitioning for a burgh.[6] Under these circumstances it is not surprising that James R. Thomson was later referred to as the 'founder of the burgh.'[7] A petition initiating moves to set up a burgh, signed by Samuel Crawford and other householders, was launched on 26 May 1886. Over the next three months Sheriff Muirhead in Dumbarton received submissions from supporters and opponents of the scheme. In an interlocutor of 25 September 1886 the Sheriff fixed the boundaries of the proposed burgh to include Yoker, Clydebank (with part of Kilbowie) and Dalmuir. The meeting, necessary under the Lindsay Act, was called for Wednesday 10 November 1886.

Like the attempt to set up a Special Drainage District, the move to establish a Police Burgh proved controversial. Fear of increased taxation in the new burgh was raised at many public meetings and in letters to the press.[8] At a public meeting in Clydebank in November it was asserted that 'there was hardly a Parochial Board in all Scotland so well managed, or where the poor rate was so low'.[9] Hence, the meeting to consider burgh status on 10 November was well attended.[10] The proposal to set up a Police Burgh was moved by E. C. C. Stanford, owner of the local chemical works, and seconded by Samuel Crawford. R. T. Napier of Napier, Shanks and Bell seconded the move against. On a show of hands after the speeches only about a dozen voted to set up a burgh with the great majority against. However, a written demand for a poll, signed by 11 ratepayers, was produced and a polling date of Saturday 13 November was set. On polling day approximately 66 per cent of 1,500 potential voters voted; 496 against and 495 for.[11] The pro-burgh lobby, however, challenged the result, claiming that two qualified ratepayers had been unable to vote as their names did not appear on the Voters Roll. Sheriff-Substitute Gebbie accepted the two votes and the majority of one against forming a burgh was transformed into a majority of one in favour. Thus, by the narrowest of margins, on Thursday 18 November 1886 Clydebank became a burgh.[12]

**FIRST ELECTED COMMISSIONERS OF THE BURGH OF CLYDEBANK
AND THEIR OFFICIALS 1886**

Standing: Chief Constable CHARLES McHARDY (Procurator Fiscal), Commissioner D. MUNRO, Mr. C. P. LEIPER (Treasurer), Commissioner S. CRAWFORD, Commissioner E. C. C. STANFORD, Commissioner J. CRAMB, Mr. JAS. JOHNSTON (Master of Works, etc.), Commissioner A. COCHRANE, Commissioner S. LECKIE, Dr. WYLIE, (Medical Officer).
Seated: Commissioner W. G. O'BEIRNE, Bailie A. NAIRN, Provost J. R. THOMSON, Bailie R. T. NAPIER, THOS. GRAHAM (Clerk), Commissioner D. WYLIE, Commissioner H. YOUNG.

Figure 3:3

Clydebank Burgh Commission

The first election of Burgh Commissioners took place on Tuesday 21 December. A number of opponents of burgh status came forward in the four wards, according to the *Lennox Herald*, 'so that a policy of economy might be inaugurated.'[13] The press reported the election as being quiet and with no particular areas of political conflict.[14] There was apparently some concern that the Commission would unduly reflect the interests of local employers, especially James Thomson.[15] Most of the candidates, however, were either local employers, their representatives or small businessmen. James Barrie, contesting the Clydebank ward, declared himself 'free from the master's screw' but failed to be elected.[16] Given their importance locally, it is not really surprising that the newly elected Commission was made up largely of employers and managers. Each of the four wards returned three members to the new Commission. The results of the first election are given in Table 3:1

Table 3:1 *Clydebank Police Commission Election 1886*

Ward	Candidate	Occupation	Votes Gained	Attitude to Burgh Formation
1 (Yoker)	R. T. Napier	Shipbuilder	208	against
	W. G. O'Beirne	Chemical Works Manager	147	?
	Donald Munro	Grocer	137	?
	D. Alexander	Grocer	134	?
	Duncan Munro	Joiner	95	against
	T. Nicol	Clydebank Shipyard Employee	92	?
	A. Johnston	Grocer	18	?
2 (Clydebank)	J. R. Thomson	Shipbuilder	295	for
	S. Crawford	Clydebank Shipyard Manager	226	for
	E. C. C. Stanford	Chemical Works Owner	200	for
	W. Hannah	Auctioneer	117	?
	J. Barrie	House Factor	113	?
3 (Kilbowie)	D. Cramb	Singer Foreman	No contest	?
	S. Leckie	Grocer	No contest	?
	D. Wylie	Singer Foreman	No contest	?
4 (Dalmuir	A. Nairn	Clyde Trust Works Manager	225	?
	H. Young Jnr.	Singer Superintendent	212	for
	A. Cochrane	—	190	?
	J. H. Biles	Marine Architect	91	?

Source: Compiled from *Glasgow Herald, Lennox Herald, Dumbarton Observer, Clydebank and Renfrew Press* 1886-91.

The first meeting of the Commission in Clydebank Public Hall on 27 December 1886 elected James R. Thomson as Provost and Messrs Napier and Nairn as Bailies. The meeting then moved to a more contentious issue, that of the name of the new burgh. Local jealousies and anxieties about upstart Clydebank's possible domination over older Dalmuir and Yoker had played some part in the opposition to the proposal to form a burgh, and this concern reappeared in the debate on possible names. Edward Stanford and Samuel Leckie suggested Clydebank in view of the growing importance of the area and its shipyard of the same name. Bailies Napier and Nairn preferred to avoid emphasising one particular locality within the burgh and suggested Kilbowie instead because, 'It is the only name that will give satisfaction to the whole burgh'. On a division, four Commissioners (Napier, Nairn, Cochrane and Young) voted for Kilbowie, Commissioner Munro abstained and the remaining seven voted for Clydebank.[17] Thus the burgh gained the name by which it became famous. The choice of this name reflected the importance of the shipyard and its owner in promoting urban growth in the area, and James R. Thomson's active participation and influence in the movement to have a burgh established.

The powers and duties of the newly established Commission were defined by the Lindsay Act of 1862. The Commissioners could raise rates, appoint officials and make provision for lighting, paving, cleansing and drainage, and the supply of water. They were able to take action to promote public health, such as the building of sewers and the control of slaughterhouses. They were also empowered to license hackney carriages, suppress vagrancy and ensure the policing of public houses. Their powers were extended by the Burgh Police (Scotland) Act of 1892, especially in relation to public health and building control. The 1892 Act provided the basis for local government in Clydebank until long after 1914. The Town Councils (Scotland) Act 1900 changed the authority's title from Clydebank Police Commission to Clydebank Town Council.

One of the first actions of the new Commissioners was to appoint officials. At the meeting of 27 December 1886, Thomas Graham was appointed Clerk of the burgh. Soon after, other major appointments were made, Charles Leiper as Treasurer, Dr John Wylie as Medical Officer of Health and James Johnston as Master of Works, Sanitary Inspector and Cleansing Inspector. In January 1887 the Police Commission set up four committees to oversee particular duties. These committees were Finance Law and Parliamentary Bills; Streets, Roads and Buildings; Sanitary and Lighting.[18] Naturally, with the passage of time, the growth of the burgh and the extension of the Commission's powers and duties further officials were appointed and new committees established, such as the town's librarian in 1913 and the Halls and Baths Committee in 1901.

It was the duty of these officials and committees to supervise burgh activity in particular areas. Perhaps the most immediate of these was cleansing and sanitation — after all, inadequate sanitation had been the catalyst of the movement to have the Clydebank area formed into a burgh. However, expectations of improvement were not fulfilled at first and, indeed, dissatisfaction with appointed cleansing contractors continued until the Council itself took over responsibility in 1902. The Council also acted to improve and extend the town's sewers. Boquhanran Burn and its culvert continued to cause concern until at least 1895 despite frequent cleansing and threats of legal action against its proprietors. The Commission also compelled proprietors to build new sewers, and occasionally took control of private drains and sewers. By 1890 it had five main outfall sewers and their subsidiaries constructed, and in 1903 connections were made to the main sewer being built through the burgh to the Glasgow Corporation Sewage Works which opened in Dalmuir in May 1904.[19] The provision of water to the rapidly expanding burgh proved to be a bone of contention. Despite frequent attempts the burgh failed to wrest control of the supply from Old Kilpatrick Parochial Board until 1906. Burgh roads did not become a direct responsibility of the Police Commission until after 1891. The 1890s saw the beginning of a programme of road widening and improvement which was, at times of depression, used as one method of relieving unemployment. The *Clydebank Press* of 30 December 1893 reported that the burgh was employing 100 men at 2/- a day to widen roads, but though many more had applied no more could be employed on grounds of cost.

Despite periods of occasional depression the burgh economy was generally buoyant and this was reflected in the Council's construction of public buildings and of leisure facilities, some of the latter with the assistance of generous benefactors Provost Young first proposed the construction of municipal buildings in 1893[20] and, after a plebiscite of local ratepayers, on 26 April 1898 it was agreed to go ahead with the construction of municipal buildings, halls and baths on land on Dumbarton Road acquired in 1889. The foundation stone for the burgh buildings was laid on 23 June 1900 and they were opened on 13 March 1902. Shortly after, on 6 May 1902, the Hall Street Baths were opened.[21]

An important area of burgh activity lay in the extension of the burgh boundaries. The population of Clydebank had risen to 18,670 in 1901. By the beginning of the new century it was argued that extension was necessary because there was little suitable building land left within the existing boundaries of the

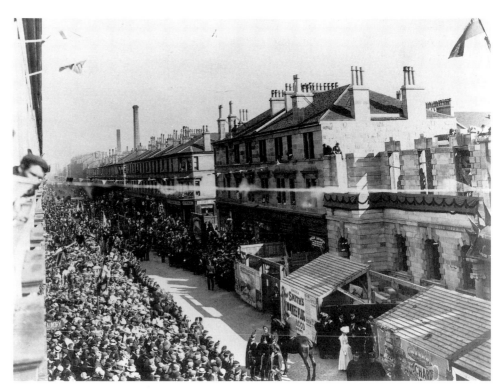

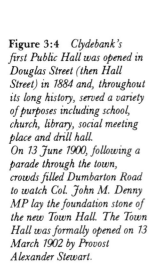

Figure 3:4 Clydebank's first Public Hall was opened in Douglas Street (then Hall Street) in 1884 and, throughout its long history, served a variety of purposes including school, church, library, social meeting place and drill hall.
On 13 June 1900, following a parade through the town, crowds filled Dumbarton Road to watch Col. John M. Denny MP lay the foundation stone of the new Town Hall. The Town Hall was formally opened on 13 March 1902 by Provost Alexander Stewart.

town. An attempt to include Radnor Park in the burgh in 1890 was unsuccessful as was the attempt to annexe North Dalmuir and Radnor Park in 1900-01. However, in 1906 the burgh boundaries were extended to include Radnor Park despite the opposition of its ratepayers who feared a rates increase. Radnor Park became the fifth ward of the burgh and added almost 9,000 to the town's population.[22]

The Commissioners and Town Councillors presiding over the period whilst Clydebank gained its nickname of the 'risingest burgh' undertook considerable municipal activity. Much had been achieved in the development of the

Figure 3:5 Looking west along Dumbarton Road this view was taken after the opening of the Town Hall in 1902 and before the extension of the tramway to Dalmuir in 1904. Note the absence of the Town Hall clock which was not added until 1931 along with the war memorial situated in the west wall on Hall Street.

infrastructure, public health measures, leisure provision and public services, such as the Fire Brigade established in 1887. However, much remained to be done. Some potential areas of municipal activity, such as the provision of housing were largely untouched before 1914, even although housing might have been built under the Housing of the Working Classes Act of 1890. As expectations changed with the passage of time demands for broader municipal action became more insistent and were reflected in the political life of the town.

Political Parties and Pressure Groups

Party politics as such played little part in municipal politics before 1914. There was a strong tide of opinion that party should play no part in Town Council activity. In 1892 the local Liberal Party was reported to have considered it inadvisable to link politics with municipal work in the burgh.[23] This comment was typical of the period. However, other reports clearly show the party affiliations of Town Council members and candidates. Many pre-war provosts such as Provosts Spite, Stewart and Taylor were Liberal, while Bailies Hogg and Balfour were Conservatives. Party labels did not formally enter into press reports of local politics until after the emergence of the Independent Labour Party (ILP). The first working-man candidate stood for the Council in 1892 but the ILP enjoyed no electoral success until 1906 when two ILP councillors were returned.

Several factors explain the limited impact of Labour candidates before 1914. One factor was the youth of the group — the Clydebank ILP branch was formed in 1894[24] — and consequent lack of experience and organisation. Secondly, Scottish working class loyalties lay mainly with the Liberal Party over this period.[25] Thirdly, a considerable proportion of Clydebank's citizens were Roman Catholic,[26] often of Irish descent, and at this stage the Roman Catholic church opposed Socialism.[27] Lastly, rightly or wrongly, a feeling existed in Clydebank that the Labour grouping was connected with the liquor trade, a significant political factor in a town with a strong temperance movement. The slight impact of Labour is underlined by the lack of public interest in local elections. The local press commented on lack of enthusiasm amongst electors in 1892, 1900, 1909 and 1913. Wards were often won without a contest; only one ward was contested in 1888, 1896, 1898, 1903, 1905 and 1909, and there were no contests in any ward in 1887, 1891 and 1899. As a result, up to the First World War the local authority remained firmly in the hands of local employers or managers.

However, if party played a limited role in local politics, pressure groups were very active at both municipal and parliamentary levels. Housing became an increasingly important issue, and political pressure groups developed in Clydebank as elsewhere in Clydeside at this time.[28] In Clydebank, the problem was not so much one of slum housing by contemporary standards, although unsatisfactory housing conditions certainly existed. Rather, as the town's population grew, the problem was a lack of sufficient houses of a type and at a rental level suited to the majority of the townspeople. Pressure groups were formed to demand action in the housing sphere. A Tenant's Defence Association was formed in 1899, a Garden Suburb Association in 1910 and a Tenants Protective Association in 1912. In addition, a Housing Committee arose in 1900 after conferences of various interested groups such as the local Friendly Societies, Co-operative Societies and the ILP. In 1901 and 1902 a Housing Committee supporter stood, albeit unsuccessfully, for the Town Council, while the Tenants Association petitioned for municipal housing. Little was achieved. The Council did set up a Housing of the Working Classes Committee but only 28 Council houses were built under the 1890 Act before 1914.[29]

The temperance movement was another active pressure group which, despite

Figure 3:6 *In spite of the influence of the temperance movement many areas were well supplied with hostelries. This view shows Colin Robb standing in front of his premises on the north side of Glasgow Road, Yoker, on the site presently occupied by the Lovat Arms. The inn, a single-thatched roof cottage comprising a small parlour and a bar, was a popular haunt of cattle drovers in its earlier days.*

its large membership, failed to achieve its aims. Between 1889 and 1914 the number of official outlets for the sale of alcohol rose with the population, from 13 in 1889 to 33 in 1914, and cases of shebeening came before the local courts.[30] The emerging Labour Party apparently lost support on account of its supposed local links with the drinks trade.[31] In 1897 local temperance organisations formed the Progressive Union which nominated or approved candidates for some years. However, after 1900 Progressive Union activity tailed off locally. Thereafter temperance action tended to be restricted to the holding of meetings to oppose any increase in licences, and the drumming up of support for temperance legislation. Religious groupings also played their part in politics but more directly in parliamentary politics than municipal affairs.

From 1886 to 1914 Clydebank Burgh was part of the Dunbartonshire constituency and, as its population rose, an increasingly important part. The burgh itself was described as a Liberal stronghold in 1895[32] but the county seat was mainly Conservative over the period. The Liberals held the seat for 11 out of 28 years, between 1892-5 and from 1906-14. The parliamentary electorate was smaller than the municipal electorate. Only adult male householders had the vote until 1918 when universal male suffrage and the first instalment of female suffrage were introduced. By far the most controversial issue in parliamentary politics before 1914 was Ireland, and it was in this arena that religion played its most obvious part in Clydebank politics.[33]

Liberal attempts from the 1880s to give Home Rule to Ireland brought the party strong support from local branches of Irish nationalist organisations such as the Irish National League (INL) and later the United Irish League (UIL). There were links between these organisations and local Catholic clergy. Father, later Canon, Montgomery gave active support to the INL and so, indirectly, to the Liberals. A particular object of the Catholic Social Union, formed in 1898, was the registration of all Catholic voters in the district.[34] There is less evidence of organised Orange political activity but in 1906 members of the Halls True Blue LOL No 177 Lodge were urged to do their very best to return a Unionist to represent Dunbartonshire in Parliament.[35] The Irish Home Rule controversy apparently aided recruitment to the Orange movement. While there had been three lodges in Clydebank in 1897, it was claimed in 1908 that there were six adult lodges and one juvenile lodge.[36] In July 1908 the *Clydebank Press* reported that 350 Clydebank Orangemen were involved in a demonstration in Dumbarton, whilst in June 1908, 400 adults and 100 juveniles took part in the annual parade of Clydebank's No. 26 Lodge.[37] Occasionally Loyalist-Nationalist rivalry led to friction. In April 1886 the *Lennox Herald* reported a riot in Hamilton Terrace, Yoker, involving Orangemen and Catholics. There were a great many casualties and 21 people were detained by the police.[38] Further disturbances were reported in the *Clydebank Press* in December 1893, May 1894, October 1902 and August 1908.

The Irish question was certainly the most explosive national political issue in Clydebank before 1914. Although the formation of the burgh was hotly contested a general political consensus existed in municipal politics. Commissioners concentrated on administrative activity such as the development of burgh sanitation and water supply. Local employers dominated the Council over the period. The early 1900s, however, saw the first real cracks in the consensus. Growing support for Labour and the activities of housing pressure groups gave pointers to post-1914 political developments in Clydebank.

CHAPTER FOUR

Social Trends, 1886-1914

The new Burgh of Clydebank boasted a population of over 5,000 in 1886. By 1913 Clydebank's population had risen to over 43,000. The pace of the town's growth had earned it the nickname of 'the risingest burgh.' However, the influx of people into Clydebank to work in its developing shipbuilding industry and at Singer's factory made considerable demands on the new burgh in terms of social provision. The following sections on housing, health and welfare, education, religion, and leisure and recreation outline the major trends in the town's development.

Housing

Until 1871, the area surrounding Barns o' Clyde was largely rural and sparsely populated, dotted with country mansions, farm buildings, and little clusters of

Figure 4:1 *Late nineteenth-century view of thatched cottages on Dumbarton Road, Dalmuir which housed workers from the adjacent print works (beyond cottages on the right). The Duntocher Burn bridge is on the right and the Ross Memorial Church was later built on the site of the adjacent cottages. Mountblow Road is just out of the picture in the left foreground and the Dalmuir Quoiting Green is just beyond the cottages. The imposing tower of the Singer clock can be seen in the background.*

cottages which housed the workforces of small industries in Dalmuir, Whitecrook and Yoker.[1] However, when J. & G. Thomson decided to build homes for some of their workers next to the new Clydebank Shipyard's main gate on the south side of the Glasgow Road, they chose to erect tenements, the traditional form of urban housing in the West of Scotland. 'Thomson's Buildings' were two blocks of four storey buildings, which contained 126 flats and accommodated around 700 people after they were completed in 1872.[2] The tenements became the centre of a new industrial village, which grew rapidly after 1875 as building tradesmen, businessmen, lawyers and other trustees for heritable estates, and a variety of individuals and institutions seeking a 'solid' investment in land and property, acquired ground near the shipyard and built more houses for Thomson's employees.

The neighbouring countryside altered dramatically in appearance between 1871 and 1886. Thomson built only a score of new dwellings during these years, but in the early 1880s sold ground and made loans to property developers to build nearly 150 tenement homes which were erected in Cunard, Clyde and Union Streets and in Columba and Rosebery Places. The firm then leased the houses and sub-let them to men from their yard. Other builders erected tenements on their own account opposite the shipyard (and the new foundry which opened there in 1883) in the area lying between Hume and Canal Streets. Thomson's workers were also able to find accommodation further along Glasgow and Dumbarton Roads in new tenements as far west as Swindon Street.[3]

The building boom was not fuelled by the demand for homes from Thomson's workers alone. The Clyde Navigation Trust built six new tenements in Dalmuir in 1874, in what became Nairn Street, for 40 men from the repair yard. Napier, Shanks & Bell established a new shipyard at the western end of Yoker in 1877, and by 1886 there were dozens of tenements in the area lying between Elgin Street and Hamilton Terrace, providing homes for members of the shipbuilders' labour force. The construction of the Singer factory in Kilbowie provided an even greater impetus to housebuilding further north of the river. The American company built only two tenements to accommodate about 60 foremen, watchmen and firemen near the works. Property developers were quick to start work on many more, on Kilbowie Road and the roads leading off this main thoroughfare, as far north as Graham Street, as well as in the small village of Radnor Park, on top of Kilbowie Hill.[4] Thousands of Singer's employees travelled to the factory each day from their homes in Glasgow and the Vale of Leven, and there were so many men seeking homes closer to their workplace that the new houses were soon filled. The new Burgh of Clydebank boasted a population of over 5,000 in 1886, and there were about 1,000 houses within an area which, in 1871, had been inhabited by just 800 people and had contained little more than 100 dwellings.[5] The population continued to grow rapidly during the 20 years which followed the formation of the burgh, as the expansion of Clydebank's existing industries and the setting up of new ones created thousands of jobs. Land not taken up by industry and new parks was quickly bought up and built on by property developers.

The vast majority of the houses built in Clydebank after 1871 were tenement flats, mostly two apartment 'room and kitchens' and many one apartment 'single ends',[6] but there were other varieties of housing in the burgh. Villas began to appear along Duntocher Road after the opening of the Glasgow, Dumbarton & Helensburgh Railway, and Dalmuir Station, in 1858.

They were purchased or rented by business and professional men seeking homes in the country, away from the smog and bustle of Glasgow, but within easy reach, by train, of their offices in the city centre.[7] The Clyde Navigation Trust built seven villas in what became Reith Place, for senior staff from the repair yard in Dalmuir, and villas, detached and semi-detached houses and cottages, and 'cottage tenements' of two storeys, were built to accommodate managers and senior foremen from the shipyards.[8] Many of these 'gaffers' and senior members of staff were English or Irish, and were unaccustomed to and disliked tenement housing, and the shipyard owners came to believe that it was not a good thing for men in positions of authority to live cheek by jowl with those they supervised at work each day.[9] During the 1870s, some men from Thomson's yard enlisted the financial support of a building society and built cottage-style homes for themselves in Hamilton and Cameron Places.[10] John Brown & Co. built the Atlas Cottages in 1904, and William Beardmore & Co. bought and built a large number of cottages and villas in Dalmuir after 1905, but the senior men from the shipyards usually bought or rented their 'superior dwellings' from other property developers.[11] So, too, did the foremen and office staff who came to Clydebank to work for Singer and other new industries after 1886, as well as those from the professions, businessmen, and the prosperous traders, who became more numerous as the burgh grew in prosperity and population. By 1914 Clydebank's 'desirable residences' were concentrated in The Crescent and close to Beardmore's yard in Dalmuir, in the area of Upper Dalmuir lying to the east of Duntocher Road, in Montrose Street, around the western end of Barns Street in Whitecrook, and near John Brown's works and Rothesay Dock.[12] Most of these houses had their own gardens, single rather than shared entrances, and contained three or more rooms. They provided houses for the more well-to-do members of the community, but even prosperous 'Bankies' usually rented their accommodation. In 1913, Clydebank's Sanitary Inspector reported that less than 300 houses, or 3.4 per cent of those in the burgh, were owner-occupied.[13]

The housebuilding boom in Clydebank continued during the opening years of the twentieth century, and 1,700 new homes were built there between 1901 and 1906, providing a total of just under 5,000 to accommodate a population which rose from 18,654 to over 26,000 during the same period.[14] Nevertheless, the question of housing provision caused great concern among burgh officials. Because of the high demand for houses from the thousands of workers who still commuted to Clydebank each day, new houses were quickly snapped up and rents were comparatively high. The pressure for homes, and high rents, encouraged over-

Figure 4:2 *Rear of Old Church Place, Old Kilpatrick around 1907. In the background is the gable end of Hogg's building where the Ettrick Bar and car park now stand.*

crowding — from 1886 to 1906, an average of just over five people lived in each house in the burgh — and overcrowding was a factor in the high rate of incidences of infectious diseases.[15] Only further housebuilding could ease the shortage of accommodation and its attendant problems, but by 1906 there were only 62 acres within the original burgh boundaries which were free and considered to be suitable for housing.[16] The determination of Clydebank's officials to annexe adjoining lands in 1906 was due, to a considerable extent, to the perceived need for more land for new homes in the burgh.

The extension of Clydebank's boundaries in 1906 brought 542 acres of land, around 2,000 houses and nearly 10,000 people into the burgh.[17] The largest new housing estate in the annexed areas was just south of the village of Radnor Park. Robert McAlpine & Sons had returned to Clydebank in 1904 to build the first of a series of massive extensions to the Singer factory. As the demand for houses in the area remained high, and the prospects for the continued prosperity of Clydebank's industries seemed good, the firm decided to invest in 140 acres of land on the west side of Kilbowie Hill, just beyond the burgh boundary at that time, and to build houses there.[18] By 1906, McAlpine had built 151 tenements and a few semi-detached houses, and could offer 1,200 homes for let in the area bounded by Kilbowie Road, Second Avenue, First Terrace and Crown Avenue.[19] The estate soon acquired the nickname 'The Holy City', because the view from the south of the white roughcasted, flat-roofed buildings, stretching in long terraces across the slope of the hill, reminded observers of postcard pictures of Jerusalem.[20] The Holy City had its critics. Burgh officials claimed that McAlpine chose the site to avoid having to pay the burgh's rates, even though most of their tenants worked in Clydebank and used its municipal services. They complained, too, that by building beyond the jurisdiction of the burgh's Dean of Guild Court, the firm was able to use materials and build to specifications which would not have been permitted in Clydebank. McAlpine supporters responded by saying that the Holy City houses offered equally high standards of comfort, sanitation and shelter as those in the burgh, and pointed out that the average annual rent for a McAlpine home was just £9, £2.10s less than the average in Clydebank.[21] Rents in the Holy

Figure 4:3 *This view shows the nearly completed Holy City from the south looking towards First Terrace. Radnor Street is on the left and the band are playing in a bandstand gifted to the community by Robert McAlpine.*

City remained lower than the burgh average after the estate became part of the fifth ward of Clydebank in 1906.[22]

Tenement building came to a virtual standstill in Clydebank after the onset of a deep recession in the local shipbuilding and engineering trades in 1907.[23] Even in 1911, when the local economy had begun to recover from the effects of the slump, a staggering 1,340 of the 8,658 houses in the burgh lay empty.[24] The slow rate of housebuilding did not have too great an effect on overcrowding at first — because of unemployment, many men and their families left the burgh, and Clydebank's population rose only slightly to 37,548 in 1911.[25] However, investors' faith in the future of Clydebank's industrial progress had been shaken by the depression, at a time when other opportunities for investment, offering greater returns than house rents, were opening up.[26] McAlpine, the largest landlord in the burgh, built few tenements after 1906, and concentrated instead on creating a small estate of cottage tenements and concrete villas on land to the west of the Holy City, in what was christened 'The Better Land'.[27] The Town Council, which built 25 houses in Barns and Richmond Streets in 1906, found difficulty at first in attracting tenants to the new housing and proved unwilling to show a lead to private developers by building more before the end of the First World War.[28] Only William Beardmore & Co. embarked on major housebuilding ventures after 1907. The firm purchased some villas and tenements near the Dalmuir Naval Construction Works, but paid builders to erect the majority of the 274 homes they owned in 1914, in the area lying between Scott and Dunn Streets and in Agamemnon Street.[29] In 1914, Beardmore set up the Dalmuir and West of Scotland Estates Co. to build more tenements, and the new company started work that year on the first of 51 new tenement buildings which were erected in new streets around Castle Square by 1918.[30]

A great deal of attention has been focussed on Clydebank's housing problems during the 1920s, and explanations for these problems have been sought in the peculiar difficulties faced by property owners and builders during the First World War. Yet Clydebank's housing situation had caused concern since the 1880s and remained as a blight on the generally prosperous image of Scotland's 'risingest burgh'. The houses themselves were generally of a good standard for the day, as most of the buildings were less than 20 years old in 1914. The Dean of Guild Court had been largely successful in preventing shoddy, 'jerry-built' homes being erected, and ensuring that new houses were adequately supplied with drainage and, after 1899, with a separate water closet for each family.[31] But it proved

Figure 4:4 *By the late nineteenth century the north side of Dumbarton Road had taken on a typical urban appearance. The need to provide housing for the workers of the newly established Beardmore shipyard resulted in the company, along with other speculative builders, instigating a speedy building programme. By the end of the First World War further tenements had been built on the south side of Dumbarton Road, thus completing a landscape which remained virtually unchanged until the Blitz.*

impossible to control overcrowding. The recovery of Clydebank's industries and the renewed growth of the population was not accompanied by a revival of housebuilding, and only 50 new houses were built in 1912 and 1913.[32] By 1913, there were just over 8,000 houses for a population which had risen to over 43,000.[33] It was reported that 38 per cent of 'Bankies' lived in houses where there were more than three people to each room, and only 31 per cent lived less than two to a room, while the average number of people to each room in the burgh was 2.32 — figures which were worse than the equivalent average for Glasgow, or for Scotland as a whole.[34] A short burst of renewed housebuilding activities in 1914 and 1915 did little to alleviate the situation, because of an influx of men and women to work in the burgh's munitions industries during the war.[35] When there was no improvement in the situation after 1918, and tenants were faced with higher rents for their overcrowded 'homes fit for heroes to live in', it was little wonder that housing became a controversial and emotive political issue in Clydebank during the 1920s.

Health and Welfare

Health care has been a fundamental concern of society since pre-biblical times. In Scotland, the 1845 Poor Law Amendment Act established a network of Parochial Boards, each empowered to appoint one or more medical officers to treat the sick poor of an individual parish. In order to meet the needs of an expanding population Old Kilpatrick made separate appointments to the western and northern districts. The loss of the Parochial Board minutes prior to 1868[36] makes it difficult to chart the development of medical services, although we do know that at least eight doctors fulfilled the role of parochial or sanitary medical officer (PMO) in the period 1855 to 1880.[37]

The first sign of the continuity which became a feature of the Clydebank medical scene was the appointment as PMO of Dr Adam Gilmour of Duntocher in

SPLENDID OPENING FOR A YOUNG MEDICAL MAN.

Figure 4:5 *Reproduced from* Punch *1848.*

June 1866. After his death in 1895 the vacancy was filled by his son, Dr John Gilmour, who was later joined by his sister, also a Glasgow medical graduate.[38] A similar evolution can be traced in the town of Clydebank itself. Recognising the opportunities afforded by J. & G. Thomson's expanding shipyard, and by the incipient removal of Singer's works from Glasgow to Kilbowie, Dr James Stevenson — himself the son of an engineer — put up his plate in Clydebank shortly after he qualified in 1878. Within a few years Stevenson had established himself as medical officer to the North British Chemical Company works and to a number of Friendly Societies with members in the shipyard. On the resignation in 1897 of Dr John Wylie, medical officer to the Burgh since its formation, Stevenson was the only local practitioner to possess the requisite Diploma in Public Health, and thus replaced Wylie without the irritation of competing against other candidates.[39]

Before his lamented death in 1910 Stevenson had the satisfaction of taking his two sons, James (MB ChB, 1906) and William (MB ChB, 1908) into partnership with him.[40] By this date the single-handed practitioner of 1880 had been replaced by 11 doctors in Clydebank proper, with half as many again located in the parish as a whole. Some constituted a fairly transient population, either failing to establish a successful practice or passing on to more lucrative pastures. A significant number, including those like the Stevensons who were returning to their native heath, remained to form a stable nucleus devoting the bulk of their careers to the Burgh of Clydebank.

Figure 4:6 *Dr James Stevenson, Medical Officer for the Parish of Old Kilpatrick 1895-1909 and Medical Officer for the Burgh of Clydebank in succession to Dr Wylie, 1897-1909.*

Health care under the Poor Law had two fundamental aims: it was intended to provide basic medical relief for sick paupers at minimum cost and to prevent the spread of infectious diseases. In the early years of the Old Kilpatrick Parochial Board the majority of problems in both of these spheres appear to have centred on the village of Duntocher. After the arrival of Thomson's shipyard in the early 1870s this focus began to change. On 7 January 1873 the Board, acting in its capacity as a Local Authority under the Public Health (Scotland) Act of 1867, granted permission for a 50-person common lodging house at the Clydebank Shipbuilding Yard. Within a decade sanitary conditions in the burgeoning town were a major cause for concern. The investigation of a fever outbreak in Clydebank led to a scathing indictment by Dr Gilmour in November 1883 of the conditions prevailing in Keyden, Strang & Co.'s property, where the privies were 'simply disgraceful'. The facilities at Canal Street were no better in Gilmour's estimation and 'the wonder to me is how the people can use them at all, but I suppose it is only necessity that compels them.'[41] In the following year Gilmour's colleague, Dr John Cameron, highlighted an equally alarming tendency when he reported his concern over an outbreak of scarlet fever, exacerbated by careless parents in the densely crowded tenements who allowed their children to mingle freely with their compatriots while in the grip of scarlatina.[42]

Other hazards followed in the wake of urbanisation and industrialisation. Many young widows were admitted to the poor roll, often as a result of losing their husbands in some industrial accident, and the incidence of mental illness, classified bluntly as insanity, appears to rise in the shipyard community during the 1880s.[43] Time and again, however, attention would return to the problem of infection.

Attention thus far has been focussed on family doctors and on statutory measures to deal with paupers and with sanitation. Hospital treatment for the majority of the working population — the 'respectable poor' — was provided in the voluntary hospitals or infirmaries, funded primarily by philanthropic subscriptions aided by employees' contributions from industrial and other works. The earliest of these large acute general hospitals were established in the major population centres such as Glasgow, Greenock and Paisley. A more modest alternative, suited to smaller communities, sprang to prominence in the west of Scotland in the 1890s with the opening of cottage hospitals in towns such as

Dumbarton (1890), Johnstone (1893), Helensburgh (1895) and Rothesay (1897).

Clydebank's failure to join this movement can be explained by the special relationship which it enjoyed with the Glasgow Western Infirmary. From 1891 onwards the Infirmary admitted more patients from Clydebank than from any other area outwith the Glasgow boundaries, including such great population centres as Paisley. In return, the Clydebank workforce at Thomson's (later John Brown's) shipyard and Singer's factory responded magnificently. From 1887 onwards their annual subscriptions were surpassed only by those from the Fairfield's yard, and those three stood head and shoulders above all others in their support for the Infirmary. With the arrival of Beardmore's works at Dalmuir in 1906 the Western gained another substantial Clydebank contributor.

In addition to these donations by organised labour, Clydebank was in the forefront when the Western introduced a system of 'Honorary Local Treasurers' in the early 1880s to solicit funds from interested individuals living outwith Glasgow. Charles Leiper, a local banker, accepted this challenge on behalf of 'Clydebank' in 1884. Although the sums raised were modest in comparison with those obtained in the yards, Leiper's initiative was a significant one. His first annual list of subscribers, compiled two years before the formation of the burgh, included names from Dalmuir, Duntocher and Yoker, as well as from Clydebank itself. Clearly, the care of the inhabitants of the parish of Old Kilpatrick was, for the future, to be masterminded from Clydebank.[44]

On the instructions of the Local Government Board (overseers of the Poor Law) the Parochial Board in the early 1870s actively sought temporary accommodation for a hospital to meet the needs of a threatened outbreak of cholera; the proximity of foreign vessels moored at Bowling lent a certain urgency to such plans. As early as 1874 — prompted by an outbreak of smallpox and possibly hastened by the rapid population growth around the nascent industrial community — the Board began to give serious consideration to the erection of an infectious diseases hospital, possibly in combination with the authorities in Dumbarton, Cardross and Bonhill. By June 1876 these plans had been abandoned in favour of an arrangement with Maryhill, Hillhead and Partick Joint Hospital, opened at Knightswood in the following year.[45] The Board also availed itself of the services of the Belvidere Fever Hospital in Glasgow, though not always with satisfactory results. In June 1881 an outbreak of scarlatina in Milton was traced back to a patient discharged home from Belvidere with parts of her clothing not properly disinfected.[46] The parochial doctors were not amused.

One consequence of the granting of burgh status was the attempt by the Commissioners for Clydebank to be designated as the local authority, against the wishes of the Parochial Board. In January 1893 this was enough of a reality to enable the burgh sanitary committee to draw up plans for a 12 or 16-bed infectious (ID) hospital, stimulated by fresh warnings of possible epidemics of smallpox and cholera. It was also estimated that such an amenity would be cheaper than the current arrangements with Knightswood. In the event, the announced withdrawal (through lack of accommodation) of facilities at Knightswood in January 1894 hastened the search for an alternative. In the same month the Renfrew Commissioners proposed a joint hospital to be erected by the burghs of Renfrew and Clydebank and by the Upper District of Renfrew County Council.[47] A site was acquired at Blawarthill and an agreement drawn up to share the costs and the management in proportion to the respective populations. On this basis Clydebank was obliged to meet 57 per cent of the bills and in return provided eight of the 14 hospital board members.[48] Problems with tradesmen and subcontractors delayed completion of the 30-bed hospital, which was formally opened in February 1897. Making the best of this involuntary and frustrating delay, the hospital committee erected a plaque at the entrance to commemorate the purely fortuitous conjunction with Queen Victoria's Diamond Jubilee. It was perhaps an indication

Figure 4:7 *Originally built as an infectious diseases hospital, the function of the Renfrew and Clydebank Joint Hospital at Blawarthill was extended shortly after the inception of the NHS and its transfer of responsibility to the Western Regional Hospital Board, to include TB, chest and isolation beds. In 1967 Blawarthill was converted to a geriatric hospital.*

of the Commissioners' priorities that the decision to proceed with the erection of Clydebank's municipal buildings was announced three weeks *after* the admission of the first patient to the new fever hospital.[49]

In the course of the next five years Blawarthill developed an enviable reputation for the quality of training afforded its nurses, with no fewer than three appointed as matrons of English fever hospitals by September 1902. Encouraged by the success of the venture, and by the necessity of expanding the service, the Clydebank representatives proposed a 54-bed extension in April 1902. Initially opposed by Renfrew Town Council, who fell into line after the intervention of the Local Government Board in the spring of 1903, the plans were ultimately scaled down to provide an additional 34 beds. The new wards were opened on 13 October 1906, at a ceremony graced by the provision of 'cake and wine, with tea, etc.'.[50] The timing could hardly have been bettered. Little more than six weeks later, on 29 November 1906, the Burgh of Clydebank was extended to incorporate Kilbowie, Radnor Park and North Dalmuir, thus increasing the population from c26,000 to c36,000 overnight. Two months later the network of ID hospitals in Dunbartonshire was again extended with the opening of the 22-bed Duntocher Hospital. Funded jointly by Milngavie Town Council and by Dunbarton County Council, Duntocher was designed by R. A. Bryden, architect of numerous hospital buildings including Lennox Joint ID (now Birdston) Hospital and Blawarthill.[51]

The creation of the Burgh of Clydebank coincided with the national expansion of public health provision and, in particular, the development of an extensive local network of infectious diseases hospitals. This period also brought a marked rise in the number of Scottish medical practitioners; 1886 was, again coincidentally, the first year in which the University of Glasgow capped more than 100 medical graduates. Both of these factors were crucial to the development of Clydebank's medical services in the first two decades of the burgh's existence. Few of the inhabitants, however, had any inkling in 1907 of the fundamental changes to be introduced by the 1911 National Insurance Act.

Education

When, in April 1873, the Old Kilpatrick School Board held its first meeting, the population of the parish was a mere 6,247. There were 1,167 children of school age (5-13 years), but more than a third were not attending any school. Of those, 240

Figure 4:8 *View of Clydebank Terrace, referred to locally as 'Thomson's Buildings', one of two blocks of four storey tenements built adjacent to the main shipyard gate by J. & G. Thomson for their workers. It was in this building, at No. 13, that Mrs Pitblado ran her Clydebank Adventure School (also known as 'Pitbluidy's Schule') for the children of the workers.*

were unable to read and a larger number were unable to write. There were nine existing one-teacher schools, ranging from the three church foundations (of the Free Church and the Catholic Church, and the parish school conducted under the aegis of the Church of Scotland), to three small adventure schools conducted by married women. The Education (Scotland) Act of 1872 required elected school boards in every parish and burgh to provide adequate elementary schooling for all children aged five to 13 years and moreover, to compel their attendance.

The Board's members, elected triennially, were well placed to carry out these objectives. Throughout its history, from 1873 until 1919, the Board was dominated by a combination of the industrial, landowning and religious leaders of the community; early chairmen were James White (later Lord Overtoun), Captain R. D. Buchanan (who conducted his own Episcopalian school in Dunglass Castle), and James R. Thomson (chairman of the shipyard of J. and G. Thomson). Industrialists and landowners occupied around four of the seven Board seats until 1900 when men and women from the professions assumed leadership: people like Dr James Stevenson, medical officer of health for Old Kilpatrick Parish and Clydebank Burgh at the turn of the century.

The clergy were well represented. There was always a Catholic priest and a Church of Scotland minister, and others were drawn from the Free Church, the United Presbyterian Church and the Congregational Evangelical Union. With the exception of Labour, candidates for the Board did not stand as representing the normal political parties, but, instead, their churches. The Board joined two other institutions of local government which were dominated by religious divisions: the Board of Heritors and the Parochial Board. These three authorities were closely connected; indeed, the School Board's first Clerk and Treasurer was Robert Barr, the Parochial Board's Inspector of the Poor.

The Board members, as in many small Scottish parishes, ran the educational affairs in the early years very much themselves. They were not given to much forward planning; school holidays were set two weeks beforehand. With virtually no administrators, these were money-conscious and often penny-pinching managers. They conducted most of the complicated and sensitive negotiations over the transfer of schools, and personally worked on the plans for new schools.

The early years were relatively easy, with the number of eligible children in the parish increasing modestly from 1,167 to 1,483 between 1873 and 1879. The existing one-teacher schools had to be used in the early years, though a new building was acquired in Clydebank, the 'Bothy School', a low stone building with few windows where the teacher, John Fulton (who was to go on to be the leading head teacher in the parish), was said to have had to knock out a window himself. The schools taken over by the Board were Protestant church schools. The adventure schools, including the room-and-kitchen school run by Mrs Pitblado for shipyard workers' children, were poorly regarded by the state system and closed. The Catholic Church, fearing that its distinctive religious teaching would suffer under Presbyterian control, elected not to participate, and the Catholic school at Duntocher, like all other Catholic schools in Scotland, stayed out of the school-board system. However, Catholic members were elected to enable the Board to supervise compulsory attendance of all children whether at state, church or private schools.

Under Old Kilpatrick Board, the teachers collected and kept pupils' fees, and the Government education grant came to them directly; the Board merely paid the teachers an additional small emolument, drawn from the rates. Education was a cottage industry under the Board. The aims were modest: to get pupils through the doors, and to teach then the three Rs (and a fourth — religion). Apart from the

Figure 4:9 *The 'Bothy School' was the first school in Clydebank run under the auspices of the Old Kilpatrick School Board. Situated at the north-east corner of the Thomson shipyard, it was opened in 1873 and provided schooling until the new purpose-built school in Kilbowie Road was completed.*

Clerk and Treasurer, the only other non-teaching official to be employed was Donald McMurphy, the School Board Officer. His primary task was to inculcate habits of school attendance in the parish's children and their parents. This was one of the thornier problems for the Scottish school boards in the 1870s and 1880s — and one, incidentally, that did not arise in England and Wales until compulsory education was introduced there in 1880. The attendance rate on the formation of the Board in 1873 was under 60 per cent. In July of that year, handbills were distributed telling parents that compulsory classes 'will be enforced throughout the Parish from and after the 11th August next' when the schools re-opened after the holidays. The handbills also told parents the fees they would be obliged to pay. The sums were substantial for working-class households, ranging from 10d. per month for Standards (Primary years) I, II and III, 1/- for Standards IV and V, to 1/3d. for Standard VI.[53] Parents too poor to pay had to apply to the Parochial Board for assistance — a demeaning experience for many 'respectable' parents and guardians who fought hard to raise children without recourse to 'the Parish'.

The coming of compulsory education was far from welcome to many parents and children. Previously, education had been taken principally during winter months, leaving spring and summer months free for older children, i.e. those above nine years of age, to seek employment. Above this age children became highly employable in all manner of industries and commercial undertakings. The income children could generate, though modest, was a vital supplement to working-class families. Because of this, poverty was a compelling reason for children's non-attendance. Fees continued to be charged until 1889 (with girls being charged more than boys until 1881), placing parents in a 'Catch 22' situation: being required by law to send their children to school, yet being unable in many cases to set aside the money needed. The Board became progressively less lenient in dealing with this issue. In 1873, it waived fees in the case of one parent, stipulating:

> 'In respect that he has ten of a family, the eldest only eleven years of age, and that his wages are only 24/- a week, the Teacher has granted the request on the distinct understanding that should many more applications of the like nature be made the privilege would be withdrawn.'[54]

But in 1878 John Fulton complained to the Board that many of his children were not paying their fees; this was important to him, as two-thirds of teachers' income at that time came directly from that source. In response, the Board told him 'to refuse admittance, and then let the Attendance Officer deal with the parents under the [Education] Act'.[55] Working children were ordered back to school. One mother in 1879 was too impoverished to pay her daughter's school fees, but the Parochial Board refused poor relief because her estranged husband had taken up residence in another parish. The Board often acted like an old-fashioned kirk session. One defaulting father failed to appear in 1876, but his wife had to listen while the Rev John Stark vilified him as a drunkard.

It is not surprising in these circumstances that there was a high level of 'defaulting'. At one peak, in the winter of 1882-3, there were 303 defaulting children in the parish; only 57 per cent of pupils at Duntocher Roman Catholic School were in attendance on an average day. Hundreds of parents were summoned to special defaulters' meetings. Defaulters — legally the parents, not the children — were summoned before the Board, and failure to ensure their children's attendance led to prosecution. At the JPs' court in Dumbarton they could expect in 1894 to be fined five or ten shillings or seven days in gaol; if they lived in the burgh the Clydebank Police Court fined 15 shillings to one pound or up to ten days imprisonment. It was not merely amongst poor families that defaulting was prevalent. Of 104 adults summoned between June 1899 and March 1900 because their children or wards were not attending school, 66 were semi-skilled or unskilled

Figure 4:10 *Clydebank's first purpose-built school situated to the west of Kilbowie Road on land feued from Alexander Dunn Pattison. Within 10 years of its opening in 1876 it had become inadequate to meet the needs of the rapidly growing population. In this view, John Fulton, Headmaster, can be seen alongside pupils in the school playground.*

workers (including 54 labourers), 11 were widows, and 26 were skilled workers (including 14 riveters, drillers, riggers and fitters).

Rapid demographic change made the School Board's task more difficult. The parish population stood at 6,247 in 1873, rising modestly to 7,514 in 1879, but then shot up to 14,584 in 1888 and to 23,698 in 1897. The rise was most acute in the eastern end of the parish — in Yoker, Dalmuir, Duntocher, Radnor Park and especially Clydebank itself — where the numbers rose from 1,674 in 1882 to 9,395 in 1897. In terms of children of school age, the numbers rose from 1,167 in 1873 to 5,402 in 1900; in Clydebank the numbers increased eightfold in the last 18 years of the century.

Not only did the schools taken over in 1873 become quickly insufficient, but even the comfortable and well-built Board schools were overcrowded. The major crisis came at the peak of population growth in 1885 when nearly 1,300 houses were being constructed in Clydebank, Dalmuir and Radnor Park. The Board admitted that 'the Compulsory clauses [of the Education Act] have already become inoperative in these portions of the parish'.[56] Her Majesty's Inspector of Schools, William Jolly, wrote of Clydebank School in February 1886:

> 'I found the school very much overcrowded; 430 being present, with accommodation for 408, and an average of 440. Temporary relief is urgently and immediately required and is easily available in a neighbouring hall. The ventilation was *very bad*, all the worse with the crowding . . . . The floor was very dirty in all the rooms and should be better and more frequently washed. The Girls' Offices [toilets] were wet and dirty . . .'[57]

Schools were constantly being changed. Clydebank school was rebuilt in 1886-8 to a grand design with magnificent staircase, chandeliers, and busts of the members of the 1873 Board. Some £20,000 was spent on it, the dream of the Rev John Stark following the American idea of the large central school. But other facilities suffered. Temporary schools were almost constantly in use in the late nineteenth century: one at Dalmuir Masonic Lodge (a school started by the community for which the Board, after several years of pressure, was forced to pay), a large shop ('Mr Leckie's') in Kilbowie Road, and St Columba's Church (which held the Elgin Street School infant class in 1897).

Even after 1900 the expansion of schools was slow. For the Catholic Church, still outside the state system, Duntocher School was joined by one at Our Holy Redeemer's in 1889 (replaced six years later, and with an annexe for senior pupils

Figure 4:11 *A member of the first School Board in 1873 until his death in 1889, the Rev. John Stark of the Duntocher West UF Church probably had the greatest influence on early education in the burgh. In 1886, after much debate about future educational requirements, the decision was taken to replace the Clydebank School, which was too small, with a larger school, capable of holding 1500 pupils. The new school turned out to be a showpiece, costing £20,000 instead of the original £13,000 and this, along with the original argument that the new school was too large, led enraged ratepayers to march through the streets in protest. The Rev. Stark then had the dubious distinction of having his effigy burned by the angry mob. The new school was opened in 1888 but it was not until after Stark's death in 1889 that he was proved correct and recognised as the great innovator he was.*

opened in 1913). The Old Kilpatrick Board was equally slow, even as government signalled the need to expand facilities — especially secondary schooling. Whilst new elementary schools were opened at Radnor Park (1900), Boquhanran (1906) and Dalmuir (a replacement, opened 1908), it was not until 1911 that a separate annexe for post-elementary, or 'Higher Grade' education was added to Clydebank School. To this centre, some 40 advanced pupils came from all over Old Kilpatrick parish to be trained to compete for scholarships, to go on, eventually, to Glasgow University. But Clydebank produced few scholarship boys before 1914, and the town had a reputation for low educational standards. The first graduate teacher was not appointed until 1889, and pupil teachers and low-paid assistants were the mainstay of the profession in the burgh until the 1910s.

The Clydebank schools were notorious with the government inspectors for their dirtiness and want of proper lavatory facilities (dry closets being still the norm until the 1890s). The educational regime had an overbearing preoccupation with rigid discipline — quietness in class being deemed more worthy than ability to think or even read and write. The cane was apparently much used, and the Board was so disturbed by the number of complaints from parents that it was banned and a tawse (or belt) supplied in each school. Matters were not assisted by low-quality government inspectors who, before 1900, issued reports like one of 1890 on Clydebank School which chided the teacher, 'talking was much indulged in throughout changes [of lesson], a habit that must be cured to gain the highest grant in future.'[58] In response, the teacher installed in the classroom, at his own expense, a harmonium to 'assist the marching'. Success was rewarded at the next inspection:

'Discipline becomes firmer and was generally very creditable, except for talking in some classes, and irregularities in the playground. Class drill has also improved'.[59]

But by 1899 inspectors were demanding different results; it was discovered that one teacher had kept a class going over the same reading book, again and again, for a year and a half — a book from which 'all freshness and interest have long vanished'. Teachers were being asked by the early years of this century to inculcate 'intelligence' in their pupils. But despite the abolition of pupil teachers in 1906, the unwillingness of the School Board to increase spending substantially meant that it was not until after the First World War that the Clydebank schools started to open up significant opportunities for educational advancement.

Figure 4:12 *Circa 1900 Our Holy Redeemer's Church moved from Kilbowie Road to a site on Glasgow Road on which they erected a two storey building which served as both church and school. In 1902 the present building, seen above, was erected, at which time the former premises (seen behind the new church) was wholly utilised as a school.*

Religion[60]

Long before the establishment of 'Tamson's Toon' in the 1880s, the district was religiously diverse. The Church of Scotland, the established state church, was represented by the Parish Kirk at Old Kilpatrick. Due to shortage of church accommodation, the refusal of the heritors (landowners) to build churches for villagers in the east end of the parish, and the failure to consult parishioners about the choice of new ministers, dissenting Presbyterian congregations were formed by disgruntled evangelical textile workers, colliers and tradesmen: the Secession and Relief Churches in the late eighteenth century, and Free Churches at the Disruption of 18 May 1843 when about a third of the clergy and adherents of the Church of Scotland walked out. In addition, William Dunn's cotton mills at Faifley, Duntocher and Hardgate had attracted a Catholic community of some 750 Irish immigrants, leading to the foundation of St Mary's Catholic Chapel-school, Duntocher, in 1841.

But urbanisation in the south-east of the parish after 1875 necessitated a spate of church-building for the incoming population from Govan, Glasgow and elsewhere. Between 1872 and 1897, practically all the new churches were built on or very close to Dumbarton and Glasgow Roads: such as St James' Church of Scotland (1876); the Union Church (1877), an unusual foundation run jointly by the Free and United Presbyterian Churches, and locally called the 'Standalane Kirk'; the Hamilton Free Church of Scotland (1884); the Methodist Church (1887); the first Our Holy Redeemer's Catholic Church (1889) at the foot of Kilbowie Road; Morison Memorial Evangelical Union Church (1892); the Baptist Church (1892); North Bank Street Free Church (1896); St Columba's Scottish Episcopal Church (1896); and the Clydebank West Free Church (1897). In nearly every case, these churches were built after small congregations had met together for a few years in hired halls, schools, or in members' homes.

From the start, Clydebank churches were affected by the continuous renewal of the built-up area. After the initial wave of church-building in the 1880s, three

Figure 4:13 *At the time of the Disruption in 1843 the Rev. Matthew Barclay resigned his charge at the Old Kilpatrick Parish Church and, along with a large proportion of his congregation, formed the Barclay Free Church. A very popular man, Barclay was very active in local affairs, especially in the field of education, and on his death in 1865 he bequeathed a sum of money to set up a trust for educational purposes. This view, taken from the old wooden canal bridge, shows the Barclay Church and Manse on the corner of Dumbarton Road and Barclay Street, Old Kilpatrick.*

Figure 4:14 *The second oldest church in the burgh after St. James', the original Union Church was situated on the north side of Dumbarton Road, west of the 'Caley' bridge at 'Standalane'. Completed in 1877, it was demolished in 1892 to make way for the new North British Railway and a new church was built directly opposite on the south side of Dumbarton Road.*

congregations were bought out and moved by the North British Railway Company in 1893-5 to make way for the Dalmuir line: Our Holy Redeemer's, the Union Church and the Episcopal congregation in Canal Street. Church-building continued as the burgh grew. The United Presbyterians were the first to arrive on Kilbowie Hill, followed in 1897 by St John's-on-the-Hill Church of Scotland with a Church in 1904. St Stephen's RC Church in Dalmuir was built in 1907-9. Radnor Park Church of Scotland started in 1895, its congregation almost doubling with the erection of McAlpine's 'Holy City' in 1905-6, and Radnor Park Congregational Church in 1909, with a replacement church in 1911.

In a religious census carried out in 1891, there were 11 places of worship in the burgh with a total membership-adherence of 4,745 (or 72 per cent of the adult population), with those attending at least once on a Sunday numbering 3,760 (or 56 per cent).[61] With this kind of support, the churches were mighty bastions of 'respectability', attacking 'rough' and 'immoral' activities like drinking alcohol. An unofficial plebiscite in 1893 seemed to show that 66 per cent of adults in the burgh were opposed to the granting of more drinks licences.[62] The law supported the puritanism of the churches; drunkenness on the Sabbath was much more severely dealt with than on any other day of the week, with the Fiscal demanding in 1900 that two men found drunk and incapable outside Hamilton Memorial Church suffer the 'full penalty' due in 'a Sunday case' — a forty shilling fine or 21 days in prison.[63] In 1909, the United Free Church Presbytery attacked the Caledonian Railway Company's extension of Sunday train and steam-boat travel from the East of Scotland to the Clyde coast as 'an unwarranted encroachment on the Sabbath rest of their employees'.[64]

The influence of religion was extended by the role of religious voluntary organisations which were aimed at different age-groups and sexes. For the young there were the Bands of Hope attached to nearly every Protestant congregation in the burgh, providing at weekday evening meetings lectures on the benefits of teetotalism, with all members taking the pledge of total abstinence. For Catholic children (and adults) there was the equivalent League of the Cross — the earliest Clydebank branch formed in 1888 at Our Holy Redeemer's, meeting in a special League Hall at the foot of Kilbowie Road; by 1895 the branch had 350 members. Total abstinence was mandatory at the turn of the century in the Foundry Boys' and Girls' Society and in the Boys' Brigade.

The temperance theme was implicit in virtually every one of the enormous range of religious organisations formed in the burgh before the First World War: the YMCA, YWCA and Young Men's and Girls' Guilds, the Women's Guild (Church of Scotland), the Free Church Guild, the Gospel Temperance Association (Union Church), and a glut of literary societies. So also with friendly and benefit societies: the Sons of Temperance with a branch in Radnor Park by 1909, the Independent Order of Rechabites with a tent, 'The Hope of the Hill', at Radnor Park, the Order of Druids, the Mistletoe Lodge, meeting in the shipyard dining hall, and the International Order of Good Templars which had a branch at Radnor Park United Presbyterian Church. The Lodge organisation was important amongst male artisans, and assisted in the creation of group identity and the promotion of moral values of thrift, self-help and religious respectability. It also provided ethnic and religious identity. Amongst Catholics there were the Order of Hibernians and the Irish National Foresters with meetings usually presided over by the local priests.

Religious organisations provided a varied diet of pastimes. There were talks by ministers and lay speakers. In 1893, a course of six lectures to the Hamilton Memorial Free Church Guild tackled the controversial subject of recent Egyptian archaeological exploration which was challenging the literal interpretation of the Bible. There were Saturday and holiday excursions. In 1891, the Union Church picnic took the 8.10am. train from Kilbowie to Balloch and thence by steamer to Luss, whilst Radnor Park Church's Sunday-school excursion in the same year took 300 children and a brass band to Garscadden House where games and races were held in the grounds. By far the most common form of entertainment, though, was the musical evening of sacred songs and instrumental tunes. The Free Church Mothers' Meeting in December 1894 entertained 300 working-class women to tea with recitations and songs from the Mission Choir. Similarly, though at a different

Figure 4:15 *This view of the 'Holy City' shows the recently built Radnor Park Congregational Church on the left. Originally meeting in members' houses, the first church was opened in 1909 in First Terrace. It rapidly became too small and the above church was opened in Green Street in 1911.*

social level, the leading lights in the Clydebank YWCA held a 'tea' of sacred music and addresses in March 1900 at the North British Station Hotel, presided over by the wife of the British Linen Bank manager and with Lady Overtoun the principal speaker. 'Respectable' leisure between 1890 and 1914 was composed of a hectic succession of such evenings — often purely long programmes of songs, solos, duets, and selections on the violin and piano — always conducted, as the *Clydebank Press* assured readers who might be concerned at the growth of levity in religion, with 'a high tone'.

Despite the importance of the churches in the community between the 1870s and 1914, religion was being affected by major changes in popular taste. Whilst the Sabbath remained a fairly puritanical affair in Scotland, secular leisure on other days was growing. The churches tried to compete with the 'sports revolution'; in April 1905, Morison Memorial EU Congregational Church established a Cycling Club, with the first Saturday 'run' to Dumbarton. The demand for 'light entertainment', and especially music, was forcing the churches to increase the use of brass bands and instrumental music; this was nowhere more apparent than in the celebration of New Year with the institution of not only watchnight services but also 'socials' — the one at the Union Church on Hogmanay 1894 being organised by the Gospel Temperance Association. Hogmanay was a favoured day for weddings, and the churches held wild celebration in check. A correspondent to the *Press* reported in 1901 that, 'on the whole, I would like to impress on your readers that the bringing in of the New Year in Clydebank was seemly and decorous.'[65]

Another change being felt in Clydebank was the increasing celebration of the Christian year. Old Kilpatrick Free Church conducted its first Harvest Thanksgiving service in 1893, and it was predicted that 'they are not likely to be the last of the kind in the district'.[66] Until the mid 1890s, only the Catholic and Episcopal churches conducted special Christmas Eve watchnight and Christmas Day services, and for the majority of people it was an ordinary working day. Clearly, there was anticipation of change, though disappointment at the lack of it, as in the following *Press* report:

'Christmas Day of 1894 has come and gone, but during the past week there has been little in the burgh to indicate that we have once more been passing through the season of "peace on earth and good will to men." Shops and shopwindows have been subjected to but slight attempts at decoration, while some merchants of the old school have forborne entirely to recognise the occasion in this respect; and those few members of our working classes who are fortunate enough to have employment, have pursued their daily tasks as usual . . . . The schools, too, remained open . . .'[67]

Six years later some Presbyterian churches had instituted watchnight services, shops were decorated for Christmas with 'caves' (now 'grottoes'), and Christmas trees were being erected. The giving of Christmas presents was being strongly encouraged by shopkeepers who gave guidance to the inexperienced as to what were suitable presents for each member of the family.

But traditional forms of religion remained important. Religious revivalism, which had affected Scottish communities periodically throughout the nineteenth century, was promoted from the earliest days of Clydebank's history by evangelical organisations. In the summer of 1886 and again in 1891, Mr T. W. Canning of a London-based organisation held two months of 'tent services' on the Old Show Ground, Clydebank, and at Gilmour's Mill, Duntocher — 'open-air tea and testimony' events 'well-attended and greatly blessed by God in the saving of many souls'.[68] In 1905 the Welsh revival of Evan Roberts was brought to the burgh by various Welsh evangelists, enjoying packed services of 'testimony' at the Morison Memorial Church. Revivalists continued to troop to the burgh — some from as far away as New York. Religious ideas and customs remained strong despite the great advance of liberal thinking and secular habits at the turn of the century.

Leisure and Recreation

Religion and the temperance movement played the greatest role in organised leisure during this early period, catering for both the spiritual and recreational needs of the community. Although leisure was often work-related or individually pursued, clubs, societies, excursions, soirees, lectures, lantern slide shows and, later, films were all provided under the auspices of the churches and the various temperance associations. Concerts, usually featuring songs, recitations and instrumental selections of a religious nature were held regularly and were presented by local church choirs, elocutionists and musicians as well as nationally and, occasionally, internationally known artistes. Attendances were often very high with over 800 people attending a St James' Parish Church concert in 1891.[69]

By the 1890s at least three churches had rambling clubs, and literary and lecture societies were numerous, the St James' Literary Society (1878) being the most successful and certainly the longest running. Children were also well catered for through Sabbath School activities, Kinderspiels and the Bands of Hope. The highlights for the children were probably the annual picnics, usually to fairly local places such as Cochno, and each attended by hundreds of people from the different congregations in the area. After the formation of the PSA (Pleasant Sunday Afternoon) by the Morison Memorial Church in 1905,[70] other churches quickly followed suit (the ILP being the only non-church organisation to do so) and many more activities, such as cycling and swimming were introduced. In 1909 the Morison Memorial Church set up Clydebank's first camera club.[71]

The late nineteenth century saw the beginnings of the uniformed youth organisations, which attracted large numbers of young people. The Boys' Brigade, founded in 1883, spread rapidly, and locally many companies were formed and disbanded between 1886 and 1909. The formation of the Boy Scout movement in 1907 resulted in a temporary slowing down of BB membership, but by the 1920s there were six local companies, i.e. 1st, 2nd and 3rd Clydebank, 1st and 2nd Old Kilpatrick and 1st Duntocher. Little is known about the early Boy Scout movement, but by 1909 three troops were registered locally, ie. the 42nd Glasgow (1st Clydebank), the 57th Glasgow (5th Clydebank) and the 84th Glasgow (3rd Clydebank). In 1910 Clydebank transferred from the Glasgow District to the

Figure 4:16 *1st Dalmuir Girl Guides Company on parade in 1927.*

Dunbarton County District resulting in the change from Glasgow to Clydebank company numbers. About this time the 1st Clydebank Troop re-formed as the 1st Clydebank (Singer Alpine) and by 1917 the 1st Dalnottar, 1st Duntocher, 2nd Clydebank and 4th Clydebank were in existence. During the First World War scouts from all over Britain, including Clydebank, gave valuable service to their country by acting as coastguards. The only Girl Guide company during this period seems to have been the Baden Powell (Radnor Park) Girl Guides who met in a hall in Third Terrace, and the the Old Kilpatrick Company which was formed in 1920.

At the turn of the century the municipal authority increased its role in leisure provision, and in 1902 the opening of the Town Hall provided a great improvement in facilities for all kinds of entertainment. The Hall Street Baths were opened in the same year and the Clydebank Amateur Swimming Club was immediately formed, increasing its membership from 44 to 210 during its first session. The Club's first annual gala was held in this inaugural year and by 1905 a water polo team was established, although it was unable to play matches in the new baths as the pool size was inadequate, a problem which grew more pressing in later years.

Figure 4:17 *The opening of the new Public Park in Dalmuir on 1 September, 1906 was a very grand affair. The festivities commenced with a huge parade of decorated floats, bands, marchers and local dignitaries which made its way along Dumbarton Road and up Mountblow Road to a temporary bridge at the "Dam Breast" on the Duntocher Burn. This was to become the western entrance to the Park and here Lady Overtoun cut a ceremonial ribbon before the crowds proceeded to a higher point in the Park where a platform had been erected for the official opening. This was done by Lord Overtoun, whose gift of £5,000 towards the cost of the Park certainly speeded up the provision of this popular amenity.*

In Dalmuir, on 1 September 1906, the burgh's first public park was opened by Lord and Lady Overtoun, the ground having been bought with money gifted by Lord Overtoun.[72] The following June, the fountain, a gift from ex-Provost Leckie, was erected, and the following month, the bandstand, a gift from Mr J. Dundas White MP, was opened. This bandstand was removed to Whitecrook Park in 1935 and again in 1983 to Three Queens Square where it was restored to its former beauty. A further 12½ acres, including Dalmuir House, were added to the park in 1908, the first of many future extensions. The park quickly became a focal point for the burgh with regular concerts and rallies and political gatherings, such as those held during the 1920s Rent Strike and the annual May Day celebrations.

Prior to the opening of the Public Library in Dumbarton Road, both Duntocher and Clydebank had part-time subscription libraries. Clydebank subscription library opened in 1879 utilising, at various times, a classroom in Clydebank School in Kilbowie Road and the Public Hall in Douglas Street, whilst the Duntocher library reopened in 1893 after many years closure and continued in fits and starts for several years. In 1880 Lawrence Watt was appointed to the voluntary post of librarian of Clydebank, a position he held until 1913 when the Public Library opened. In 1910, after much acrimonious debate, the Town Council agreed to accept a gift of £10,000 offered by Andrew Carnegie on condition that it adopted the Public Library Act. The new Clydebank library was officially opened in October 1913 with Harry G. Pincott as the first librarian, a position he held until his death in 1945.

In addition to the church affiliated societies there were many cultural organisations. For those of Highland origin several Highland Associations existed from the 1880s. In 1887, the first annual Highland Games were held, the earliest ones taking place at Hamilton Park, home of Clydebank FC, then Whitecrook Farm, before moving to the original Kilbowie Football Ground. Burns lovers had a choice of six clubs, Hardgate, probably the oldest club, being formed in 1866. The Barns o' Clyde Club, closely associated with the shipyard in its early years, was established in 1894 and had the longest existence, followed by the Duntocher Heron Club (1897), the Kilbowie Jolly Beggars Club (1897-8) and the Old Kilpatrick Club (c1900). In the early 1890s the Dalmuir Club disbanded, but in 1909 a group of people held a Burns Supper and continued to do so each year until 1914 when a vote was taken to form a fully constituted club. This club became the long established Dalmuir and Clydebank Burns Club.

Music also had wide appeal as was evident by the number of musical organisations in the area. Several lasted only a short time whilst others, such as the Clydebank Select Choir (1887), Clydebank and District Choral Union (1897-8), Clydebank and District Harmonic Society (1897) and the Clydebank Amateur Operatic and Dramatic Club (c1909) were amongst the more successful and longest lived. The jewel in the crown, however, was the Clydebank Male Voice Choir which has an interesting origin. In 1900 members of the Clydebank Rovers Rambling Club gathered at Central Station to bid farewell to a colleague who was emigrating. As they raised their voices in song to give their friend a rousing send-off, Charles Rennie was so impressed by their voices that he decided to form them into a male voice choir. The new choir made its public debut in 1901 as the Clydebank Rovers Male Voice Choir, but the following year 'Rovers' was dropped from its

Figure 4:18 *Lawrence Watt, a timekeeper in the Clydebank Shipyard for 60 years, held the position of librarian of the Clydebank Subscription Library from 1880-1913. In addition to his interest in the library, he was a very active member of the local community until his death in January 1939. He was auditor to the Clydebank Co-operative Society, a Past Master of the Loyal Order of Ancient Shepherds and an active member of the Union Church. He was best known, however, as a botanist, especially for his work on the flora of Dunbartonshire, and enjoyed a considerable national reputation. In 1932 he presented his herbarium to Clydebank High School.*

Figure 4:19 *The Clydebank Rovers 'De'ils Own' 8th annual outing to Inverbeg in 1905.*

name and it became the Clydebank Male Voice Choir. In 1905 the choir made the first of its many appearances at the St. Andrew's Halls, Glasgow. Under the conductorship of Thomas Allwood (1909-1919) the Choir progressed to its first competition, winning second place at the Glasgow Exhibition Festival in 1911, followed in 1912 by the Kilmarnock Cup, the first of many future successes.

The district also boasted several bands and orchestras including the Clydebank and District Orchestra, ILP Orchestra, Kilbowie Orchestra and, of course, the bands of the many uniformed youth organisations. The Salvation Army Band and Clydebank RC Band were amongst the most prominent of the religious bands. Although formed in 1914, the Singer Pipe Band did not really establish itself until the 1920s. However, probably the best known today are the Duntocher Brass (or Silver) Band, the Clydebank Burgh Band (Clydebank Brass Band until 1906) and the Singer Pipe Band. Originating around 1829 as the Spinners Band, a change of name led to the formation of the Duntocher Brass Band in the mid 1870s. When the Singer factory moved to Kilbowie, many men from areas with a strong brass band tradition followed and joined the Duntocher Band, which was closest to their new homes. Eventually the majority of the players were from Clydebank and Radnor Park. Later, when Singer offered them free practice premises nearer home in the Kilbowie Dining Hall, not surprisingly the Clydebank and Radnor Park men accepted. At the beginning of 1889 they abandoned Duntocher, taking their instruments with them.

However, certain Duntocher people contended that the instruments belonged to the Band and not to the individual players, and, after futile peaceful attempts at getting them back, in August 1889 they decided to retrieve them, by force if necessary. A large contingent marched from Duntocher to the Kilbowie Dining Hall where the defectors were practising, to demand the return of the instruments. According to James Hunter, bandmaster, when this was refused, 'the others then rushed on them and there was a general melee. [He] was seized by the throat and two others were kicked. There was a great deal of cursing and swearing, and there were between 200 and 300 people outside.'[73] On their march back to Duntocher feelings were high, and for the remainder of the night large crowds patrolled the streets of Duntocher. Eighteen people were arrested, while two Duntocher men were fined 10/6 each for assault and 14 were fined 5/- each for breach of the peace.[74] Later, a civil case was brought at Dumbarton Sheriff Court for the return of the instruments. Duntocher won the case, a decision which was later upheld at an

Figure 4:20 *As well as enjoying considerable success in numerous competitions since their foundation, the Clydebank Burgh Band have been present at almost every significant occasion in the history of the Burgh.*

appeal in the Court of Session. The Duntocher Band continued, playing at the many local functions, but it never really had any great competitive success during this period. However, the losers in the dispute, the Clydebank Burgh Band, became very successful, winning the Scottish Amateur Band Association Championship seven times between 1896 and 1910. Left with nothing, its early years were a struggle raising cash for new instruments and uniforms, but in 1895 it won second place at the first Scottish Amateur Band Association Championship and first place the following year. The band was well on its way to becoming one of the foremost bands in Scotland.

To encourage the study of natural science and archaeology the Old Kilpatrick Naturalist and Antiquarian Society was formed in 1887. It was responsible for setting up a small museum in the newly opened Gavinburn School which, under the care of the headmaster, became a useful addition to the school's resources. Horticulture was enjoyed by many enthusiasts and in 1889 the Old Kilpatrick Horticultural Society was formed, surviving until around 1907 but reforming in 1913 as the Old Kilpatrick Horticultural and Industrial Society. The annual show was quite an event in the year's calendar, drawing entrants from all over the surrounding area. With such a high density of tenement housing many people had to rent garden plots and this led to the establishing of several allotment societies. The Clydebank Allotment Society, formed at the turn of the century, was one of the earliest. During the First World War people throughout the country were actively encouraged to grow vegetables to help alleviate food shortages and Clydebank played its part with enthusiasm. From the latter half of the war, allotment societies mushroomed, and the Clydebank and District Garden Plots Association was one of the first to be formed in 1916.

Undoubtedly the most popular indoor entertainment was theatre, a tradition in which Clydebank was particularly rich. Many well known names from the world of variety visited the town, playing to large and enthusiastic audiences. In 1902 Clydebank's first purpose-built theatre, the Gaiety in North Elgin Street, was opened. Renamed the New Gaiety after renovation in 1908, in addition to the usual variety acts, Mr A. W. Pickard, the new proprietor, introduced regular bioscope entertainments. At Prince George's Bioscope (later Municipal Pictures) in the Town Hall films of local events were particularly popular, with audiences scanning

Figure 4:21 *The Gaiety Theatre in North Elgin Street was Clydebank's first purpose-built theatre and opened on 27 January 1902 with seating for 1,400 people. In 1927 it was converted to the Bank Cinema, the main entrance being then relocated in Glasgow Road. Taken around the start of the First World War, this photograph shows the staff outside the entrance to the theatre.*

the screen for 'kent' faces. Bioscope and cinematograph entertainments had been gradually introduced into other forms of entertainment as crowd-pulling novelties but, by 1917, after the New Gaiety had been converted to a full-time cinema, the Empire in Glasgow Road was advertised as the last remaining theatre, films having almost completely replaced live variety shows. The Co-operative Hall in Hume Street held regular film shows between 1914 and 1916, operating variously under the names Vimograph, Picture Palace and Premier Pictures whilst, around 1913, the Graham Street Roller Skating Rink was converted to the Cinem Varieties, changing its name in 1915 to the Palace. The Pavilion Theatre at the foot of Kilbowie Road opened in 1919 and, further up, opposite Singer Station, stood the New Kinema. Duntocher's cinema enthusiasts could visit the local Public Hall to watch the latest films, while Dalmuir had two picture houses, the Napoleon Star at the rear of Glenruther Terrace and, further along Dumbarton Road, the Dalmuir Picture House which opened in 1915. One local gentleman recalls that, as a boy, to spin out the time, words of Harry Lauder's songs were projected on to the screen, and, with the lady pianist hammering out the tune, they 'beltit it oot' with great gusto![76]

Not surprisingly, sport attracted large numbers of people. There were numerous billiard halls, wrestling was held in the Public Hall (later the Drill Hall) in Douglas Street and by 1905 week long contests were a regular feature in the Gaiety Theatre. Travelling boxing booths visited the town and roller skating saw a boom around 1910 with the Graham Street Rink and the Empire, Agamemnon Street, competing for skaters. Outdoor sports, however, predominated and cycling and rambling were among the most popular of the earliest pastimes with several clubs forming from the 1890s onwards.

The oldest bowling club in the district is Yoker which was founded in 1850 by the Harvey brothers of the Yoker distillery. Dalmuir Bowling and Tennis Club and Clydebank Bowling and Quoiting Club were opened in 1884, Dalmuir pipping Clydebank to the post by four months. In 1886 the younger members of the Dalmuir Club asked to take over the smaller green for tennis courts and a branch club was formed, being extended and improved five years later. In June 1908 the

Figure 4:22 *View of the 'Tower', one of several magnificent villas erected on Duntocher Road (formerly 'The Hill') by speculative builders in the 1870s for 'well-to-do' businessmen. In 1908, the then owners, ex-Provost and Mrs Alexander Stewart, hosted a glorious garden party, held to raise funds for the Dalmuir Tennis Club.*

Clydebank Press had a vivid description of a fund raising garden party for the tennis club held by ex-Provost and Mrs Stewart in the grounds of their house, the 'Tower', which lay adjacent to the courts in Duntocher Road:

> 'Ladies looked fresh and fascinating in their fashionable frills and furbelows and the gentlemen, in straw hats and tennis suits, added not a little to the brilliance of the scene.'[77]

Clydebank Bowling and Quoiting Club was opened on ground leased by James R. Thomson from Miss Hamilton of Barns and Cochno, the club not being formed until 1885, the year following the opening. It was established principally for workers of the shipyard but was open to the public on payment of a higher fee. In 1899 an unused quoiting green, along with some ground which had been purchased, was opened as an additional bowling green. In the pre-war years the club was very successful, winning the County Cup five times. The next two bowling greens to open, Old Kilpatrick and Radnor Park, did so in 1907 although Old Kilpatrick had had a club prior to the present one. Situated adjacent to the old Boquhanran School, Radnor Park Bowling Club was built with profits from the McAlpine Public House Trust and opened in June 1907. Robert McAlpine, Sen. performed the opening ceremony at which he stated that he always knew fine things could be done with the profit from drink and he hoped the green would be a means of keeping men from temptation.[78]

Cricket had a larger following than today with five clubs in existence at various times. These were the Clydebank Cricket Club which opened in 1894, Clydebank Primrose, Old Kilpatrick and Bowling, Dalmuir (1914) and Willowbank United, which played at Millbrae, Yoker, and was the forerunner of the later Millbrae Cricket Club. Curling was played at Yoker, Duntocher and Dalmuir whilst Clydebank, Old Kilpatrick and Duntocher all had quoiting clubs. Hardgate could boast two clubs, Hardgate Quoiting Club and Hardgate Victoria Quoiting Club. Golfers had the choice of two courses, one at Old Kilpatrick which has long since disappeared, and the other, Clydebank and District Golf Club, at Hardgate, which was opened in June 1905. Clydebank has the distinction of being the home of the first open athletics club in Scotland. In 1885 the Clydebank branch of the

Figure 4:23 *Although latterly in decline, the sport of quoiting was for many years a popular outdoor activity, with players from five local clubs competing in friendly inter-club rivalry or in West of Scotland competitions. This group of quoiters assembled on the knowes in Hardgate belonged to one of the two Hardgate clubs — an area which proved to be the last bastion of the sport locally.*

Clydesdale Harriers held their first cross country run, starting at the Black Bull Inn, Milngavie and covering 13 miles. Due to changes in Scottish Amateur Athletics Association regulations after the First World War, the Clydesdale Harriers decided to settle in Clydebank and for many years had a strong influence on athletics in Scotland, providing several internationalists and gaining a high reputation throughout the country.[79]

Not surprisingly, however, football, both juvenile and junior, attracted a large following and in the 1870s Yoker, Dalmuir and Duntocher all had teams.[80] In 1886 the original Yoker team disbanded but the following year Yoker Athletic was formed. By the turn of the century Yoker Athletic, Duntocher Harp, Dalmuir Thistle and Clydebank Athletic were among the many teams in the area. At first Yoker Athletic played at Harvey's Land (owned by the Harveys of Yoker Distillery) but until the mid 1890s the team had to move around each year, until a home was found at Hamilton Park, Whitecrook, providing a permanent base for approximately a decade. Around 1904-5 the team settled into its final ground, Holm Park, where it remains to this day. Winning the Western Junior League Championship in 1905-6 and the Glasgow Junior League Championship in 1908-9 were its greatest achievements in this early period.

Formed from a splinter group of Duntocher Hibs FC, Duntocher FC played its first games in the 1899-1900 season at the ground of Old Kilpatrick Juniors before moving to the first Kilbowie Park in Clydebank. With this move the team was re-named Clydebank Juniors FC. The Juniors had many notable successes during this period, winning the Dunbartonshire Charity Cup twice and the Kirkwood Shield and Partick Police Cup once each. Several players went on to play at senior level, one of the most successful being local boy 'Patsy' Gallacher who went on to play for Glasgow Celtic, Falkirk and Ireland.

The first Clydebank FC was formed in 1888, participating in the Scottish and Dunbartonshire Cups and instigating the Buchanan Cup. The team played at another Hamilton Park which was situated between Belmont Street and Canal Street, but, following a reasonably good 1891-2 season and after only one home match the following season, it had to vacate this ground due to the extension of the railway line. Unable to find an alternative site all future games were played away from home and the team finished the season with only one point. That season saw the demise of the club but it was briefly resurrected for one season around 1899, playing alongside Yoker Athletic at the Whitecrook Hamilton Park.

The third Clydebank FC was formed in 1914. Set up as a limited company the share issue proved very popular locally and within three months the club possessed one of the best grounds in Scotland, Clydeholm, opposite Yoker Athletic's Holm Park. Never hugely successful on the field, its best result was in a friendly against a Celtic select featuring 'Patsy' Gallacher, which they won by five goals to three. A more inopportune year than 1914 could not have been chosen to launch a new football club and inevitably the war took its toll on the team. Reorganisation of the Scottish League saw Clydebank out for two seasons and competing in the Western League which it won in the 1916-17 season. This championship helped it get elected to the one-division Scottish League and here it remained for five years, unable to finish any season higher than fifth place.

By the end of this early period the influence of the church was gradually declining. The war and the growing popularity of more secular and modern forms of entertainment had their effects, although the temperance influence remained strong throughout. The cinema was soon to reach its 'golden era'; sports such as boxing and football were to witness a boom and the Town Council would play a greater role in recreational provision. All of these factors were to change the future leisure pursuits of the people.

Part Two

The Town in War and Peace, 1914-1945

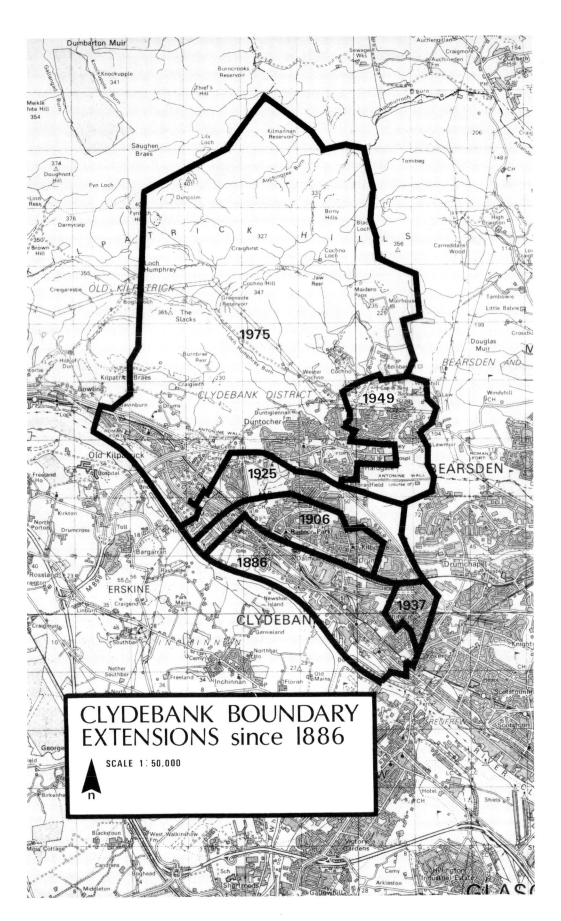

CLYDEBANK BOUNDARY
EXTENSIONS since 1886

SCALE 1 : 50,000

N

Figure 5:1 *Clydebank boundary extensions since 1886.*

CHAPTER FIVE

The Shipyards at War, 1914-18

John Brown

Every shipbuilder knew that the huge demands for merchant and naval tonnage that saw launchings on the Clyde double in scale between 1910 and 1913 to reach the record level of 756,976 tons, could not last. The huge extensions in capacity that had been brought into being to meet the demand would sooner or later outstrip the market and idle times would return. There were signs of such a downturn in early 1914, but the outbreak of the First World War abruptly halted any downswing, and for the next five years the resources of the shipbuilders were strained to near breaking point to meet the needs of Britain at war.

As one of a small number of naval yards, Clydebank became an Admiralty controlled dockyard; this was formally the case with effect from 12 July 1915.[1] Between 1914 and 1918 all but five vessels built were for the Admiralty. These included two merchant vessels on the stocks at the outbreak of war which were completed and converted to war work, the *Ormonde* in 1917 as a troopship, and the *Platypus* in 1916 as a depot ship. The other three merchant vessels built were standard cargo boats for the Shipping Controller. The achievement of the Clydebank yard was impressive. Between 1914 and 1918 the yard launched 45 warships: these comprised one battleship, the *Barham* in 1914; two battlecruisers, the *Repulse* in 1916, and the *Hood* in 1918; two light cruisers, *Canterbury* and *Ceres*, and one seaplane carrier, the *Pegasus* in 1917, the first such vessel to be built. Somewhat surprisingly for a yard specialising in warships, Clydebank also built three of the E-class submarines in 1916.[2]

However, the main part of Clydebank's output was 35 destroyers, fast vessels increasingly called into use for convoy duty to protect merchantmen and hunt the submarines that wreaked such havoc on the sea lanes. Clydebank, in fact, built more destroyers than any other yard in Britain during the war. The entire Clydebank contribution was put in context by the *Glasgow Herald* which published a list comparing the main Clydeside company production records during the First World War.

Table 5:1   *Clydeside War Production*

Yard 1914-18	No. of Vessels	Displacement Tons	HP
Clydebank	47	155,153	1,563,300
Fairfield	43	136,270	1,157,570
Dalmuir	69	118,080	634,290
Scott	33	52,099	651,350
Yarrow	48	37,554	613,900
Denny	46	36,456	666,900
Others	195	223,795	814,820
TOTAL	481	759,407	6,102,330

Source: Glasgow Herald, 28 December 1918

According to this source, the Clydebank yard produced one fifth of all war construction on the Clyde, and one quarter of the engine horsepower installed during the hostilities.[3] The yard records give a slightly different picture: the tonnage launched to the end of 1918 was 149,891 displacement tons with a horsepower of 1,314,500. Three other vessels were not launched till 1919, bringing the wartime programme to 159,231 tons and 1,448,500 HP. In addition, the merchant vessels contributed a further 33,912 gross tons and 22,650 HP. The 159,231 displacement tons is approximately equivalent in labour and materials input to around 400,000 gross tons of merchant shipping. In merchant equivalent tons, Clydebank built and launched a workload of something like 80,000 tons of ships in each of the five years of war. This huge defence effort fully employed the resources of the Clydebank yard. It was fortunate that John Brown & Co. had expended over £800,000 in equipment and improvements in the decade before the war, for the pressure of work left little opportunity for demolishing old plant and installing new equipment during the war. In fact, the Clydebank yard spent only £79,000 in net additions to capital during the war. This inevitably meant an accelerating rate of obsolescence and a deterioration of the capital stock of the company.

Figure 5:2   *Construction work on the battle cruiser* Hood *which, when launched in 1918, was the largest warship in the world. On 24 May 1941 she was blown up while engaging the German battleship* Bismarck.

But on the bright side, if pressure of work and poor government depreciation allowances did not encourage much capital investment during the hostilities, the naval contracts represented a mighty transfusion of profitability. Since the Clydebank yard was treated as part of the entire John Brown empire for balance sheet purposes, it is not easy to give a clear view of the profits earned. The books do, however, allow a calculation of profit on each individual contract. On this basis it is possible to calculate that the 44 Admiralty ordered vessels returned a profit of £1,392,335 to Clydebank between 1914 and 1918. Like all the warship builders, Clydebank was a very profitable yard during the war, and had large cash reserves at its disposal at the end of the hostilities, even after making provision for the Excess Profits Tax introduced in 1915.[4]

Because Clydebank was an Admiralty controlled yard throughout the conflict, the yard management had priority claims on manpower and materials to meet the wartime orders. In spite of the fact that thousands of shipyard workers initially volunteered for military service, their losses were quickly made up by transferring men from merchant yards which did not get much of a share of Admiralty business before 1916. Employment in the Clydebank yard consequently remained at a high average level of about 9,700 men, almost exactly the figure in employment in 1913 at the peak of the peacetime building boom. The influx of men from other areas presented a problem of accommodation. John Brown had contracted for two new blocks of workmen's tenements providing accommodation for 186 families at a cost of £49,773 in 1915; the builder was Mr Leslie Kirk.[5] Further accommodation was undertaken for under-foremen in 1915. Later that year Thomas Bell sought the agreement of the Board to assist a local purveying contractor, Mr John Russell, to erect a large workmen's restaurant adjacent to the shipyard gate at a cost of £2,000. The pressure on housing was intense and by mid-1916 Bell was intimating a need for further accommodation, and plans were drawn up to build another 23 tenements on company ground in Dumbarton Road at the west end of the shipyard.[7] While part of the construction was a necessary response to emergency war needs, the building of cottages for foremen and under-foremen was, as Thomas Bell stated, 'not all philanthropy, but hard headed business to separate the foremen from the men'.[8]

While the Clydebank yard did not lose its supply of labour during the war, it eventually had to give up the services of its Managing Director for a time. In 1917, Thomas Bell was called to London to serve as Deputy Controller of Dockyards and Warshipbuilding at the Admiralty. He was responsible for the building, repair and maintenance programmes of all naval craft and armed merchant vessels. His service was recognized with the award of the KBE in 1918. The war was kind to the Clydebank yard. It emerged from it highly profitable and flush with cash reserves. Its reputation had been enhanced and, because of its type of work — mainly in smaller vessels like destroyers — it had not been tempted into heavy capital outlays or great expansions of capacity during the war years. It was fighting fit for the peace; its neighbour and rival at Dalmuir was not so fortunate.

Beardmore

Both the Admiralty and the War Office were totally unprepared for the outbreak of war in August 1914.[9] There were no plans for increasing the production of munitions vital for the prosecution of anything more than a very short campaign. With little consideration of the production problem caused by the haemorrhage of skilled manpower as men flocked to join the colours, orders for shells, mines and field equipment were hurriedly placed with established armaments manufacturers, including William Beardmore & Co. and John Brown & Co. Within a matter of days of the beginning of hostilities, 60-pounder shells and fuses

Figure 5:3 *Sir Thomas Bell 1865-1952. Associated with the shipyard for 60 years, Bell became, at the age of 44, Managing Director, a position he held for 26 years.*

Figure 5:4 *A Mark VII 6-inch howitzer and carriage at Parkhead in 1918.*

were being manufactured at Dalmuir. By the end of September, when the shortage of heavy field guns at the front became critical, William Beardmore willingly volunteered to install plant at Dalmuir to assemble 18-pounder field guns and six- and eight-inch howitzers.[10] The Admiralty, as hard pressed as the War Office, placed orders with Dalmuir for 24 *BE2C* type aeroplanes, 500 Leon mines, two L-class destroyers, and two E-class submarines. With the exception of the destroyers, these contracts were planned to enlarge the company's expertise as preparation for future commissions. As an interim measure the cabinetmakers and mechanical engineering shops were converted and extended for aircraft production. During 1915 work began on the construction of a separate seaplane shed and a range of shops for assembling howitzers.[11]

In attempting to meet these huge commitments, William Beardmore was quickly confronted by a lack of skilled men. In common with other Clydeside employers he sought to overcome this problem by breaking down demarcation barriers between the various trades. The craft unions, sensing that their position was threatened, protested and simultaneously demanded an increase in wages to cover the rise in the cost of living. Negotiations collapsed in January 1915 and in mid-February the Beardmore workforce came out on strike, led by David Kirkwood, the chairman of the shop stewards committee. They found little public sympathy for their cause and on 1 March they accepted a rise of 1d an hour instead of the 2d they had demanded. Their action infuriated the Government, and by the end of the month Lloyd George had devised a scheme to impose controls on all the armament companies engaged in munitions work and on their workforces. Legislation was delayed until the end of May and six weeks later William Beardmore & Co. was declared a controlled establishment. This allowed the company to enforce dilution to raise the output of field guns from Dalmuir, which had fallen seriously behind schedule. The new unions resisted this high-handed action and the company refused to use their powers without their agreement. The argument over dilution continued throughout the rest of the year, complicated by a rent strike in Glasgow, Clydebank and other towns, in protest against recent increases. Matters were brought to a head during a visit to Glasgow by Lloyd George at the end of December 1915 in an effort to find a solution. When this failed, a dilution scheme for Beardmore was pushed through which guaranteed the position of David Kirkwood and the shop stewards. Instead of honouring this arrangement, William Beardmore and his managers used it as a vehicle for crushing the power of the unions in the company, ordering David Kirkwood not to leave his bench throughout working hours without permission. On 17 March 1916 the workers in the howitzer shops at Dalmuir and Parkhead came out on strike, precipitating widespread unrest throughout Glasgow. The Government responded quickly and David Kirkwood and two other Beardmore shop stewards were deported to Edinburgh. After some ineffective protest the strike collapsed, and by 4 April everyone was back at work, except for 68 employees at Dalmuir.[12]

With the formation of the Ministry of Munitions, the role of the armaments companies changed and greater emphasis was placed on research and development. William Beardmore enthusiastically formed an aeroplane design department at Dalmuir with Lieutenant G. T. Richards, an Inspector of Naval Aircraft, as its head. Between 1915 and 1918 five prototype aircraft, *WBI-V*, were produced. Only one of these, the *WBIII*, a modified *Sopwith Pup* for flying from aircraft carriers, was successful. One hundred were built at Dalmuir in 1917-18 for the carrier *Argos*, converted from the liner *Conte Rosso* which had been under construction in the yard at the beginning of the war. By the end of the war the aeroplane workshops at Dalmuir had turned out 650 planes, including 80 *Sopwith Pups* and 20 *Handley Page VI 1500* heavy bombers. To test these planes, an aerodrome was laid out nearby the works.[13] The Dalmuir aeroplane design department was also involved in the construction of *24r*, one of the new 23-class airship, originated by Vickers. The manufacture of the components and their sub-assembly was carried out in hurriedly constructed galleries in the recently-built seaplane shed. The final assembly was to take place in a new airship shed across the river at Inchinnan in Renfrewshire, paid for by the Admiralty. The *24r* was completed in October 1917, followed nine months later by the improved *R27*. The contract for *R28* was cancelled in the autumn of 1917 to make way for the *R34*, modelled on the Zeppelin *L33* that had recently been brought down over Essex. Neither the *R34* nor three further contracts for the *R36, R40* and *R41* were completed before the end of the war.[14]

Figure 5:5 Argos
in the fitting-out basin at Dalmuir in 1918. This vessel was the world's first through-deck aircraft carrier and had begun life, before her conversion for wartime use, as the liner Conte Rosso.

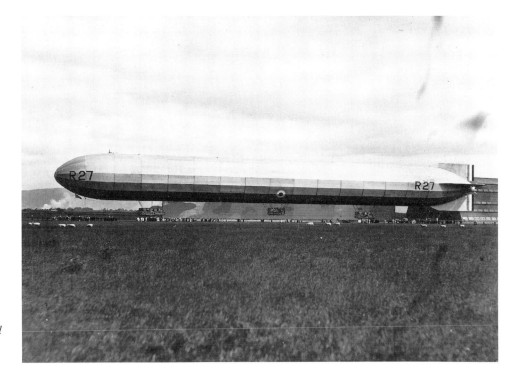

Figure 5:6 *Ever ready to expand and diversify, Beardmore commenced airship construction across the river at Inchinnan. In this view the airship R27 is seen as she was in June 1918. Whilst airship construction proved relatively unsuccessful the Beardmore-built R34 successfully completed the first ever double crossing of the Atlantic by an airship.*

At the same time as Dalmuir became involved in airship construction, William Beardmore & Co. were invited to perfect light bomb and bullet-proof armour plate for the experimental 'landship' or tank. After the success of tanks at Delville Wood, near Beauquesne, in September 1916, orders were placed for almost 1,000 tanks. Early in 1917 Beardmore undertook to build 50 mark IV tanks at Dalmuir. A shed was put up for this purpose, but no further orders followed as the War Office wanted the plant to concentrate on the assembly of spherical Hotchkiss- and Lewis-gun mountings for tanks. By the end of the war Dalmuir had produced over 20,000 such mountings.[15]

The diversification into the manufacture of these new weapons was achieved to the detriment of Dalmuir's original role as a shipyard. Contracts were placed with Beardmore in 1915 for only two M-class destroyers, two R-class destroyers, a Hawkins class cruiser and two further E-class submarines. This pattern was repeated in 1916 with the inclusion of one of the novel, but impractical, steam-powered K-class submarines. The Admiralty were more concerned that Dalmuir should devote its engineering resources to the construction of gun mountings rather than ships. The developing naval crisis of 1917 led to a revision of their policy and the volume of orders was raised. At the same time funds were advanced to extend the naval gun shop at Dalmuir to build mountings for the greatly enlarged naval and merchant shipbuilding programmes.[16]

By the armistice in November 1918 the yard had delivered 69 vessels (including 33 barges for the War Office) comprising 118,089 tons and 634,290 indicated horsepower, the third largest wartime output on the Clyde. The plant was physically almost twice as large as it had been at the outbreak of war.[17] Over £800,000 had been spent on new facilities, mostly tailored to specific wartime requirements like airframe construction and howitzer assembly. After the poor results of the pre-war years, the plant had become very profitable from 1914, with returns reaching £500,000 in 1918-1919.[18] The wartime extensions at Dalmuir were only part of a massive expansion of the whole of William Beardmore's business empire. At a staff victory dinner for all departments held in April 1919, Lord Weir dubbed Sir William a Field Marshall of Industry for his contribution to the war

Figure 5:7 *Front cover of the souvenir menu of the 'Staff Victory Dinner' held at the Grosvenor Restaurant.*

effort — 'It was sufficient for Sir William to know that the country needed something and he felt that he could make it. He made his plans, he produced what was wanted, he went ahead and did the work, and when it was done it was early enough then to talk about finance'.[19] However, Sir William had failed to generate a management structure capable of controlling his vastly extended enterprise.

CHAPTER SIX

Clydebank Politics in War and Peace

First World War

The outbreak of war in 1914 brought boom conditions to Clydebank's shipyards although, initially at least, the disruption of foreign trade caused problems for the workers at the Singer factory. Over the war years the town's population continued to grow as workers moved to find jobs in Clydebank.[1] Support for the war effort led to considerable numbers of local volunteers joining the armed forces. However, there was also opposition to the war and to the introduction of conscription in 1916. Such opposition locally came from the ILP. Early in 1916, the Trades Council, which had a considerable number of ILP members, voted by 18 to 2 with four abstentions against conscription[2], while the ILP urgently pressed for careful consideration of the recent enemy peace offer in December 1916.[3] The ILP were refused permission to meet to welcome the 1917 Revolution in Russia. A leading ILP member, Police Judge McDonald, declared that permission had been refused because 'the Soldiers and Workmen's Council have boldy declared in their manifesto for peace at an early date, and that without annexations or indemnities.'[4]

The ILP was active in other areas during the war years. As early as August 1914 the *Clydebank Leader* reported that the ILP and the Trades Council had formed a committee to organise meetings to protest at food price increases. Organised protest on the price issue soon developed. In January 1915 the *Clydebank Press* reported an ILP meeting at which the speaker, John A. Fraser, claimed that 'the working classes were being absolutely exploited by the commercial classes', and a resolution was passed urging the Government to control the price of food and other necessities.[5] Even the introduction of rationing later in the war did not totally remove concern on this issue. The ILP were also involved, together with the Trades Council, the Ward Committees and the Tenants Protective Association, in a movement to oppose rent increases. The wartime population influx had exacerbated an already serious housing shortage and landlords took the opportunity to raise rents. Late 1914 and 1915 saw a sustained and well supported campaign of protest meetings and demonstrations at which landlords and factors were denounced as exploiters, and resolutions were passed demanding Government action.[6] In April 1915 the Clydebank Trades Council was the first on

Figure 6:1 *Although primarily active in the field of politics, the ILP found time to involve itself in more leisurely pursuits. In this view the ILP orchestra is caught between performances.*

Clydeside to pass a resolution calling for the establishment of Fair Rent Courts, and in the following month a Fair Rent League was set up.[7] There were suggestions of a Rent Strike but little came of this at that time. Agitation on rents, however, did not die down until the freezing of rents by the 1915 Increase of Rent and Mortgage Interest (War Restrictions) Act.

Some pre-war pressure groups, such as the temperance movement, remained active during the war. The movement was encouraged by the government-imposed restrictions on public house opening hours in August 1915. Nationalist support for an independent Ireland continued, but, curiously enough, the Easter Rising of 1916 received no recorded local support. Division 417 of the Ancient Order of Hibernians went so far as to unanimously pass a resolution condemning 'the foolish and criminal action of the Sinn Fein Society in Dublin' in May 1916.[8]

Outside of ILP propaganda, party political activity fell subordinate to the war effort. No contested elections took place at the local elections of November 1914 and, thereafter, as nationally, local and parliamentary elections were suspended for the duration of the war. It was argued that a political truce should exist until the end of the war, and at the 25th Annual Meeting of the local Liberal Association in 1917 it was reported that 'there had been no propaganda during the past year.'[9] Members of the two main political parties of the day, the Liberal and Conservative parties, worked together in a variety of official and semi-official activities. Liberals and Conservatives organised recruiting campaigns in the early years of the war. Town Council members, such as Provost Taylor, took part in the local rationing committee and the military tribunal vetting applications for exemption from conscription. Such activity drew some criticism but apparently did not unduly damage the Council, while indeed, the Council occasionally supported local protests on prices and housing. In February 1915 the Town Council passed a resolution in favour of government control of food and coal supplies, the reduction of prices, and preventing 'unscrupulous landlords from raising rents.'[10] Similarly, in February 1918 a council deputation went to Edinburgh to put pressure on the Secretary of State for Scotland to assist with the town's housing problem.[11]

The general election of 1918 provided the first test of political opinion after the war and was the first election to take place under universal male suffrage and limited female suffrage. From 1918 Clydebank and Dumbarton formed the inter-war constituency of the Dumbarton Burghs. As approximately two-thirds of the electors lived in Clydebank, the town had a predominant voice in the election of the local MP. In December 1918 the coalition candidate was the Liberal Provost John Taylor of Clydebank, while David Kirkwood, a prominent left-wing trade union activist, was the first Labour candidate for the burgh. John Taylor defeated Kirkwood by 11,734 votes to 10,566. However, the closeness of the result served notice of the emergence of Labour as a serious challenger in Clydebank politics.

The Inter-war Years
Protest Politics

The years 1919-1939 saw substantial change in Clydebank, in terms of politics, economy and housing. The town suffered periods of very severe unemployment in the early 1920s and early 1930s, when the traditional industries of shipbuilding and engineering came under considerable pressure. Acute housing problems remained. The existing housing stock was inadequate for the population which had risen to around 46,000. The problem of overcrowding was only partly remedied by the intermittent house building activities of the Town Council. These social and economic problems gave rise to a number of vociferous protest movements through the 1920s and 1930s, the most famous of which was the Clydebank Rent Strike. The history of the Clydebank Rent Strike is given elsewhere in this book, but its roots lay in the dashing of hopes for improved housing in the post-war 'Land fit for Heroes', and even more in the severe economic difficulties surrounding the deep depression affecting the town in the early 1920s. A political protest element was involved, as the election of a Housing Association representative to the Town Council in 1923-25 shows.

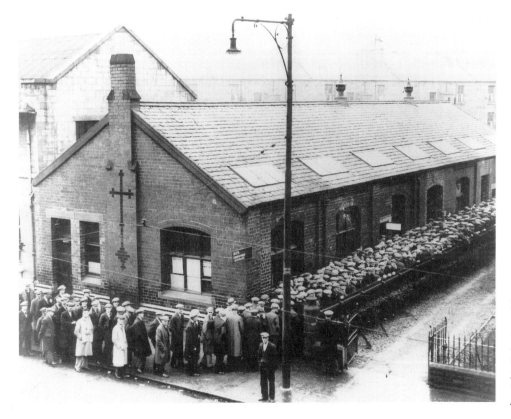

Figure 6:2 *This scene at the old employment labour exchange (formerly Our Holy Redeemer's Church) was all too common during the 'depression' years and was a stark reminder of the effects of periods of fluctuating markets.*

71

The economic recession also gave rise to pressure groups to assist the unemployed. Such activity was concentrated in the early 1920s and the early 1930s when unemployment was at its worst, although it was not confined to those years. A Clydebank Unemployed Workers Committee was set up in 1921 to assist the unemployed and to put pressure on the local authorities to do likewise.[12] It organised deputations, marches and demonstrations in September 1921, August 1923, March 1924 and August 1925 to ask for Parish Council financial and other assistance to be improved, but without much success. By the mid 1920s this local body had merged into the National Unemployed Workers Movement (NUWM). As employment prospects brightened in the late 1920s the movement tailed off but it became active again following the economic downturn of the early 1930s. The NUWM put demands to the Town Council, such as those of January 1933 asking for 1/- per week extra for dependent children, a bag of coal per week, free milk for children under school age, and public work schemes.[13] For a time the NUWM urged the dropping of the Means Test. This would have been illegal action and was ruled out by the Town Council, but the Council did petition the Government against the Means Test in January 1932.

Active membership of the NUWM was never claimed to be more than 600.[14] The movement had close links with the local Communist Party, which led local Labour politicians to boycott the movement thus diminishing its influence.[15] The Communist connection extended to a joint local election platform offered by three NUWM and two Communist candidates in November 1931.[16] The candidates came bottom of the poll. On the whole, the NUWM, which faded as the economic outlook improved from the mid 1930s, had limited influence. However, this was not the impression that existed in some quarters at the time. In 1933 T. Baird Duffy wrote to the *Clydebank Press* claiming, 'Revolution. This is what the NUWM advocate. This is their ruling passion and principle'.[17] The Rent Strike drew a parallel reaction. In the 1920s a *Times* editorial described the Rent Strikers as having a 'Communistic and cut-throat policy'.[18] Such views reflected the widespread contemporary belief that all of Clydeside was 'Red' and a hot-bed of support for left-wing revolution in Britain. Clydebank shared in this reputation. On 2 October 1931 the *Clydebank Press* published a letter from 'Sensitive' suggesting that it change its name to Hilltown because Clydebank 'has become a synonym with revolution and Bolshevism to the world at large'. Modern historians such as T. C. Smout[19] and Christopher Andrew[20] have now concluded that 'Red Clydeside' was largely a myth. However, during the inter-war period politics in Clydebank underwent a shift to the left, although not a revolutionary shift, as the increasing success of the Labour Party at local and parliamentary elections shows.

Parliamentary and Local Elections

The post-war breakthrough for Labour came first in the parliamentary arena. In 1918 the Coalition Liberal John Taylor defeated Labour's David Kirkwood by a majority of 1,168. At the next general election in 1922, with 16,397 votes, David Kirkwood had a majority of 7,290 over Taylor. In this result, Clydebank was following national trends as the working-class vote swung away from the Liberal Party to the Labour Party. As nationally, there was a swing from Liberal to Labour by Irish Catholic voters after the establishment of the Irish Free State. The Liberal Party nationally and locally was riven by splits. The local Labour Party was well organised at constituency, town and ward levels. An important local factor in Kirkwood's success was the rent agitation of the period. The local branch of the Scottish Labour Housing Association organised a campaign of opposition to John Taylor from 1920, accusing him of going back on promises to oppose measures resulting in rent increases. In 1920 Taylor received 890 postcards from Association

Figure 6:3   *David Kirkwood addressing a rally of the National Unemployed Workers Movement.*

members calling on him to honour his 1918 election pledge, 'Vote for Provost Taylor and No Increase in Rents'.[21] Certainly, in January 1923 the *Clydebank Press* attributed Taylor's defeat to the rent question.[22]

David Kirkwood remained constituency MP for the rest of the inter-war years, retaining his seat even in 1931 when the Labour Party suffered a great electoral setback nationally. Kirkwood had a fiery reputation as a leading member of the wartime Clyde Shop Stewards' Movement and a prominent member of the ILP. In a Commons Committee in 1923 he concluded his speech with a threat that 'the Socialist republic would be established at the point of the bayonet',[23] and he was involved in scenes in the House of Commons in 1923, 1925 and 1927. However, Kirkwood mellowed as time passed and eventually became a member of the House of Lords. A Clydebank Communist, William Waddell, attacked him in 1929 for not being radical enough.[24] Kirkwood was fervently anti-Communist. It was reported that at the 1930 conference of the League Against Imperialism, 'Mr Kirkwood denounced the Communists and said that they did not represent the working classes'.[25] On account of its Communist links Kirkwood refused to support the NUWM, while he refused to participate in the ILP split from the Labour Party in the 1930s. Thus it seems that Kirkwood was less of an extremist than he might appear at first sight although he contributed greatly to Clydebank's 'radical' reputation of the inter-war years. A local children's rhyme of the period reflected Kirkwood's local popularity and reputation:

> 'Vote, vote, vote for Davie Kirkwood,
> Vote, vote, vote for all his men,
> Then we'll buy a penny gun,
> And we'll make the Tories run,
> And you'll never see a Tory again.'[26]

Labour had a more gradual impact on local government. From 1920 to 1939 Clydebank was divided into five wards, with minor boundary changes in 1925 and 1933. Each ward was represented by three councillors until the reorganisation of local government in 1929 increased that number to four. Normally, one third or, after 1929, one quarter, of the councillors retired each year. Table 6:1 summarises the results of the elections from 1920 to 1939. The table shows that Clydebank was under Moderate control until November 1934, with the exception of the brief Labour administration of 1924-25.

Table 6:1   *Clydebank Town Council Membership 1920-1939*

Year	Moderate	Labour	Independent	Communists	Other	Control of Council
1920	10?	5	—	—	—	Moderate
1921	11?	4	—	—	—	M
1922	12?	3	—	—	—	M
1923	10?	4	—	—	1 Housing Assoc.	M
1924	6?	8	—	—	1 HA	Labour
1925	5	9	—	—	1 HA	L
1926	9	5	1	—	—	M
1927	11	3	1	—	—	M
1928	12	2	1	—	—	M
1929	12	3	—	—	—	M
1930	13	5	2	—	—	M
1931	13	5	2	—	—	M
1932	13	4	3	—	—	M
1933	11	6	3	—	—	M
1934	10	8	2	—	—	M/Indep
1935	7	11	2	—	—	Labour
1936	6	12	1	1	—	L
1937	7	11	1	1	—	L
1938	5	13	1	1	—	L
1939	5	12	3	—	—	L

Source: Compiled from (a) *Clydebank Press* 1919-39.
(b) *Clydebank Town Council Minutes* 1919-39
(c) *Clydebank Town Council Abstracts of Accounts* 1919-39.

The Moderate Party was essentially an anti-Socialist group. Although including many Conservative supporters, a number of Moderate councillors, such as Bailie Barclay, were associated with the local Liberal Party, and in 1935 a Moderate candidate at the local elections claimed not to represent any one particular party, sect or creed.[27] The party was organised by the Citizens' Council, whose membership was made up of mainly small businessmen and whose chief political function seems to have been the selection of candidates for local elections. The monthly meetings of the Council were as often social and educational as political. On 27 February 1931, the *Clydebank Press* reported a meeting at which the Assistant Sanitary Inspector read a paper on the adulteration of food.

Up to a point the manifestos of Moderate candidates were similar to those of the Labour Party, referring to promoting house building, a suitable level of rents and improved public health. However, Moderate candidates laid more stress on the need for economy and efficiency, particularly at times of depression. In 1933 a Moderate candidate, J. McKenzie, suggested that 'the time is not opportune for grandiose municipal schemes'.[28] In line with the national economy drive, in October 1931 the Council discussed cuts, for instance, in relief to the unemployed and in municipal employees' wages. Eleven Moderates and one Independent voted for the cuts, two Moderates abstained, and five Labour and one Independent

Figure 6:4 *On Saturday 25 April 1925 Provost Samuel MacDonald formally opened the model yachting pond in Whitecrook Park, constructed by unemployed workers during the period of heavy unemployment.*

voted against the cuts.[29] Not only did the Council agree to reduce assistance to the unemployed in 1931, it also virtually halted the progressive housebuilding programme of the 1920s, raised rates and refused to cut council house rents. Labour election propaganda opposed such actions, and from 1931 Moderate control of the Council was eroded.

The break in Moderate control in the 1920s was only temporary and owed much to the Rent Strike. However, as the Rent Strike faded, older political loyalties reasserted themselves, while there was disappointment with the limited achievements of the brief Labour Administration as is shown in the letter from 'Another Trades Unionist' to the *Clydebank Press* in May 1924:

> 'When one comes to think of the promises made for the securing of votes and compares it with the work done, he is forced to compare the Labour party's attitude in our Council with the pawnbroker's shop — full of unredeemed pledges.'[30]

However, Labour took control again in November 1934 at a time when the town was moving out of depression. More favourable economic circumstances allowed for the implementation of Labour policies, such as renewing large-scale house-building in the late 1930s at North Kilbowie. However, Labour could not implement all of its promises. Labour had proposed to lower municipal rents and this became something of an embarrassment to the party when, in power, it proved unwilling to take such action as it would involve breaking the law. Although the election of a Labour Council in 1934 and the continued election of David Kirkwood as Labour MP ran against national political trends, Clydebank, even at times of economic crisis, rejected illegal action and concentrated on the solution of problems by traditional means.[31]

The Approach of War

The possibility of the outbreak of another war in Europe was clear by the mid 1930s. At the same time groups campaigning for peace were becoming increasingly prominent.[32] Both collectively and individually, members of Clydebank Town Council gave considerable support to the anti-war movement in the burgh and nationally. The Council contributed financially to the peace cause. In May 1937 £20 was given to the British National Committee of the International Peace Campaign, while in September 1930 a £5 donation was made to the Clydebank Peace Council.[33] Town Councillors attended peace conferences — Provost Martin represented the Council at meetings of the Scottish Peace Congress and the International Peace Campaign in Edinburgh and London on three occasions in 1937, and in the same year Bailies Wood and Brown attended the annual meeting of the Scottish Peace Council in Edinburgh.[34]

The Town Council's support for the cause of peace was not simply passive. It acted to show the strength of its beliefs. In common with a number of other local authorities such as Wick and Tranent,[35] it refused to participate in the Government's voluntary Air Raid Precaution (ARP) scheme, introduced in August 1935. The refusal, led by Labour Councillors Davidson and Downie, was repeated on several occasions.[36] The reasons given for this action ranged from the claim that 'it was preposterous to think that this town could erect adequate shelter from bombs', to the view that 'precautionary measures created the war psychology'.[37] Yet, as in other areas, the Council was not prepared to break the law. After legislation to compel ARP planning by local authorities was introduced in late 1937, Clydebank fell into line. In March 1938 a sub-committee was established to form an ARP scheme and this was upgraded to a full ARP committee in September 1938.[38] Indeed, the historian of the Clydebank Blitz considers that ARP organisation was not seriously affected by the Council's stand. It pushed ahead strongly after legislation was introduced and was able to profit from the experience of other authorities.[39]

Some criticism was directed at the Council's peace policy. On several occasions between 1935 and 1937 Moderate councillors attempted without success to get the Council's policy on air raid precautions reversed. However, a body of evidence suggests that the Council's policy was in keeping with the feelings of many Clydebank citizens. The local attitude to the peace question was quantified in the League of Nations Union 'Peace Ballot', the National Declaration on the League of Nations and Armaments, in May 1935. The Union was a peace society which favoured arbitration and multi-lateral disarmament. Its local president, John Peacock, was assisted in organising some 500 canvassers by Mrs Hyslop, a prominent local Communist Party member and Town Councillor by co-option in 1937. The results of the ballot, in which 40 per cent of local electors took part, showed, as nationally, over 90 per cent support for the League of Nations, disarmament and economic sanctions against aggressor nations. Only 66 per cent voted in favour of military measures against aggressors.[40] Further evidence of anti-war sentiment in Clydebank can be seen in the establishment of a local Peace Council which, by 1937, was said to represent 34 organisations including trade unions, church guilds, cooperative parties and war committees. It organised Peace Weeks in 1937 and 1938, featuring meetings, posters and anti-war films.[41] The ILP held an anti-war conference in October 1935,[42] and the Clydebank Mutual Service Association, originally established in the early 1930s to help the unemployed, was involved in staging a local author, W. H. Atkinson's anti-war play *Death Cloud* in February 1936.[43] Labour, which spearheaded the policy, maintained a majority in local elections. At a public meeting in January 1938 only 12 members from a large audience volunteered to train in ARP matters.[44] Indeed, even in August 1939, the

Clydebank Press published a claim that the burgh was 'well over 800 short' in local defence services.[45]

Second World War

War came in 1939 and Clydebank suffered greatly. Political activity was considerably reduced in the war years when, as during the First World War, elections were suspended. Vacancies in the Town Council were filled by co-option for the duration of hostilities. The Council maintained its ordinary administrative activities, overseeing cleansing, lighting, public health and so on. In 1942 it established a committee to consider the Beveridge Report on the social services which, in the following year, recommended support in principle for the report's findings.[46] Even house building was continued, though at a slower pace than before the war with, for example, current building at Whitecrook being considered by the Housing Committee in December 1944.[47] Yet the Council also had additional duties and responsibilities, many of which were placed upon it by the Government as a result of the emergency. The town's ARP activity came under the supervision of the ARP Committee. An estimated 40 per cent of local children were evacuated in September 1939[48] under the Government scheme administered by local authority personnel. The Council appointed some of its members to form a Food Control Committee with representatives of local traders and trade unions in the first month of the war.[49]

Perhaps the most pressing of the Council's wartime administrative duties was organising repairs to war damaged buildings under the Housing (Emergency Powers) Act 1939. The German Blitz of March 1941, which resulted in over 500 deaths, left only eight houses in the burgh undamaged.[50] An already difficult housing problem was made considerably worse. As Bailie Braes, the Convenor of the Housing Committee, commented in March 1945:

> '. . . even prior to the war 50% of the houses in the burgh had been overcrowded. Added to this we had lost 30% of our houses in the blitz. The conditions under which some of our people are living can only be described as horrible.'[51]

Clearly, in attempting to fulfil its responsibilities under the 1939 Act the Council faced many problems, some of which, such as the supply of materials, lay beyond its control. As a result much remained to be done in 1945.

Political party activity, though at a generally subdued level, was continued throughout the war. The Citizens' Council endorsed R. B. Cornock in his attempt to be co-opted to the Council in 1941.[52] In June 1943 the Trades and Labour Council was given permission to hold a demonstration to celebrate the second anniversary of Russia's entry into the war.[53] In the same year the local branch of the Communist Party held a meeting to hear a report on the Scottish Congress of the party[54], while in 1944 the Labour Party was allowed to hold a May Day demonstration.[55] Some limited opposition to the war and all it entailed continued into 1940 when the No Conscription League and the ILP held anti-war meetings.[56] However, unlike the First World War, these were the only reported expressions of such sentiments in the burgh. Of more immediate concern to burgh citizens were complaints on the inadequacy of air-raid shelter accommodation provided under Council supervision. A public meeting in 1941 attended by 60 local people criticised the Council for not providing adequate shelter.[57] As on other occasions, the Council maintained that policy on the provision of air-raid shelters was a Government rather than a local authority responsibility.

Despite the very difficult problems facing the town during the war years its political structure was preserved. The local administration performed its regular and emergency duties as well as possible in the circumstances. Political life generally continued, though in a restricted form. The Council did, however, attempt to plan for the post-war future. An exhibition was held in December 1943 to show the Council's intentions for rebuilding the burgh at the end of hostilities,[58] while the Committee on the Beveridge Report pointed the way to the post-war social planning undertaken by the 1945 Labour Government.

CHAPTER SEVEN

The Clydebank Rent Strike

The famous Clydebank Rent Strike is generally believed to have begun after the First World War, but its roots lay deeper in the history of Clydeside. There were many isolated cases of groups of tenants withholding rents in several British cities prior to 1914.[1] They chose this course of action to protest against what they considered to be excessive increases demanded by their landlords or, like 200 tenants in Radnor Park's Holy City estate in September 1905, to put pressure on the owners of their houses to carry out what they considered to be essential improvements or repairs.[2] These sporadic and generally brief incidents attracted little attention in the national press, but they did stimulate public interest in the formation of tenants' rights organisations, which were particularly well supported in the Glasgow area, and seem to have provided inspiration for the more widely-publicised and prolonged rent strikes which broke out all over Britain during the First World War.[3]

The 'Rent Wars' of 1915 were fought mainly in industrial areas of Britain, where landlords were able to exploit the shortages of accommodation, created by the influx of men and women seeking work in the munitions industries, by raising rents. Opposition to rent increases was particularly strong on Clydeside,[4] and some Clydebank tenants played a part in the rent strike movement, in protest against rent increases of up to 13 per cent in the burgh.[5] However, anti-landlord agitation died down in Clydebank, and in most British towns and cities, after the Government rushed through the Rent and Mortgage Interest (War Restrictions) Act in December. The 1915 Act pegged the standard rate of interest, as well as the rents of small houses (in Scotland, of houses let for £30 or less per annum), at the levels which existed in August 1914. The provisions of the Act were to remain in force until six months after the end of the war, and tenants were generally satisfied with the protection offered by the legislation.

There was little housebuilding activity in Britain between 1915 and 1918, and the quality of much of the existing housing stock declined because the landlords found repair and maintenance costs prohibitively expensive. The Government realised that there would be a further deterioration in the physical conditions of existing buildings after the war if rents remained pegged at 1914 levels, but that the complete removal of controls would result in vast increases in areas where houses were in greatest demand, and in dire financial hardship for hundreds of thousands of families.[6] In an attempt to compromise between the demands of landlords for increases which would cover their costs, estimated to have risen by 180 per cent during the war,[7] and of the tenants, who claimed that wages had not risen by sufficient amounts to compensate for the higher costs of living,[8] the Government introduced the Increase of Rent and Mortgage Interest (Restrictions) Act of 1919. The 1919 Act permitted increases of up to 10 per cent on the standard rent of 1914, while extending rent controls to pre-war houses with rentals of up to £60. However, it was only a stop-gap measure. More comprehensive legislation was forthcoming in the Rent and Mortgage Interest (Restrictions) Act of July 1920. The 1920 Act permitted rent increases of 15 per cent immediately, and of a further 25 per cent once essential repairs had been carried out on a controlled house. It offered landlords less than most had demanded, but it was also roundly condemned by the tenants' organisations, trades unions and opposition politicians for offering too much to propertied interests.[9] Clydebank, hitherto on the periphery of the Rent Wars, became the main battleground of the renewed legal struggle between landlord and tenant in Scotland.

Widespread public protests against the partial relaxation of rent controls began after the passing of the 1919 Act, and 5,000 Clydebank tenants joined others all over Scotland in signing a covenant declaring their intention to pay no more than the standard rent of 1914.[10] In August 1920 the Scottish Labour Housing Association, which had branches all over Scotland, called for a general 24 hour strike.[11] In Clydebank, only the Singer plant was able to work normally on 23 August, the day of the strike,[12] and large demonstrations were held in the burgh on 28 August, the day when the factors, the landlords' agents, could collect the first payment of new rents under the 1920 Act.[13] The following week, crowds of women were reported to have followed the factors' clerks, jeering at them, as they attempted to collect the increased rents in the Holy City.[14] At first, only a small minority of Clydebank's tenants seem to have withheld the increased rent.[15] However, as a severe post-war depression in the engineering and shipbuilding trades deepened, and the Clydebank Housing Association's campaign to promote and organise a rent strike progressed, resistance to the demands of the landlords grew.

There were 500 registered unemployed in Clydebank at the end of 1919, but the number grew to 5,000 during 1920 and 1921, rising slightly by the end of 1922, and many more men and women were put on short-time working.[16] At a time when the queues were lengthening at the local employment exchange and rents were rising, the membership of the Clydebank's Housing Association, a branch of the SLHA, rose from 400 in 1919 to over 2,000 in 1920, and to 4,000 people in 1921.[17] The CHA attracted support by its energetic efforts to explain to tenants their rights under the law, but also by offering expert legal assistance to tenants threatened with eviction because they had not paid the increased rents. Officials of the SLHA were able to offer assistance to striking tenants in other parts of Scotland, but nowhere was the legal battle conducted so successfully as in Clydebank.

The CHA's organiser, a retired iron-turner from Dalmuir named Andrew Leiper, made a close study of Britain's rent laws, and he and the Association's legal adviser, David D. Cormack, were able to exploit a number of loopholes while defending tenants served with ejectment summonses for failing to pay the increases. Initially, the most effective defence was on the grounds of the invalidity of notices. Most Scottish factors informed tenants of the new rents in 1920 by sending them notices of intention to increase rent (commonly known as 'notices of increase'). Leiper and Cormack argued in Dumbarton Sheriff Court that, under Scots law, a landlord entered into a contract with his tenants, whereby the latter agreed to pay an agreed rent for his home. Any demand for a new rent required entering into a new contract, but this contract could not be legally valid unless the old one, under which the old rent was paid, was ended by a notice to terminate the tenancy (or 'notice to quit').[18] This point of law may have been overlooked by the property owners and factors, but it is more likely that they deliberately ignored it,

Figure 7:1 *Clydebank Housing Association organiser, Andrew Leiper, one of the most prominent activists during the Rent Strike campaign.*

because of the time, trouble and expense involved in drawing up and sending out thousands of notices to quit, and in the assumption that notices to quit would be considered mere technicalities by apathetic tenants and by a sympathetic judiciary.[19] Their confidence was boosted by a test case brought before Glasgow Sheriff Court in September 1920, where Councillor Emmanuel Shinwell appeared to challenge an ejectment summons brought against him for non-payment of increased rent. The Sheriff dismissed Shinwell's defence, which was based on the alleged incompetence of the notice of increase, but Shinwell's failure to escape eviction was due in part to his lack of skill in presenting his own case, as well as to the Sheriff's benign treatment of the factor's case.[20] Leiper and Cormack were far more successful in conducting the defences of Clydebank tenants. In Dumbarton Sheriff Court, Sheriff-Substitute Alexander Menzies agreed with Cormack that a Clydebank tenant need not pay increased rent, as the man had received no notice to quit before the notice of increase, and the new rent was therefore illegal.[21] He ruled consistently in favour of the tenants in cases brought before him thereafter, and the CHA was quick to publicise the fact that, in Clydebank at least, most tenants need pay only standard rent, without fear of eviction.[22]

Menzies' decisions at Dumbarton Sheriff Court had far-reaching implications. If the notices of increase were indeed illegal, then tenants need not pay higher rents, and could take action to recover any sums in excess of the standard rent which they had paid since the passing of the 1919 Act. Some 'Bankies' refused to pay any rent at all, until the legal situation was clarified. For these reasons, the Glasgow Property Owners and Factors Association took a test case from Clydebank, Kerr v Bryde, to the Sheriff-Principal's court in Stirling, and then to the Court of Session in Edinburgh, only to find Menzies' ruling upheld.[23] Finally, on 3 November 1922, a further appeal was heard in the House of Lords. To the dismay of the landlords and factors, the highest court in the land confirmed the rulings of the Scottish courts by finding in favour of the tenant, Dugald Bryde.[24] The effects of these decisions were dramatic. By December 1922, 20,000 Glaswegians were said to be on rent strike, and tens of thousands of tenants in other parts of Scotland were also witholding all, or in most cases some, of their rents.[25] The collection of increased rent became virtually impossible in Clydebank, as the Kerr v Bryde decision confirmed that 75 per cent of the notices of increase served in the burgh were invalid.[26]

The House of Lords' decision was a triumph for Andrew Leiper, David Cormack and the leadership of the CHA. However, the Government was already preparing fresh legislation on rents, and responded immediately to the Kerr v Bryde decision in order to prevent chaos in Clydebank and the spread of the rent strike. The Onslow Committee reported on the problems which had arisen in collecting increased rents, and its recommendations were incorporated in two new Acts. The Rent Restrictions (Notices of Increase) Act of June 1923 stated that, from 1 December 1922, a notice of increase 'shall have effect and shall be deemed always to have had effect as if it were or had been also a notice to terminate the existing tenancy'. This ruling was intended not only to remove the basis for Cormack's and Leiper's defences of Clydebank tenants, which were now meeting with success all over the country, but to compel all tenants to pay the increased rent from December 1922. Those tenants who had paid only the 'standard' rent of 1914 were not made liable for arrears in respect of unpaid increases from the period before December but, cruelly, those who had paid the extra sums were not entitled to recover the 'illegal' increases. The new Act did little to encourage popular respect for the law.

The Notices of Increase Act was followed in July 1923 by the latest Increase of Rent and Mortgate Interest Restrictions Act, which prolonged the life of the 1920 Act until June 1925 and gave the county court the power to amend an invalid notice and to rule that it 'shall have effect and be deemed *to have had effect* [my italics] as a valid notice'. The new legislation seemed to cover over the cracks in existing rent law, and to prevent tenants from rushing to apply for rebates in respect of increased rents paid before the Kerr v Bryde decision, and property owners and factors hoped that enforcement of the 1923 Acts would put an end to the troublesome activities of the CHA. However, the Government could not legislate for the actions of Leiper and Cormack, and they promptly made a nonsense of the new rent laws.

The CHA encouraged Clydebank's tenants to ignore the fresh batches of notices of increases which were served after the passing of the 1923 Acts, and the factors returned to Dumbarton Sheriff Court to seek ejectment warrants against some rent strikers to set an example. Cormack surprised them by arguing that the latest notices were also invalid, because they were served by the factors even though the 1923 Notices of Increase Act stipulated that they must bear the names and addresses of the landlords. The factors' legal representatives argued that this was yet another attempt to frustrate the intentions of the law, based on an unimportant technicality, but Sheriff-Substitute Menzies refused to accept that the factors, acting as the owner's agents, could legally serve notices.[27] As 90 per cent of the latest batch of notices had been served by the factors, the CHA was able to have most of the latest eviction cases thrown out of court.[28] The crusty old Sheriff-Substitute then rubbed salt into the factors' and owners' wounds. He agreed that he had the power, under the 1923 Rent Act, to amend and validate the invalid notices. However, he refused to do so in the Small Debts Court, and ruled that the factors must take the notices to the Sheriff Court. As the presentation of petitions to the higher court was far more expensive, he effectively placed another obstruction in the path of those who sought to obtain authority to evict striking tenants.[29]

Between 1914 and August 1924, only nine Clydebank tenants (including, in January 1924, the celebrated Dugald Bryde) were evicted from their homes, all for failing to pay even the standard rent.[30] The landlords were generally unwilling to evict those who were unemployed or who, through no fault of their own, could no longer keep up their payments. Aside from humanitarian considerations, they knew that there were considerable expenses involved in obtaining an ejectment decree and carrying out an eviction, and that it became virtually impossible to recover arrears once a tenant was put out of his home.[31] However, Clydebank's property owners began to sustain serious losses after the announcement of the Kerr v Bryde decision in the House of Lords. Sir Robert McAlpine & Sons collected just £15,562 from their tenants during the year beginning 1 November 1922, less than they had received annually before 1920, when their rents were increased by 30-40 per cent.[32] The firm had to write off £4,469 in rents and £2,205 in occupiers rates, which it had failed to collect prior to December 1922, after the Kerr v Bryde decision and the 1923 Notices Act.[33] More than 150 tenants of the Dalmuir and West of Scotland Estate Co were behind with their rent by November 1923, and arrears amounted to £5,324,[34] while 155 of John Brown's 633 tenants were paying less than the full rent, and 17 were paying no rent at all, in March 1924.[35] Clydebank's factors complained in August 1924 that 60 per cent of the tenants in the burgh were withholding at least part of their rents, and they estimated that the total sum in arrears amounted to the staggering sum of £220,000, more than the annual rental value of Clydebank's housing and equivalent to about £4 million at 1988 prices.[36] Led by David Patterson, a leading factor and property owner, the landlords decided the time had come to break the rent strike by launching a campaign of mass evictions.

Early in 1924, 456 ejectment decrees were obtained in Dumbarton Sheriff Court. They were allowed to lapse when William Adamson, Secretary for Scotland in the recently-formed Labour Government, arranged a truce so that the Government and local authorities could try to find a compromise solution to the rent problem.[37] However, the attempt to end the 'rent war' came to naught in Clydebank, where the CHA refused to accept the validity of any demands in excess

THE CLYDEBANK RENT STRIKE

of standard rent, and about two dozen evictions went ahead in Radnor Park, Dalmuir and in the centre of Clydebank.[38] The focus of press attention now switched from the legal battles in the courts to the streets of Clydebank.

Leiper was influential in setting up a Tenants' Vigilante Committee in 1924.[39] The Vigilantes arranged for obstruction of the sheriff's officers when they arrived to evict a tenant, and they were aided by 'scouts' recruited largely from the ranks of the local National Unemployed Workers' Movement. The Vigilante Scouts patrolled the burgh boundaries on bicycles and reported back to the neighbourhood in which evictions were scheduled, when the sheriff officers approached.[40] Twelve large bells were obtained and the ladies of the Vigilante Committee would ring them to summon their women neighbours, and any men in the vicinity, to the house where an eviction was to take place.[41] The women jeered the sheriff officers, and blocked streets and close mouths, or packed into the evictee's house, to make the eviction as difficult as possible to carry out. On many occasions, nameplates were changed and tenants temporarily swopped houses to confuse the sheriff's officers. If a family was evicted, neighbours sometimes broke into the house and put back the furniture.[42] Reports in the national press of lawless street demonstrations were exaggerated and caused great offence in the burgh, and one of the few incidents involving physical violence occurred when angry tenants assaulted a group of reporters covering an eviction.[43]

In January 1925, the new Conservative Secretary for Scotland, Sir John Gilmour, arranged a second truce in Clydebank, and the CHA's propaganda campaign and the spate of evictions came to a brief halt.[44] The truce was arranged to allow the Government Commission on Rent Restriction Acts, presided over by Lord Constable, to take evidence in a more restrained atmosphere. The Constable Commission was appointed to investigate the difficulties in carrying out the terms of the Rent Acts in the industrial areas of the West of Scotland, and took evidence in the five areas of greatest opposition to rent increases, in Glasgow, Greenock, Paisley, the Hamilton district and the Dumbarton area.[45] The members, Lord Constable, Patrick Dollan from the tenants' side and James Steel for the factors, took evidence in Clydebank in February 1925 and issued their reports in June. The majority report (Dollan issued his own) found that a prolonged depression during the early 1920s had resulted in real financial hardship in Clydebank, as in other industrial areas, and that, despite an upturn in the economy, 'the worker is much worse off than he was in 1920 and not so well off as he was in 1914'. Rents in Clydebank were reported to be higher than those in comparable areas of Glasgow, and the increases in occupiers' as well as owners' rates in the burgh were considered to be very steep. However, Clydebank's houses were of comparatively recent construction and were considered to offer a relatively high standard of accommodation. Joblessness was no longer a serious problem in the burgh, according to the report, although the average number of unemployed registered over 1925 was 3,098. Clydebank was said to have fared no worse, and had probably suffered less from the effects of the post-war depression, than other industrial communities. The majority report concluded that the longevity of and the wide support for the rent strike in Clydebank was due partly to high unemployment and high rates in the burgh, but mostly to the extraordinarily successful legal campaign waged by the CHA at Dumbarton Sheriff Court. It recommended that the Government take legal action to simplify the form of notices of increase, thus eliminating the confusion which arose in serving them and which had been so successfully exploited by Leiper, Cormack and their associates.[46]

The Rent and Mortgage Interest (Restrictions Continuation) Act of 28 May 1925 did little more than continue the lives of the 1920 and 1923 Acts, while the text of the Rent Restrictions (Scotland) Bill was savaged during its first reading in July, as it failed to deal realistically with the problems which had arisen in Clydebank and which the Constable Commission had identified as requiring remedial action.[47] The factors and owners, despairing of new legislation which would assist them, embarked on a new campaign to break the rent strike. Like other property owners, Sir Robert McAlpine & Sons were being put under pressure from the Inland Revenue and the rating authorities to settle their own arrears, despite their protestations that it was unfair to tax rents and demand occupiers' rates which, while owing in theory, could not be collected from tenants.[48] By August 1925, the arrears of rent in McAlpine's houses in Clydebank, and a few tenements in Greenock, totalled about £50,000. This figure included sums written off as irrecoverable after the Kerr v Bryde decision, but not the £5,000 claimed as a rebate for occupiers' rates the firm had paid but not recovered from striking tenants.[49] The firm, which had promised to accept the standard rent until the legal position was clarified, decided that the time had come to take vigorous action against the most brazen defaulters. Ejectment warrants against 26 Holy City tenants, some of whom had paid no rent for up to three years and all of whom were in arrears with the standard rent, were obtained in November 1925.[50] When it was realised that the firm would carry out the evictions, many of the other striking tenants came to an arrangement with McAlpine, promising to pay the increases, and to settle their arrears by weekly instalments, in return for an assurance that the defaulting tenants and their families would not be evicted.[51] Other landlords instructed their factors to obtain new ejectment warrants, and there was a new spate of evictions in the burgh.[52]

In March 1926, 3,000 Clydebank tenants were in arrears even with the standard rent, and it was 'generally agreed that a very considerable portion of the arrears of rent has now become irrecoverable in fact though not in law'.[53] The CHA continued to contest the factors' efforts to evict strikers, and the Vigilante Committee continued to organise obstructive demonstrations at the scenes of evictions, but the Rent Strike began to lose its momentum. The Dalmuir and West of Scotland Estates Co. received a report from its factor in April, stating that rents were being collected more easily,[54] while McAlpine's income from rents, which reached the lowest level since the pre-war years during their financial year from November 1922, had recovered considerably by the end of 1926.[55] The drop in unemployment in the burgh, from an average of 3,488 in 1926 to 1,687 the following year, and to 1,581 in 1928,[56] had an effect — many people had only fallen into arrears with their rents because the family breadwinner had lost his job. But the most significant reason for the flagging support of the strike was the change in the attitude of the courts.

At the end of 1925, the Glasgow Property Owners and Factors Association decided to make full use of their legal rights, and took a series of appeals from Dumbarton Sheriff Court.[57] Sheriff-Principal James Macphail overturned Menzies' ruling in the most important case, McKeller v McMaster, in a judgement which implied that landlords need not serve notices of increase before raising rents, but need only alter the figure in the rent books to notify the tenants of increases.[58] He found consistently in favour of the factors and owners in other test cases, and the Court of Session upheld his judgement when the CHA appealed.[59] Menzies had to bow to the weight of opinion from above, and refused to hear technical objections to notices of increase in rent cases brought to his court.[60] The CHA's financial resources were stretched to the limit by the expense of contesting actions in the higher courts, and it was unable to challenge many of the owners' and factors' appeals.[61] Meanwhile, it became easier to obtain ejectment warrants against striking tenants, and evictions became more numerous. The first rent strikers to be evicted were offered new council houses in 1924,[62] but there were none to offer to tenants evicted at the end of 1925 and in 1926. Many homeless families were forced to live with friends, and some actually lived in tents in McLean's Park, until the Town Council acquired some old railway carriages and converted them into temporary homes.[63] As the CHA's court-room successes became more rare, as

Figure 7:2 *Towards the end of the Rent Strike the tide was turning against the CHA and, increasingly, tenants withholding rent found themselves evicted and, accordingly, homeless. In the above photograph, Councillor Jean Rae, a noted campaigner in her own right, is seen with tenants temporarily housed in the old railway carriages.*

locals could see the misery of families made homeless for withholding rent, and as unemployment fell and more people had the means to pay the higher rents, and to make arrangements to pay off arrears, so support for the Rent Strike ebbed away.

One of the few victories for the CHA in 1926 came after Andrew Leiper was threatened with eviction for non-payment of increased rent. At Dumbarton Sheriff Court, he easily exposed a number of flaws in the case of the factor's representative, and the proceedings against him were abandoned.[64] However, the CHA was firmly on the defensive, and it suffered two crushing blows in July 1927. First, the Court of Session upheld Macphail's judgement in Clydebank Investment Co. v Marshall, a final attempt by the CHA to establish the right to challenge incorrect notices. The decision seemed to end any hopes of further successes for the CHA on the notices issue, as did the judges' assertion that sheriffs should in future interpret the laws on rent 'benignantly and not malignantly': in other words, that they should pay greater attention to the intention of the law than to errors made in framing it.[65] Then, on 21 July, Andrew Leiper stepped accidentally in front of a motor-car in Dumbarton Road, sustaining serious injuries from which he died in hospital on 9 August.[66] The tragic loss of the most prominent official of the CHA, and the cumulative effects of the Court of Session decisions, effectively ended the Clydebank Rent Strike. Some tenants continued to withhold rents, and the CHA continued to support them, but they provided only minor problems for the owners and factors. On 27 January 1928, the Dalmuir and West of Scotland Estates Co.'s factor reported 'that the difficulty with the tenants had now been got over and the rents were coming in satisfactorily'.[67] McAlpine's financial secretary noted on 12 March that 'the position of the landlords in regard to notices issued under the Rent Restrictions Acts has been materially improved as the result of certain decisions given in the Court of Session and the application thereof in the Sheriff Courts — particularly in that of Dumbarton. The payment of increased rent is now generally recognised as legal and there is a willingness on the part of the tenants to pay such increased rent wherever their financial circumstances so permit'.[68]

The CHA and its supporters won many victories, but they failed to win the 'Rent War'. Theirs was a remarkable struggle, in which the law was exploited by ordinary people to frustrate the intentions of the law-makers. A large portion of the rent arrears was never recovered by the landlords, and the court-room successes of the CHA enabled thousands of 'Bankies' to make substantial savings in their costs of living, and in some cases to live rent-free, during the hard times of the severe post-war depression.[69] However, the campaign for pre-war rents had little support from MPs at Westminster, and even the leadership of the ILP conceded, by 1923, that the landlords must be allowed to make some increases in rent.[70]

With no hope of parliamentary action to reform the laws on rent in the tenants' favour, men such as Leiper and Cormack could fight only for short-term gains for the tenants they represented. Those gains were won at a price. Many small landlords were unable or unwilling to maintain and repair their pre-war houses when rents were withheld, and this had an adverse effect on the quality of Clydebank's housing stock. Sensational and often ludicrously exaggerated newspaper reports of mass evictions, violent street demonstrations and virtual anarchy in the burgh, did much to put Clydebank on the map at the heart of the 'Red Clydeside', frightening off potential investors who might have built new houses and created new industries there.

CHAPTER EIGHT

Social Trends, 1914-1945

The period 1914-45 was one of great international upheaval during which two World Wars were fought and the economies of the industrialised world were devastated by deep inter-war depression. Naturally such dramatic historic events took their toll upon Clydebank as elsewhere. Before 1914 Clydebank's social structures had had to face up to the demands of rapid industrial growth. Both wars saw an inflow of workers into the town, placing additional strain on resources such as housing. Clydebank itself suffered great destruction during the 1941 Blitz. Previous chapters on the shipyards at war, political developments in Clydebank and the Rent Strike have already examined aspects of economic, social and political change in the town. The following sections on housing, health, education, religion and leisure and recreation specifically examine local developments in these areas over 1914-45.

Housing

The history of housing in Clydebank in the inter-war years was dominated by two features. The first was the political agitation and confrontation between tenants, private landlords and the courts over rent-increases and evictions, a legacy of the wartime rent strikes throughout Clydeside. The second feature was the attempt by local government to fulfil the role of the provider of working-class housing imposed upon it by post-war Government legislation. This need was heightened by the abdication by builders and landlords of their traditional role as providers of new housing. Whilst private ownership and rental continued to dominate the housing market throughout the inter-war years, speculative building accounted for only 112 houses — less than 5% of the total built between 1918 and 1939.[1] Rent restrictions, mortgage restrictions, and the spectre of a massive subsidised public building programme robbed the housing market of what little logic it possessed for the majority of private investors. The physical transformation of the burgh which occurred in these years was thus effected through the medium of the local authority — inexperienced in building and housing management, and at loggerheads for much of the period with the authorities which controlled the building programme. The consequences of these indirect effects of the war on the population of Clydebank were to be felt throughout the inter-war years.

The war had seen a virtual cessation of building in the burgh. Only 955 new houses (100 of them 'Munitions Houses' provided by the Ministry of Supply for incomers) were built between 1914 and 1918 — barely adequate to meet the indigenous demand for new homes, let alone the massive pressure on the housing stock in the burgh created by the influx of munitions workers needed to meet the demands of war.[2] Post-war demographic and social trends were only to exacerbate these problems. However, unlike Glasgow, its neighbour to the east, Clydebank was not burdened by a massive problem of slum housing. The majority of housing was new by the standards of other Scottish towns, a newness which was reflected in high levels of rent. But the houses were small — the census of 1921 showed that 74 per cent of the burgh's houses (containing 72 per cent of the population) were one or two roomed. This compared with a figure of only 49 per cent for Scotland as a whole.[3] The problem thus faced by the burgh was one of a shortage of housing, and of severe overcrowding in the housing that was available. 'People who have been all their days in the burgh are compelled to seek elsewhere for lodgings', wrote R. D. Brown, the new Sanitary Inspector to the burgh in 1919. 'Young folks getting married are compelled to live in rooms or with their parents. From the health point of view, the overcrowding and difficult conditions involved constitute a serious danger . . .'[4]

The building programme that was heralded in 1919 by the passing of the Addison Act was subject to the whim of political expediency. Legislation vacillated between generous subsidies to local authorities for general needs housing, subsidies to private builders for housing for sale and rent, and subsidies for slum clearance and the relief of overcrowding.[5] Long-term planning by the Town Council was thus virtually impossible. Finance to pay for completed contracts in advance of subsidy also had to be raised. Despite attempts to fund operations through a municipal bank, the majority of the capital required (the Council spent £1,190,721 on housing between 1919 and 1940) had to be raised through negotiation with semi-public or private sources.[6] The time taken by the Scottish Office to approve layouts, plans and tenders further hindered the building process. Disagreements between Edinburgh and the Council caused further delays — many of these arose from the Council's attempts to favour local contractors with work.[7] Landowners were also obstructive — in 1926, for example, the Council accepted an offer by the local firm of John Taylor (founded by the former Provost and MP, John Taylor) to build 600 houses on the estate of North East Boquhanran, the sale of which by Sir Robert McAlpine & Sons was virtually complete. At the last moment McAlpine withdrew, seeking an increase in the agreed price of £225 per acre for the 63 acre site.[8] Subsequent to the rejection of these moves by the Council McAlpine applied to develop the estate exploiting the subsidies then available from Government; the Council sought, successfully, to block this application.[9] Such difficulties caused delays and frustrations, but the greatest problem throughout the period was the supply of building materials and skilled building labour.

The Town Council had urged the Government to 'control all building materials' as early as 1920,[10] but as late as 1938 they were still suffering from a materials crisis, thus delaying the completion of the North Kilbowie housing scheme. Built under the terms of the Housing (Scotland) Act of 1935 (designed to relieve overcrowding), the history of the North Kilbowie scheme contains many of the elements which plagued the local authority as it made its first hesitant steps into house building. The scheme, for in excess of 470 houses, had been planned as a general needs estate as early as 1931 but had been delayed in the face of severe opposition from local property-owning interests. The Property Owners' and Factors' Association, the Merchant's Association and the Clydebank and District Citizen's Council all petitioned the Secretary of State for Scotland against approval, claiming that 140 empty houses in the burgh were surplus sufficient to relieve any need for new housing.[11] The Scottish Office, despite sustained harangues in Parliament from

David Kirkwood, concluded that 'to proceed at the present time with a scheme of such magnitude' would be 'inexpedient'.[12] Revived in 1935, tenders for the scheme of 222 three apartment houses, 200 four apartment houses and 50 five apartment houses were approved in September 1936. Within weeks the tender for joinerwork had been increased 'owing to the abnormal rise in the price of timber', whilst the contractor for plasterwork refused to sign the contract with a penalty clause for late completion 'in view of the state of the market for plasterers'. Shortly after work began, the main contractor for the brickwork, Alexander A. Stuart & Co. Ltd., complained of the problems of obtaining a regular supply of bricks. By September 1937 the Town Council had sought to agree terms for a supply of 15,000 bricks per day, but still Stuart, plagued either by a shortage of bricks or bricklayers (many of whom, he claimed, were enticed to work for Glasgow Corporation who paid a guaranteed 51 week year), failed to make progress. By November there were still no completed houses; Stuart was relieved of the contract and tenders for completion were readvertised with the Council seeking to take over the entire work itself.[13] The scheme was not to be completed until 1943.

One way of overcoming the chronic shortage of building materials and delays in completions was to experiment in new methods of construction. The Government, although it preferred orthodox methods, encouraged such experimentation.[14] In its first scheme at East Kilbowie the Council used concrete blocks as the main material in half of the 46 blocks of 160 houses.[15] A bolder experiment took place on the West Kilbowie scheme where the 170 bungalows erected by the local contractor Leslie Kirk Ltd. were constructed from reinforced concrete to the designs of a local man, Thomas Rae. Rae, Superintendent to the Clydebank and District Water Trust, had built two experimental houses at the Cochno filter plant in 1924 by pouring concrete into wooden shutters in order to produce solid concrete walls. The shutters were then used to form the roof joists. These original houses were of four apartments, bathroom and kitchen, and built at a cost of £500. The Council obtained approval for Rae's design from the Scottish Board of Health and adapted them to provide 34 two apartment bungalows, 82 of three and 54 of four apartments. The estimated cost for these was £296, £345 and £390 respectively.[16] The Council also looked to non-traditional methods developed by commercial concerns, one of which (the Atholl steel house) was a product of the burgh's own industry. The first of these steel-framed and steel-walled houses was built in Beardmore Street in late 1924 — subsequently in excess of 1,000 were erected by Atholl Steel Houses Ltd., a subsidiary of Beardmore (Atholl houses were also built for railway workers in Northern France).[17] By May 1926 the Council had agreed to have 100 Atholl houses built at Whitecrook; in addition 120 other non-traditional homes were built there. The average cost of these three apartment flatted units was £405.[18]

The problems of continuity of labour supply were less easily solved at a time of shortages of skilled workers and frequent industrial disputes. A further issue was the extent to which housing contracts could be used to reduce the growing number of unemployed in the burgh. Speaking in Parliament on the first North Kilbowie scheme, James Maxton had urged that it 'was not only needed for housing purposes . . .' but also to provide 'employment for workers in the district'.[19] Two methods were favoured by the Council. The first, as we have seen, was to give preference wherever possible to local contractors. Scrutiny of all tenders by the central authorities frequently obstructed this course of action although the Council sought assurances from all contractors that local labour would be used wherever possible. The second method was to conduct housing contracts using direct labour. This method was opposed by building contractors and found little favour in the Scottish Office. However, by undertaking to meet any excess cost of direct labour contracts out of its own funds, the Council was successful in negotiating agreement on a number of occasions. Direct labour was used on the East Kilbowie

Figure 8:1 *Atholl steel house; one of a number of experimental house types erected in Clydebank in the inter-war years. Following the devastation of the housing stock at the Blitz, Clydebank led the way in experimental house building programmes. Among the many types of housing tried locally were such as pre-fab construction, Myton, Kane Brickwood, Craig Atholl, Hill Presweld, Whitcon and Blackburn.*

scheme, at West Kilbowie, at Whitecrook, and at North Kilbowie.[20]

The type of housing envisaged by post-war planners was drastically at odds with what much of the burgh had known before the war. In place of high density developments of tenement houses the new houses were laid out according to the precepts of the Garden City movement; low density developments (the flatted cottage was a concession to Scottish habits) with wide streets and large gardens.[21] If the impact of the number of these new houses on the total housing stock was small — only 14 per cent of the total by 1939 — the impact on the spatial dimensions of the burgh was massive. The new residential areas running south from the A82 trunk road to Dumbarton covered an area at least twice as large as that occupied by pre-war housing. With new space came new lifestyles, supported by the luxury fittings which many of the new homes offered over their tenement counterparts. Although early schemes offered only gas for lighting and cooking, later developments incorporated both gas and electricity, bringing householders within the orbit of a galaxy of new consumer durables. For some, transition was difficult. Although the Napier Street slum clearance scheme comprised 72 tenement houses, the internal fittings were of the highest order, and a scheme was devised to charge an all inclusive rate for electricity in these all electric flats of between two shillings and two shillings and sixpence per week. Within two months, and not long after tenants were banned from keeping greyhounds, the Council noted that they were using 'an abnormal amount of electricity'. Further investigations led to accusations of abuse of this novel facility by tenants more used to meagre fires and candlelight. Subsequently, meters replaced the weekly set charge.[22]

Selection and control of tenants faced the Council with a range of problems far outwith its experience. Moreover, the most important decision in determining the likely tenant of a house, the setting of rentals, was ultimately in the power of the Scottish Office, who were by duty bound to set an economic rent. Thus the rentals of the majority of local authority housing were set at a level in excess of that which could be met by those most in need. The rents of the Rae concrete bungalows, for example, ranged from £22 per annum for a two apartment house to £32 for four apartments.[23] Local authority rents were generally higher than those in the private sector and tenants did not hold back from petitioning against them.[24] Moreover, the ability to pay rent, as opposed to need, became the main criterion used in the selection of tenants. As loans accrued and interest payments increased, the need to make the housing books balance became an imperative. In October 1925, as private landlords prepared to launch a series of evictions of rent strikers, the Council recommended 'special consideration be given to any homeless people who may be in a position *and willing to pay the rentals* of the burgh houses'.[25] Selection of tenants from suitable applicants was eventually decided by public ballot in an attempt to forestall allegations of favouritism.[26] Nonetheless, it is clear that much local authority housing in the burgh went to those in some ways least in need. An occupational profile of council tenants between 1925 and 1940 confirms this; 65 per cent of tenants were from the relatively prosperous skilled and semi-skilled groups whilst only 10 per cent came from those in the unskilled and labouring groups where wages were lowest and vulnerability to depression greatest.[27]

By 1939 the Town Council had 2,095 new homes either built or under construction. Schemes had been completed at East and West Kilbowie, Whitecrook, Parkhall, Napier Street and Mountblow. Houses were built to a high standard of amenity — 12 per cent were of two, 54 per cent of three, and 29 per cent of four apartments.[28] Three schemes, Parkhall, Mountblow and Napier Street, were all-electric and others were upgraded later.[29] Speculative builders such as McAlpine, Taylor, and Kirk had completed a small number of bungalows and villas mainly in Albert Road, Janetta Street, Drumry Road and Maxwell Road.[30] The total number built by the Council did little more than meet the requirements that had been projected as immediate needs for the burgh in 1919, but nonetheless, by 1939 a spirit of cautious optimism existed as to the progress of the burgh's housing. It was thus particularly tragic that in the space of two nights in March 1941 the achievements and experimentations of twenty years were left in ruins. 'If the war had not intervened', wrote the burgh Sanitary Inspector in 1945, 'the local authority by this time would have overtaken the housing problem . . . many of our

Figure 8:2 *Post-blitz devastation at Radnor Street, one of the areas most heavily affected by the Blitz. Among the casualties, in terms of housing, was McAlpine's 'Holy City'.*

finest houses in the burgh were demolished during the air-raids, while many of our sub-standard houses were left standing'. He concluded that the town was 'back to where we were in 1918 with the problems . . . even more acute than they were before'.[31] In all, 4,300 houses in the burgh — around 35 per cent of the total — were either destroyed or damaged beyond repair. Fewer than ten houses escaped without any damage. Scarce resources required for building new homes were directed at rebuilding old homes, often to re-house several families in conditions of grievous overcrowding.[32] To effect these repairs, and to plan for the future, the burgh appointed as a consultant the architect, Sam Bunton, 'one of the most indefatigable promoters of new ideas' in housing construction, who was to be intimately linked with the regeneration of Clydebank in the post-war years.[33]

Health and Welfare, 1912-48

A landmark in British health care was reached with the passing of Lloyd George's 1911 National Insurance Act. The Liberal measure introduced a vast contributory scheme to insure the whole working population against sickness and to offer financial help in dealing with tuberculosis and dependents in maternity cases. The Clydebank National Health Insurance Committee met for the first time under the Act on 1 August 1912, with Provost John Taylor as its first Chairman. The Committee consisted of 31 members, with representatives from the Town Council, Friendly Societies, approved Insurance Societies, voluntary contributors (i.e. people with an annual income of more than £250) and representatives from the Scottish National Health Commissioners.

The Committee was addressed by Dr Cullen from the Scottish National Health Insurance Commission. He hoped the Act 'would mark the beginning of an epoch . . . in Public Health, and that it would enormously increase the health, happiness and prosperity of the working classes and correspondingly diminish the heavy bill of sickness and misery which prevailed'.[34] The Committee met the local doctors on 30 December 1912, and agreed that it would be widely advertised throughout the burgh by posters and in the local press that insured patients should choose their doctor by 15 February 1913. By 15 March, out of an estimated 17,000 insured persons in the Committee's area, 15,087 had chosen their GPs.[35] It was agreed to allocate equally the 'undecided' patients amongst GPs willing to take more patients. The following doctors were appointed to the Committee, viz; Ernest H. Cramb (by the National Insurance Commissioners), William Stevenson (by the Town Council), and J. Stirling Robertson and John Gilmour (by the local Medical or Panel Committee). Thomas M. Strang, the part-time MOH, became adviser to the Committee. The Committee had five sub-committees, including the Sanatorium Benefit sub-committee, with, in addition, two professional committees elected by the doctors and the pharmacists. The pharmaceutical sub-committee's chairman was Thomas Guthrie who later held a variety of positions within the British Pharmaceutical Society, including the post of President from 1938-39.[36]

The National Insurance Act considerably broadened the remit of health care from that of the old Poor Law. However, the treatment and prevention of infectious diseases remained a major problem for the medical profession. The setting up of a Sanatorium Benefit sub-committee of 14 lay members under the 1911 Act reflected the threat posed by the prevalence of tuberculosis. Until the advent of streptomycin and other chemotherapy, tuberculosis led to a very high sickness and death rate. The average annual tuberculosis death rate in Clydebank in five year periods from 1909 to 1939 was 86, 54, 51, 38, 34 and 33.[37] The first half of the twentieth century saw numerous attempts to set up a sanatorium for the treatment of TB patients in Dunbartonshire but all proved unsuccessful. Some TB patients were admitted to Duntocher and Blawarthill Hospitals although they had been built as fever

Figure 8:3 *William Boyd MA, BSc, DPhil, DLitt, LLD, founder of the Clydebank Mutual Service Association and the Dalmuir Former Pupils.*

hospitals but most were sent elsewhere, to Bridge of Weir, Peebles, Stonehouse, Shotts, Longriggend or Ochil Hills. In the 1940s some patients were sent to Switzerland. Until its last meeting on 10 December 1920, the sub-committee, advised by the GPs and the MOH, decided which patients should receive sanatorium or other treatment, but afterwards the treatment of TB patients was left entirely in the hands of the doctors.

Meanwhile, from the 1940s, other infectious diseases were gradually being brought under control, particularly with the increased availability of vaccines and antibiotics. There was a changing pattern of infection. Tuberculous meningitis was always fatal until the late 1940s but nineteenth-century 'killers' such as scarlet fever were overcome. However, epidemics remained dangerous. In the influenza epidemic of 1918, Clydebank suffered a very high death rate. There were 92 deaths in the burgh in October including 40 in one week.[38] In 1921 there was one death due to typhus, one due to smallpox, and 35 from whooping cough.[39] In 1922 there was one death caused by typhoid and 32 caused by measles.[40]

The gradual improvements which occurred were due to the combined efforts of the MOHs, burgh Sanitary Inspectors, GPs, Health Visitors, District Nurses and others. Among the MOHs since the formation of the burgh were John Wylie (1886-1897), James Stevenson (1897-1909), Thomas M. Strang (1909-1936), Russell D. Martin (1936-1939) and Thomas Hunter (1939-1964). Sanitary Inspectors included Robert D. Brown, William Cunningham and William Webster.

The improvement in all these measures is shown graphically in infant death rates from 1911-1972.[41] The large variations up to 1947 were probably due to epidemics and lack of effective treatment.

Table 8:1   *Clydebank 1911-73: Infant death rate in first year of life for every 1,000 live births.*

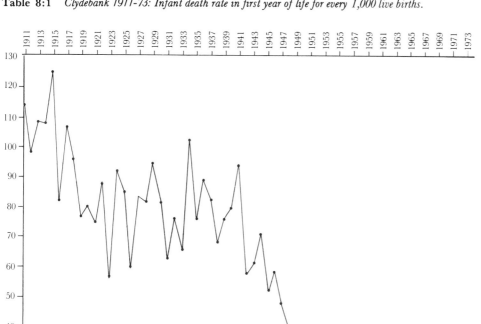

By 1912 the population of Clydebank had risen to about 38,000 and there were thirteen doctors practising and living in the area, viz: Robert C. Blyth, William Butchart, John M. Cameron, Ernest H. Cramb, John Gilmour, Andrew Downie Macphee, Patrick A. Mackay, J. Stirling Robertson, James & William Stevenson, Thomas Strang (part time MOH), J. Gemmill Thomson and Hugh Young. Two well known doctors who also practised in the town but lived in Glasgow were W. H. S. Armstrong from Scotstoun, who became Medical Superintendent of Blawarthill Hospital, and George A. Allan of Sandyford, who later became senior consultant physician in the Western Infirmary.[42]

Pioneering medical work was done by the Clydebank Mutual Service Association formed during the Depression in April 1932, by Dr William Boyd.[43] The Association aimed to give the unemployed some outside interest. A gymnasium was opened in Agamemnon Street in 1932 and in 1936 the Association opened the Clydebank Orthopaedic and Rehabilitation Clinic at 384 Dumbarton Road and a child guidance clinic.

The health of Clydebank was greatly helped in 1907 when a branch of the Queen Victoria Jubilee Institute of Nursing was formed. The branch, initially instigated by Sir Thomas and Lady Bell, supported one nurse for Central Clydebank — part of the promised financial support coming from £50 gathered in entrance fees to 'see over' the *Lusitania*, launched at John Brown the year before. Mr Park of Singer promised another £120 to employ a nurse for the Kilbowie District.[44] From their first year when the Queen's Nurses cared for 347 patients involving 8,032 visits, their nursing role grew rapidly.[45] In 1912 the burgh made notification of births compulsory, requesting that the Queen's Nurses act as Health Visitors, advising mothers at home and in clinics and attending tuberculosis patients at home.

In 1914 a Nurses Home was built at the corner of Cochno Street and Aberconway Street for the sum of £2,000. By 1916, with local practitioners and anaesthetists in attendance, tonsillectomies were being performed, 1,179 such operations being carried out in the succeeding five years.[46] In 1922 the clinic was transferred to the Dunbartonshire Education Authority. During the First World

Figure 8:4 *Among the many fund raising ventures of the period was the Clydebank & Duntocher Penny-a-Week Fund. In the above photograph Mrs Ford, the local co-ordinator, David Stewart, Manager of the Empire Pleasure Palace, Captain William Peters, Session Clerk, and boys from the 2nd Clydebank Boys' Brigade Company attached to St James' Church are seen alongside the result of this particular venture.*

Figure 8:5 *Mountblow House was built in 1767 by Robert Donald, a 'tobacco lord' and Provost of Glasgow from 1776-77. In the 19th century it was the principal of several mansions owned by William Dunn and was later sold, in 1877, by a descendant to Glasgow Corporation. Until 1893 it was the residence of James Rodger Thomson and, thereafter, was leased to the Seamen's Orphans' Institute. In 1922 it became the Mountblow Children's Home and was then used for the treatment of children under five suffering from rickets, malnutrition or debility following acute illness.*

War the Queen's Nurses staffed a creche at Singer and ran ante-natal and post-natal clinics at the Town Hall. In 1920 an Eye Clinic was set up in the Nurses Home, where Miss Garden, the Superintendent Nurse since 1907, had a staff of nine nurses. From 1928 the Nurses took part in a Singer Insurance Scheme to supply nursing care in the home for their employees. Singer and the Town Council paid the Association for these services but many nursing services were supported voluntarily. By 1937 the Queen's Nurses were performing district nursing, health visiting and midwifery, involving about 55,000 home visits and clinic attendances per annum.[47]

By the 1930s maternity provision was moving away from home births. In 1920, 25 midwives worked in Clydebank and 48 per cent of births were attended solely by them.[48] By the late 1930s fewer confinements were attended only by midwives. Some confinements took place at Homelands Maternity Hospital, Great Western Road, Glasgow and St Francis Home, Govan. On the second afternoon of the Clydebank Blitz, 14 March 1941, a considerable number of expectant women were transferred to Airthrey Castle, Bridge of Allan, a practice which continued until the late 1940s.

Sadly, the Clydebank Blitz proved a devastating test of medical services. During the Blitz many were killed or injured, only a sixth of the houses were left fit for habitation and an estimated 40,000 of the 50,000 population were evacuated in two days. First Aid posts at Elgin Street, Boquhanran and Dalmuir Schools were staffed by doctors, nurses and first aid workers, and there was also a mobile First Aid post at Milton Mains farm. Some of the injured were taken to Blawarthill Hospital which was severely damaged on the first day of the Blitz; other patients were transferred to Killearn Hospital or to Canniesburn Hospital in Bearsden. On the second night, a mobile surgical unit from Dumbarton helped with casualties in Hardgate. Details, because of the general confusion, are few, but Dr Jeffrey was at Dalmuir, Dr Thomas Hunter at the Municipal Buildings, Dr Stanley McLeish at Milton Mains, and Drs Charles Garrett and John Hilferty at Elgin Street, while ARP personnel, emergency services, St Andrew's Ambulance Association, the Women's Royal

Voluntary Services and many other volunteers assisted, performing heroically in difficult circumstances. Immediately following the Blitz, a surgery was established within the Town Hall, staffed by two doctors during the day and one overnight, giving 24 hour coverage. By the end of April, coverage was reduced to between 9.00am. and 9.00pm. Among the disruption caused by the Blitz was the damage to many of the doctors' homes and surgeries and the loss of six chemists shops.

Over the period from 1911 to 1945 health services in Clydebank had been extended. Some gains had been made in the struggle to control infectious diseases, while improvements in housing and sanitation had benefited public health. However, access to health care was still restricted and dramatic improvements both in access to medical attention and in public health awaited the foundation of the National Health Service in 1948.

Education

The period between 1914 and 1945 was one of continual change in education provision in Clydebank. As with the rest of Britain, the range, diversity and standard of schooling had to improve to keep pace with the demands of modern society. In addition, the burgh was faced with an increasing and shifting population which stretched local resources. The two World Wars produced large inflows of workers to the shipyards and war-related industries. Many brought their children, and, during the Great War especially, this necessitated an expansion of school places. Clydebank School rose to nearly 3,000 pupils with over 80 teachers, and conditions became very cramped. However, it was not merely the needs of children that had to be catered for. With expanded output from the shipyards, the School Board was called upon to increase the availability of apprenticeship training. This part of the educational service was organised in evening classes which had started in a modest way in the 1880s in the Science and Art Department of Clydebank School.

Figure 8:6 *In 1919 Dunbarton County Council assumed responsibility for education. This photograph shows the first Education Authority of the County of Dunbarton, 1919-22, outside their headquarters at Park Circus, Glasgow.*

In 1890 there had been 120 students taking science classes, with two-thirds of them studying animal physiology, mathematics, magnetism and electricity; at that time only 13 studied naval architecture, 17 machine construction and 5 'steam' engineering. However, the numbers rose steadily until 1914 when there was a sharp rise, encouraged by bonuses paid by the yards to apprentices who attended classes in the evenings.

In 1919, the Scottish school boards were abolished and replaced by directly-elected education authorities. The Dunbartonshire Authority set up local School Management Committees to supervise affairs in the various districts. The one for Old Kilpatrick was dominated by clergy; out of nine local members, five were ministers (including those of Dalmuir and Morison Memorial) and two were priests (including Father John Brotherhood). The Committee often complained that the Authority, located in distant Park Circus in Glasgow, was denying it freedom to manage; centralisation was even then being felt. The withering of local control went a stage further in 1930 with the abolition of directly-elected education authorities.[49] Responsibility for education was transferred to the County Councils, and the management of schooling passed from the hands of interested citizens (especially clergy and church people) into those of education officials.

Some important developments occurred during the 1920s and 1930s. The Scottish Education Act of 1918 which had set up the Education Authorities also permitted the inclusion of Catholic schools within the state system. The Catholic Church had tried to cope with the rapid shift of its constituency to rising industrial towns like Clydebank, but had found it difficult to meet the costs and to supply sufficient teachers. With the need emerging at the beginning of the century for the development of secondary education, negotiations were entered into for the transfer of schools on a basis that would protect the distinctive religious character of the teaching. With the 1918 Act, Clydebank's Catholic schools came under the control of the Education Authority and were put on a similar financial footing to the non-denominational schools.

The growth of Clydebank's population continued to be the greatest problem.

Figure 8:7 *Clydebank High School staff in 1925. Dr Andrew Cecil Paterson, Headmaster, is in the centre, front row, with one of Clydebank's best known teachers, Miss Janet Hogg, who taught in Clydebank from 1888-1930, on his left.*
This school was replaced by the new High School in Janetta Street, the opening of which was delayed, due to the intervention of the war, until September 1947.

However, the situation was complicated by the expansion of secondary education. In 1921, Clydebank School was divided into primary and secondary. The latter, Clydebank High School, was at the time the only wholly secondary school in Scotland, taking over 1,000 pupils drawn from all the non-denominational schools between Drumchapel and Yoker in the east to Bowling in the west. During the inter-war years, the High School offered a variety of training and qualifications, the 'Lower' and 'Higher' certificates, and the Leaving Certificate. Facilities and equipment gradually improved; by 1940, for instance, there were eight science laboratories. Whilst the High School took over the Kilbowie Road premises, the primary school was moved to a temporary building in Whitecrook. The new High School was commenced in the 1930s in North Kilbowie but war prevented it from being occupied. Post-primary provision continued to expand. New centres were created to cater for the large numbers of secondary pupils; there were centres at Dalmuir and Our Holy Redeemer's, whilst two-year courses were offered at Radnor Park, Gavinburn, Duntocher and Boquhanran. Pressure of pupils started to ease in the mid and late 1930s — partly due to the slowing down in the influx to the burgh, and partly to a decline in the birth rate. At the High School, the total number of pupils fell back to under 1,000, helping to ease overcrowding. But the resource problem was the main reason why proposals to raise the school leaving age from 14 to 15 — first mooted for 1929 — were constantly delayed.

Several important features emerged in the education system in the burgh during this period. One was the 'paper chase' — the pursuit of paper qualifications which became seen as absolutely essential for getting good jobs. The creation of different grades of secondary school made parents extremely anxious that their children should gain admission to the best, to the High School where there was opportunity to undertake the Higher Leaving Certificate for university entrance. A second major feature of secondary education was the sexual division of the curriculum. Whilst science labs were built for boys, a vast range of facilities were provided to give girls a training in domestic management. At Clydebank High School, for instance, there were by the end of the 1930s, two cookery rooms, a laundry, a needlework room, and a house at 71 Dumbarton Road where girls could be trained in 'Housewifery'. Though single girls were in demand by local employers (like Singer who provided the schools with sewing machines), the notion that 'the woman's place is in the home' was a major theme in education in the burgh. The development of the sports curriculum was another feature of the schools during the 1920s and 1930s. Facilities for physical recreation had been fairly limited before the First World War. Until 1900, the main element of recreation had been playground drill conducted by special drill instructors — usually, like Sergeant Kerr in the 1890s, drawn from retired or reserve soldiers. It was in 1900 that physical recreation first started to expand into general exercises and, within a few years, swimming classes and football. But it was only in the 1920s and 1930s that the provision of proper playing fields was attended to. In addition to swimming lessons in the municipal baths, there were, by 1940, seven acres of playing fields at Whitecrook, including three soccer pitches, two rugby pitches, three hockey pitches and a pavilion.

Perhaps most important was the transformation of education during the period from a system managed principally by church representatives, who believed in Victorian concepts of moral and religious improvement, to one conducted as an agency of the emerging welfare state. Not only had fees been abolished, but books were provided free by the 1930s. As Dr Andrew C. Paterson, Rector of Clydebank High School, wrote in 1940:

> 'Not only the child's intellect but his body is cared for. Well-planned social services have been set up whereby the school doctor periodically examines his general health, the dentist his teeth, the oculist his eyes, etc., boots and clothing are provided if the parents are necessitous and School Camps provide him with a holiday at the sea-side.'[50]

The absorption of the schools under County Council control symbolised the unification of education with other social services laid on by local and national government. Education was no longer to be left in the hands of amateurs (however well-meaning), but was to be managed in tandem with all the other duties of the civil authorities.

By 1937, there were 7,986 school pupils in Clydebank — 1,369 fewer than ten years before. The school rolls were falling most sharply in Clydebank High and Primary Schools, and especially at Elgin Street. The Catholic schools, Our Holy Redeemer's and St Stephen's, and the schools in Boquhanran, Dalmuir and Radnor Park were maintaining rough stability in size, reflecting the shift of the population centre away from the river. This was the first fall in pupil numbers experienced in Clydebank, and was allowing for consolidation of facilities. New equipment was being bought, including gramophones, and radios to permit timetabled 'wireless lessons', and new playing fields were being acquired at Dalmuir. The quality of schooling was undoubtedly improving, and Clydebank could at last claim to be keeping at the forefront of educational technology. Unfortunately the Blitz disrupted progress.[51] In the raids of March 1941, Clydebank, Radnor Park, Boquhanran, Gavinburn and Duntocher Schools were destroyed and others received slight damage. Schools suffered a loss of pupils through fatality and evacuation. Despite evacuation, by Wednesday 26 March 1941 Provost David Low's Emergency committee had met with the Scottish Education Department to discuss the provision of hutted accommodation for schooling. The accommodation shortage was further compounded by the delayed new Clydebank High School in Janetta Street and the proposal by the Department of Health, contained in a letter to the Education Committee, that, in addition to Whitecrook, the new High School and Our Holy Redeemer's might be required to be converted into workmen's hostels. Whitecrook School was converted by the SSHA Ltd. to accommodate up to 220 men employed in vital war work in the yards, engineering works, Singer and house repairs. The hostel, the first of its kind in Scotland, was opened on Friday, 25 April 1941 by Thomas Johnston, Secretary of State for Scotland. Despite evacuation, the education service

Figure 8:8 *Boquhanran Public School was opened in 1906 on the corner of Janetta Street and Albert Road. Destroyed during the Blitz the school was never replaced. This pre-First World War photograph shows a group of rather stern looking small boys with their teacher.*

Figure 8:9 *Duntocher from Goldenhill Park in the 1930s. In the foreground is the original Duntocher Trinity Church and, north of Dumbarton Road, behind the houses on the right is Duntocher Public School. Both the church and school were victims of the Blitz. Until its replacement by Goldenhill Primary School, pupils were accommodated in huts erected on the site of the blitzed school.*

continued. With the peace, children flooded back, and with damage still to be made good, and with Whitecrook School remaining a hostel until August 1946, pressure of accommodation became severe, heralding the resource difficulties that were to return to the town in the following decades.

Religion

This period witnessed the final and greatest contest between Victorian religious values and modern secular ideas — the prohibition campaign of the 1920s. Under the Temperance (Scotland) Act 1913, the electorate in every ward in the country was empowered from June 1920 to vote in plebiscites on whether they wanted to abolish all public houses and off-licences, to limit their number, or to permit licences to be issued as before. After decades of temperance activity, and with curbs on drinking during the First World War, churches, religious voluntary organisations, and temperance organisations (including most friendly societies) were convinced that the nation would support 'the abolition of the common public-house . . . which all who seek the Kingdom of God should use their utmost endeavours to secure'.[53] In Clydebank, as in the rest of Scotland, evangelicals were keyed up for the polls.

The churches were quite accustomed to electioneering. They had campaigned for church candidates for Old Kilpatrick Parish Council (and its predecessor, the Parochial Board) since 1845, and for church candidates for the Parish School Board since 1873. Thus, the first local veto plebiscite of November 1920 was preceded by eight months of efficient and fevered evangelical campaigning. Bands of Hope sent groups of sashed boys around town carrying banners, ministers preached from the pulpit on how to vote, and public meetings in the Town Hall and rallies at the gates of the 'yards' and the 'factory' were conducted by the British Women's Temperance Association and the National Citizens' Council. The Rev George Minto of Hamilton Memorial UF Church, president of the Clydebank campaign, told one meeting in the Wesleyan Hall that 'this was the Christian Church's opportunity for social service, which, if neglected, would have disastrous consequences on her future'.[53] At another meeting, he said:

> '[We are] living in a democratic age, and the voice of democracy [is] ever sounding louder and louder in our ears for change — better hours, better wages, better houses — a better and higher and truer life for every one in our land.'[54]

The issue also inspired poetry:

'Too long the dram has dragged us doon,
Its trail o' sin would reach the moon,
Crime, degradation, dearth, attune,
  The dram's dire meed;*
And frien's a' tell us Tamsontoun,
  Should strike it deid.'[55]

*'meed' — reward or wages

There was no shortage of opposition. An anti-prohibition campaign, widely considered to be financed by the drinks trade, mounted opposition rallies, bedecked pubs with posters, and claimed that the prohibitionists were trying to deprive the working man of his freedom to a drink using 'Yankee money and Yankee speakers'.[56] Moreover, the Church of Scotland was divided on the issue; the new minister at Dalmuir Church studiously avoided 'prejudicing' the no-licence issue, and his church hall was subsequently used for an anti-prohibition meeting featuring two 'Women Liberty Defenders' from Chicago.

Despite a high poll of 77 per cent, and an expectation that three of the burgh's five wards would go 'dry', the need for a 55 per cent vote for licensing restriction resulted in only Radnor Park voting 'No Licence' (by 2,505 votes to 1,869) with sufficient votes in Dalmuir for 'Limitation' (ie. a 25 per cent cut in the number of licensed premises). In all, only five pubs were abolished — a severe disappointment to the churches. However, the result was predicted by some observers who considered that the shipyard workers would not fall behind the burgh's elites during industrial and rent-strike agitation. Evangelicals called a second poll after the minimum delay — three years — but suffered a complete failure when both Dalmuir and Radnor Park voted 'wet'. These triennial plebiscites became progressively more discouraging for the temperance cause, as Table 8:2 shows. Nonetheless, over half the voters supported prohibition in 1920, and over a third in 1929, and the Town Council and magistrates supported the restriction of drinking in the burgh; in 1923, there were only 26 pubs in the town — less than half the number for towns of similar size elsewhere in Scotland. Moreover, the local authority used its discretionary powers to close pubs at 9 pm, leading to frequent raids on pubs serving illicitly at 9.30pm. The council imposed a 'dry' policy on the new housing schemes by refusing to lease land to licensees. As David Kirkwood MP told a local meeting in 1929, 'Prohibition was necessary if [we] are to have clean government, both local and national'.[57] Temperance leisure — provided by the British Women's Temperance Association, the Good Templars, the Rechabites, the Sons of Temperance and other bodies — remained prominent in the inter-war years, and few 'Bankies' born before 1930 will have failed to take the pledge in the

Table 8:2   *Local Veto Plebiscite Results, 1920-29: totals for Clydebank (5 wards)*

	% votes for No Change	% of votes for Limitation (Limitation + No L.)	% votes for No Licences
1920	49.5	50.5	50.2
1923	57.5	42.5	42.1
1926	54.2	45.8	45.5
1929[1]	64.0	36.0	35.7

[1]Only 4 wards were polled in this year.

Source: Clydebank and Renfrew Press, 19 November 1920,
      7 December 1923, 13 December 1929.

Band of Hope or the League of the Cross — surely the most widely broken solemn undertaking in Scottish history!

Important changes were underway. For one thing, religious voluntary organisations were suffering from the growth of modern forms of entertainment — notably the cinema and, by the 1930s, the radio. Feature columns in the *Clydebank Press* on these topics started to squeeze out religious items in the years before the outbreak of war. The churches tried to compete by offering ever more 'secular' entertainments. Concert parties provided a mixture of song, comedy sketches and dance: the 'Sunshine Party' at the Morison Memorial, 'The Rockets' and 'The Radiators' at the YMCA, and 'The Players' at St Columba's, whose 1938 religious drama was intended 'as an act of worship rather than as an entertainment'.[58] Church halls mushroomed around 1930 to provide expanded venues in which to stage such events — like the suite of halls opened at Hamilton Memorial in October 1929. Older forms of organisation started to wither. The Radnor Park Church Band of Hope, the largest in Dunbartonshire in the 1920s and important to the 1920 'dry' vote, closed in 1932. A second important change to emerge was council housing, but the early schemes were relatively small and near to existing churches; the main effort of church extension occurred after 1945.

Figure 8:10 *St. Stephen's Parish originated in November 1907 when the Rev. John Brotherhood set up a mission in Dalmuir. By 1909 the congregation were worshipping in this brand new church with the well loved Rev. Brotherhood as priest. The church was destroyed during the Blitz, after which the school hall was utilised until a temporary church was built around 1950. The present church was opened in 1958.*

The most profound impact on the churches came towards the end of this period — the Blitz of March 1941. The churches fared no better during the aerial bombardment than did other buildings. Amongst the churches destroyed were Duntocher Trinity, Duntocher East (church, manse and hall) and St Mary's Church in Duntocher; St Stephen's, Ross Memorial and Dalmuir Parish Church hall in Dalmuir; and the Congregational Church, manse and hall in Radnor Park. The clergy were immediately called upon to minister to the dying and the bereaved — the ministers of St James' and Ross Memorial officiated at 592 funerals during the week of the Blitz. But the wider rupture in the community was reflected in the shattering of congregational life due to loss of churches, fatalities, and dispersement of the population; at the Union Church the congregation of 1,000 people was reduced to three. Many congregations 'doubled up' in surviving church buildings, waiting for the peace before embarking on reconstruction.

Leisure and Recreation

After the 'Great War' the older established Clubs and Societies which had survived were joined by new organisations reflecting, in part, a change of leisure interests. Bodies such as the YMCA, YWCA and the Clydebank Mutual Service Association, and major employers such as Brown, Beardmore, Singer and the Clydebank Co-operative Society, joined the churches in providing a wide range of recreational facilities. In 1928, for example, Singer supported an Orchestral Association, Amateur Dramatic Club, Chess Club, Musical Association, Literary Club and Camera Club (the latter Club was formed in 1926 and was very active until its demise in 1941 when the Singer Hall was destroyed in the Blitz).[59]

The Town Council, likewise, was influential in providing recreational facilities — opening bowling greens, tennis courts and putting greens for example. On Wednesday, 21 May 1924, a municipal bowling green was opened on ground off Livingstone Street by Mrs Brown, wife of the Convenor of the Parks Committee.[60] On Saturday, 25 April 1925, Provost Samuel MacDonald opened a Model Yachting Pond at Whitecrook.[61] Golf, one of several increasingly popular sports, was not forgotten. On 23 September 1927 Miss Effie Young, sister of the Convenor of the Parks Committee, opened a temporary nine-hole golf course,[62] the full course being opened on 16 June 1928 by Sir Thomas Bell.[63] Inevitably, despite the Council's best efforts, the demand for recreational facilities was insatiable and, accordingly, some organisations became impatient. On Friday, 23 March 1923, for example, the 21st anniversary celebrations of the Clydebank Amateur Swimming Club provided a platform from which to lament the smallness of the Hall Street Public Baths, which restricted competitive swimming, forcing the water polo team to play every match away from home.[64] Some five years later a Sub-Committee recommended the construction of a new pool 75 feet by 30 feet. Plans were approved on 10 June 1929 and the Bruce Street Public Baths were opened on

CLYDEBANK AMATEUR SWIMMING CLUB Standing—J. Bruce, A. Brownlee, D. Hamilton, A. L. Reid, R. S. Alexander,
Water Polo League. Third Div. Champions, 1934 Sitting—N. H. McNab, I. Macaulay, J. Hepburn, J. Sime, R. Cameron.

Figure 8:11

103

Tuesday, 25 October 1932 by Provost John McKenzie.[65] Encouraged by this Council initiative, the water polo team won the Second Division Western District Championships for two consecutive seasons.

The numbers attending the various uniformed organisations increased during the period. By 1939 twelve Boys' Brigade Companies, nine Scout Troops, six Girl Guide Companies and several Lifeboy Teams, Cub and Brownie Packs, were active. Such provision notwithstanding, Dr William Boyd (the founder of the Clydebank Mutual Service Association) encouraged the formation of the Dalmuir Former Pupils (DFP). His vision brought together six Dalmuir youngsters, namely, Cuthbert Douse, Jimmy and Nellie Findlay, George Paterson, Agnes Kane and Helen Hutchison, whose efforts, aided by Alex Kyle, launched the DFP. Despite its title the Club was not restricted to former Dalmuir pupils and was an open mixed youth club — one of the forerunners of Community Education in Clydebank. Commencing with a once weekly PE class for boys, the DFP developed a wide range of activities, further progress only being checked by the outbreak of war and the disruption caused by the effects of the Blitz.

Culturally, every taste was catered for. Burns 'devotees' could attend several clubs, and in 1921 interest among the Highland Community revived with the formation of the Clydebank and District Highland Association. Choral music admirers were particularly well served by a wealth of choirs including the Clydebank Male Voice Choir, Clydebank Female Voice Choir, Clydebank Junior Male Voice Choir, Hardgate Male Voice Choir, Barns O' Clyde Male Voice Choir, Clydebank Choral and Operatic Society and the Beardmore (Dalmuir) Operatic Society. The Clydebank Male Voice Choir was especially successful, competing with great distinction at the Scottish musical festivals in the early twenties.[66] Thereafter the choir extended its activities to compete south of the border, notably at the Blackpool Festivals between 1928-34. Clydebank boasted a rich variety of bands; in addition to the extremely active Clydebank Burgh Band,[67] performances were given by the Duntocher Silver Band, the Clydebank RC Band and the Clydebank Concertina Band. The local pipe bands, ie., the Singer Pipe Band, the Dalmuir Parish Pipe Band and its 1923 offshoot, the Dalmuir Cameron Pipe Band, were particularly strong, the first-named being winners at the Cowal Gathering on several occasions. Amateur dramatics, always popular, received a boost in the

Figure 8:12 *For many years the district was well served by pipe bands with, in addition to the major bands such as the Singer Pipe Band, others attached to several Boys' Brigade Companies and Boy Scout Troops. In the early twenties, the Dalmuir Parish Pipe Band was the main rival to the Singer Pipe Band.*

Thirties with the reforming of the Clydebank Dramatic Group and the spread of the Glasgow-based Project Theatre Movement into Clydebank in October 1932. The local dramatic scene was further strengthened in the mid-forties with the establishment of the highly successful Clydebank Repertory Theatre.

Other popular entertainments included going to the dance halls, theatre and cinema. In the early days of the theatre, the 'bioscope' had been a novel but secondary element of the programme, but gradually the 'bioscope' (and later the 'cinematograph') displaced the 'variety act'. On Monday, 14 November 1927, for example the former Gaiety Theatre was extensively renovated, re-opening as 'The Bank' cinema. Addressing an invited audience, which included Provost J. Young and Magistrates, the Scottish Cinema & Variety Theatres Co. Ltd.'s General Manager, David B. Stewart, (formerly Manager of The Cinem and Empire theatres), commended this new venture to the audience while lamenting the demise of the once popular Gaiety Theatre and old Drill Hall evening concerts.[68] Local rivalry ensured further renovations and the spread of the 'talkies'. In June 1927 the former Empire Theatre re-opened as the Empire Cinema and on 15 December 1930 the Dalmuir Picture House was converted for sound pictures and re-opened — minus 'Roberto and his popular orchestra' — as The Regal.[69] On Monday, 14 February 1938, a new cinema — the La Scala Cinema — was opened in Graham Avenue by David Kirkwood, MP.[70] Within a few years, however, the numbers of cinemas dramatically decreased. During the Blitz the Palace was destroyed, the La Scala was damaged (for a period thereafter it was used as a furniture repository) and the Municipal Pictures, Co-op Pictures and the New Kinema foundered. On Thursday, 8 October 1942 a fire completely gutted the Pavilion Picture House.[71] The loss of the Pavilion, particularly its Sunday evening charity concerts, prompted the Council to debate the adequacy of the remaining cinemas and the possibility of Sunday opening.

Outdoors, football was the predominant sport, being strong at all levels. In the local YMCA League teams were fielded by Morison Memorial, Boquhanran Guild, Kilbowie Guild, Dalmuir YMCA, Dalnottar Rovers and Lusset Park. Juvenile football was especially strong. In May 1923 representatives from Radnor Victoria, Clydebank Corinthians, British Legion, Dalnottar Rovers, Drumchapel,

Figure 8:13 *The Empire Cinema, formerly Empire Pleasure Palace, on Glasgow Road opposite Bon Accord Place. Opened in 1914, the Empire was destroyed by fire in June 1959.*

Figure 8:14 *Yoker Athletic FC players and officials in 1933 with the Scottish Junior Cup, an achievement repeated in season 1941-42 by local rivals, Clydebank Juniors FC.*

Clydebank Celtic, Clydeview and Minerva Hibs, met in Morrison's Restaurant to discuss the formation of a Clydebank and District Juvenile League.[72] Local Junior teams, notably Yoker Athletic, were experiencing a 'golden era'. A settlement reached between the Junior and Senior League administrators enabled clubs like Yoker to hold on to outstanding players such as the 'legendary' Sam English. This settlement brought instant rewards. In season 1932-33 Yoker Athletic lifted their first ever Scottish Junior Cup, a feat matched by Clydebank Juniors in the 1941-42 season. The latter's success was all the more remarkable given their circumstances.

Figure 8:15 *Clydesdale Harriers team photograph taken outside the Hall Street Baths at the start of the 1932-33 cross-country season. After the decimation of the club in the Great War, a recovery in strength, and fortunes, had now begun.*

In season 1939-40, as Duntocher Hibs suspended their activities, the Clydebank Juniors opened their new pitch at New Kilbowie Park.[73] New Kilbowie Park was damaged in the Blitz and thereafter for a few seasons, until the re-opening of New Kilbowie Park on 31 July 1943, all matches were played away from home.[74]

On 25 March 1938 the *Clydebank Press* carried a report on the centenary of the Duntocher Curling Club. Formed from a meeting of friends at the house of James Templeton, Duntocher on 9 March 1838, Mr Templeton was elected President, David Russell, Carleith, Secretary and Robert Baird, Treasurer. Two of the newly adopted rules are worthy of quote.

Rule 6.   'Every member on being admitted shall pay the sum of 5s, and also the sum of 1s for the benefit of the old gentleman in the corner of the room in which he is admitted.'

Rule 8.   'Any member quarrelling or getting drunk on the ice shall be fined in one bottle of whiskey for the first offence, and for every offence afterwards in a bottle of rum.'

During its first century the Club played at six different ponds, at New Cut, Dalmuir, Auchenleck Farm, Hardgate, the dam, Dalmuir Park, The Crescent, Dalmuir, Carleith and finally, above Kilpatrick Station, Old Kilpatrick. Its 14 Presidents throughout this period were all well-known local gentlemen and included James R. Thomson, 1880-84, R. P. Macindoe, 1884-89, James B. Macindoe, 1889-1905, Daniel Shields, 1905-10, James Filshie, 1910-11 and the longest serving, Peter Robertson 1917-38.

Today, although without its own pond, the club is still flourishing, playing at a rink in Glasgow and, at 150 years old, is probably the oldest surviving club in the District.

Elsewhere, quoiting continued to flourish at Dalmuir, Clydebank and Hardgate, cricket at Dalmuir, Clydebank and Millbrae, and tennis at Dalmuir, Old Kilpatrick and Millbrae. In respect of the Clydesdale Harriers, the club, from the depths of 1920, began the long climb back to strength with excellent committee members such as Tom Millar, Andy McMillan and Jim Shields. Not only was the club put on a sound financial footing but the social spirit blossomed and the runners began to attain success — particularly within the ladies section. On this occasion, the War was a 'break' but not a disaster since a War Committee was formed to keep the club 'ticking over' until the cessation of hostilities.[75] Cycling also flourished in the Thirties, firstly, with the formation in October 1933 of the Lomond Roads Cycling Club and, secondly, with the formation of a Clydebank branch of the Clarion Cycling Club. The sport of boxing was very popular throughout the period. The early clubs, 'Tim' McMahon's Clydebank and District, Radnor Park, Duntocher and the Clydebank Co-operative Clubs were joined after the Blitz by Danny Wood's John Brown Welfare AAC and Jim Meechan's Clydebank Corinthians AAC. Many excellent boxing shows were mounted locally, notably wartime charity shows in aid of causes such as the 'Clydeside Distress Funds', 'Welcome Home Funds' and 'Prisoner of War Funds'. Particularly prominent was fighter-cum-promoter, Jim Meechan. On 5 July 1941, Jim, with the assistance of burgh officials David Logan, William Smith and Dr. Preston, augmented the 'Air-Raid Distress Fund', packing 2,000 spectators into Holm Park.[76] Present on that memorable occasion were Sir Harry Lauder and British Empire Fly-Weight Boxing Champion, Jackie Paterson. Afterwards, a newspaper article commented:

'Amazing folk the Clydebankers. Here they were, two thousand of them, sitting around the boxing ring, glad to lend a financial hand to aid the distress of their neighbours who'd been K.O.'d by Hitler's under-the-belt gang.'[77]

Figure 8:16 *An early production of 'The Gondoliers' by the Clydebank Choral and Operatic Society, one of the many arts groups performing in the 1940s.*

Overall, the late Thirties, with the attendant threat of war, proved difficult years for the many clubs and societies. Conscription, blackout restrictions and sequestration of property severely disrupted their activities. The greater loss, however, was occasioned by the Blitz itself. All over the district, halls, schools, club premises, uniforms and equipment were lost. Among the bands, for example, the loss of the Singer Hall and, consequently, the uniforms and equipment, led to the demise of the Singer Pipe Band. A similar misfortune almost resulted in the demise of the Duntocher Silver Band. The Clydebank Burgh Band likewise lost their Hall and £1,000 worth of equipment, but the Band (veterans of 15 Scottish Championship wins and six times winners of the Beardmore Shield) defiantly gritted their teeth and re-formed, declaring themselves the 'Clydebank Burgh, Bombed, Blasted, Burned, Blitzed, but not Busted, Brass Band'.[78] A vivid picture of the disruption caused by the Blitz is contained within the Clydebank and District Boys' Brigade Battalion *War and Peace Report 1940-1946:*

'Such accommodation as remained intact was soon in part or in whole requisitioned. Many officers were called to the Colours, or to work away from home. The blackout made it impracticable for Life Boys to meet. Even in the case of B.B. boys, parents had to be assured that arrangements had been made for the boys' safety in emergency. Supplies were scarce, or had petered out . . . . Some had joined forces to share a hall, or equipment, or staff.'[79]

For those clubs and societies that survived the war years, 'expediency' was the order of the day. Those whose facilities survived intact gladly shared with others less fortunate and this willingness to assist ensured that the loss among the ranks of the many organisations was less than it might otherwise have been.

CHAPTER NINE

Shipbuilding in Crisis, 1919-1935

John Brown

In contrast to the strong and rising demand for shipping in the years from 1910 to the end of the First World War, shipbuilding was to experience a protracted period of difficulty from 1921 to 1935. The problem was a combination of weak demand for new tonnage, together with a vast extension in the capacity of the shipbuilding industry in Britain and overseas. The war had greatly encouraged the extension of shipyards and the capacity of the British industry had grown by some 40 per cent by 1919. Then, in response to wartime losses and the immediate post-war shortage of vessels, a huge building boom saw the world merchant fleet grow rapidly from 51 million gross tons in 1919 to 65 million gross tons by 1923. This coincided with a stagnation of world trade, and world shipping capacity became a depressive drug on the shipbuilders' market. The market situation was made even worse for the big naval yards when the Washington Naval Treaty of 1921 severely restricted naval building and effectively ended the stream of Admiralty orders to yards like John Brown and Beardmore.[1]

Yet none of this was foreseen as the Armistice was signed in November 1918. Over 900 merchant vessels had been lost in the conflict, liner building had ceased for nearly five years, and cargo construction had been strictly limited as all efforts were concentrated on providing warships. Everyone recognised a backlog of repair, maintenance and pent-up demand that was waiting to be satisfied. Shipbuilders, in fact, were more anxious about scarcities of steel and men, than worried about any potential lack of orders. The warshipbuilders, however, did know that at least for a time naval building would diminish and yards like John Brown and Beardmore recognized that they would have to fill their order books in the merchant marketplace — a practice nearly forgotten in the long profitable years of naval building from before the First World War. Consequently, well before the end of hostilities, the management at Clydebank was planning its post-war construction by establishing alliances with shipowners, and associations with the suppliers of materials.

John Brown was very active in making such arrangements.[2] Being part of the steel empire of John Brown & Co., Sheffield, the Clydebank yard did not join in the various consortia of Clydeside shipbuilders that bought over the Scottish steel industry at the end of the war, although it did exchange £25,000 of shares with the North West Rivet, Bolt and Nut Co. in December 1919 to stabilize its supply of rivets, bolts and nuts.

In relation to securing orders, John Brown had made arrangements with five shipping lines by 1919. The first was secured in November 1916 when John Brown, Harland and Wolff and Fairfield jointly signed a ten-year agreement with the Canadian Pacific Railway to supply steamers. Then in 1918, John Brown concluded three berth reservation schemes; one with Lord Pirrie and the Royal Mail Group, another with the Orient Steam Navigation Co., and a third with Cunard. Finally, in 1919, John Brown extended and renewed its long-standing links with Fairfield and Cammell Laird in the Coventry Syndicate,[3] a combine designed to cooperatively seek markets and act as a sales agency for foreign naval business, and to a lesser extent for foreign merchant business. All these arrangements were made in anticipation of a large boom in merchant building at the end of hostilities; shipowners wanted to be sure they had access to berths to ensure a quick supply of new tonnage. Nor were these arrangements taken on without a commitment in capital expenditure by the shipyard. Between 1919 and 1921 John Brown poured in £316,000 in new capital additions to Clydebank to improve and modernise facilities to cope with the expected flood of new work.[4]

In the immediate post-war years these efforts were rewarded with considerable success. The agreement with Lord Pirrie delivered seven contracts to Clydebank between December 1918 and December 1920; Cunard ordered two large passenger liners, the *Franconia* and *Alaunia;* and the Canadian Pacific ordered its two Mont class liners, the *Montcalm* and the *Montclare*. All these contracts were taken at the peak of wartime and immediate post-war inflation. Clydebank, like other yards, found it could not deliver vessels in 1920 for less than three and a half or four times the price in 1913. Wages were similarly inflated. The average weekly pay per man in the yard in 1914 was £1 16 7d; in 1920 it was £4 1 11d.[5] However, by the end of 1920, the falling off in orders, and the effects of Government deflation, made this level of costs and prices untenable. The cost of materials fell quickly by 60 per cent or more by the end of 1921, but wages did not fall in line, declining by only about 40 per cent by the end of 1922. As prices tumbled in 1921, shipowners held off ordering to judge the floor in prices before placing new contracts, and because work on the stocks had been delayed by shortages, they began to suspend or even cancel work on the high-priced contracts taken up between 1918 and 1920.

By the end of 1921 Lord Pirrie had stopped the work on one vessel, the *Loch Katrine,* and had reduced the pace of building on two other vessels for Elder Dempster. Cunard suspended progress on its two liners, and men were only kept on the payroll at Clydebank by the workers agreeing to a work-sharing scheme which divided the workforce into two groups working alternate weeks. This scheme did not survive long; the workforce which had stood at 9,297 in 1920, slipped to an average weekly payroll of 6,322 employees in 1921, and was nearly cut in half to 3,653 employees in 1922.

The bright expectations of a period of prosperous activity had quickly become tarnished. Even so, work was gradually taken up again on the suspended contracts and all eventually delivered substantial profits to the yard. The contract price of the two Cunarders, *Franconia* and *Alaunia* was £2.64 million and this delivered a gross profit of £462,000, or nearly 19 per cent. Similarly the Canadian Pacific liners, *Montcalm* and *Montclare,* with a contract price of £3.3 million returned £677,000 as a contribution to profit and overheads, a rate of some 20 per cent.[6] This, however, was a bonanza that was not to be repeated. The special 'builders' friends' arrangements with the shipping lines which had provided these post-war orders did not long survive the downturn in the market. The Cunard berth booking arrangement was quickly allowed to lapse, while the death of Lord Pirrie in 1924 ended that particular source of orders; the agreement with the Canadian Pacific was not renewed when it expired in 1926.

The measures which John Brown had taken to protect itself with a big merchant order book, in anticipation of reduced naval orders, had now disappeared. This was an extremely serious problem for, against all expectation, naval orders were not simply reduced, they effectively disappeared as a source of work for the private warshipbuilding yards. The problem arose from a change in outlook in defence which saw Britain become a signatory to the Washington Naval Treaty of 1921. Under this Treaty Britain abandoned its traditional policy of ensuring that the Royal Navy had a superiority over any two other naval powers, and agreed to parity with the USA. This removed any need to build capital ships; indeed, construction was largely prohibited for a period of ten years, Britain being confined to building not more than two vessels of less than 35,000 tons within that period. As a consequence of signing this Treaty, orders for four battlecruisers — one of which had been secured by Clydebank in the spring of 1921 — were cancelled. This had a severe effect on Clydebank; after the launch of the *Enterprise* in 1919, the yard did not launch another Admiralty vessel until 1929. In the intervening decade, Clydebank, one of Britain's greatest naval yards, built only two light cruisers for the Australian navy; all the other work was merchant tonnage.

During the 1920s naval orders effectively ceased to be a serious prospect for the major shipbuilders. At the same time, the situation in the merchant market became extremely difficult. The pressure on the shipbuilders is clearly seen in the problems Clydebank met in securing orders. Between 1922 and 1928 John Brown tendered for 131 merchant contracts, but gained only 23 orders. The yard suffered substantial losses on eight of those, while the profit margin on another 12 was under 3 per cent. The net loss on the 23 contracts taken together was over £211,000. Within this, losses of £280,000 were made on three vessels for the New Zealand Shipping Co., this indicating the mistakes that could be made when contracts were taken under pressure in a buyers' market on difficult or unfavourable terms. On this occasion Sir Thomas Bell found that the owners' agent was one 'to whose rapacity there appears to be no limits'.[7]

Worse was to follow between 1929 and 1934. Merchant orders virtually dried up in 1930, and in March 1931 the Shipbuilders Employers Federation reported that only ten yards in Britain had commenced work on any new orders; some 25 yards had suspended staff and closed down temporarily. In Clydebank all eight berths were empty by September 1930, and not a single order was on the books. Closure appeared imminent.

In the second half of 1930 the outlook for John Brown was in fact much worse than the general public in Clydebank could have known. Not only was the yard without orders, but the parent company, John Brown & Co. of Sheffield, was itself on the verge of bankruptcy.[8] At the end of 1929 the Sheffield Board found that creditors holding £481,000 of the company's short term notes were unwilling to renew them and required payment. This faced the company with a major financial crisis, which threatened to destroy public confidence in John Brown & Co. A drastic financial reconstruction of the company was required. A plan was proposed to write down the ordinary share capital by £2,375,000, and to raise fresh capital through a new debenture issue. It was also proposed to merge the steel making interests of John Brown with those of their neighbour in Sheffield, Thomas Firth & Co.

In effect, the fate of the Clydebank shipyard hinged on the success of this proposal. It was ironic that the Sheffield parent, whose resources had sustained Clydebank before the First World War, should now threaten the existence of the yard. Sir Thomas Bell, confronted with this problem, calculated that in spite of losses in the merchant contracts between 1922 and 1928, earlier profits from 1918-

21, and six profitable naval orders in 1928-29, had generated a surplus of nearly £1.5 million which had been transferred to Sheffield to bolster the parent company. But, in 1930, with no new work in hand, and eight empty berths, Sir Thomas Bell's ability to extend further aid to Sheffield appeared to be limited. But at this juncture Clydebank won the order for Cunard's new giant liner, contract *No. 534*, the vessel that was to become the *Queen Mary*. It is no exaggeration to say that the reconstruction of the parent company and the survival of Clydebank were secured by this contract.

Early in 1930 Cunard had announced that it planned to inaugurate a new weekly service from London via Cherbourg to New York. All existing weekly schedules employed three vessels, but Cunard planned to make the service pay with two vessels, relying on their size and speed to ensure service and payload.[9] The announcement of this plan early in 1930, when orders were almost impossible to obtain, induced intense competition among the great liner yards — Vickers, Armstrong Whitworth, John Brown and Harland & Wolff. In May 1930 Cunard declared that it intended to place the order with Clydebank. The fact that Clydebank gained the order said a great deal for the skill of Sir Thomas Bell in concealing the financial weakness of the yard; he was indeed desperate to win the order. Even then the outcome was not certain; although the order was promised in May, the contract was not finally signed till 1 December 1930, though the yard had already ordered steel and begun laying the keel some weeks earlier.

It is difficult to exaggerate the importance of this single contract at that particular point in time. Without the Cunard order the yard was bound for closure, and with no flow of payments from Clydebank to Sheffield the financial reconstruction of the parent company could not easily proceed. In placing the order Cunard paid an advance instalment of £250,000 to Clydebank on Boxing Day 1930. Without this Christmas present the Clydebank overdraft with the Union Bank would have risen to £300,000 while the agreed limit was only £200,000. However, this timely infusion of funds saved the day; the Sheffield reconstruction proceeded smoothly and Clydebank appeared set for three to four years work in an industry elsewhere saturated with unemployment and unused capacity. Even so, this single contract did not guarantee employment for everyone. The yard had an average weekly workforce of 6,675 men in 1929. In 1930 this declined to 5,085, but in 1931, with work proceeding quickly on *No. 534,* employment was cut to an average of 3,556 men with an average weekly pay of £2 13 4d.[10]

Unfortunately, not even this level of stability was to last as the world economy slipped into financial crisis in the second half of 1931. Cunard became a victim of the uncertainty and instability, for it was financing the construction of *No. 534* by discounting bills in the money market. Such discounting depended upon the bills being accepted and guaranteed by Cunard's bankers, but in late 1931 Lloyds Bank refused to continue to stand behind the guarantee of some £3 million required. In view of this, Cunard was forced to suspend work on the vessel. Work ceased on 12 December 1931 and was not to be resumed for two years and three months on the successful negotiation of the merger between the competing transatlantic liner companies, Cunard and White Star on 3 April 1934. The Government approved of this merger and only agreed to grant financial assistance to complete *No. 534* once the terms of the merger were agreed. This was part of the Government's attempt to encourage rationalization generally in British industry at that time.

The stranded hull of *No. 534* loomed over the depressed and unemployed town of Clydebank for nearly two and a half years, symbolising the failure of the town's economic base. In the near silent yard, the workforce was down to 422 men in 1932, and averaged only 675 employees in 1933. The men retained were mainly foremen and under-foremen, and they were largely employed on the maintenance of equipment. Throughout the prolonged period of idleness, Cunard paid for maintenance, inspection, and continuous painting of the hull. Shipbuilding had

Figure 9:1 *The inevitability of No. 534 had long been foreseen, for at a dinner given on 22 February 1884 to celebrate the completion of a new engine works, John Grant, a director, visualised the launch of massive transatlantic liners such as the 534.*

ground to a halt, not only in Clydebank and on Clydeside, but throughout the whole country. In 1933 the Clyde launched only 49,000 tons of shipping and only 133,000 tons were completed in Britain, a level that was barely 5 per cent of the capacity of the industry. In the depth of this depression the Clydebank yard managed to attract only one other small order between 1931 and 1934.

The consequence of these setbacks was, not surprisingly, a collapse in the profitability of the yard. A small trading surplus of £39,000 in 1931 deteriorated to a trading loss of £44,000 in 1933. In the heart of this distress it was to be the long dormant flow of orders from the Admiralty which produced the first glimmer of reviving fortunes. The 1932-33 naval construction programme allocated 25,716 tons of shipping to Clydeside, and of this Clydebank gained orders for two vessels, the cruiser *Southampton,* and a sloop, *The Halcyon,* an order book of 10,770 tons. In

Figure 9:2 *As the workforce returned to the Clydebank Yard to resume work on the 534, the Burgh was bedecked with bunting, and pipers preceded the returning workers.*

1934 a further 37,285 tons of Admiralty work came to the Clyde, and John Brown won a share of another sloop and two destroyers totalling 3,650 tons. This turnaround arose from a worsening of the European political climate. In October 1933 Germany withdrew from the Geneva Disarmament Conference and from the League of Nations. In response, the British government set up a Defence Review Committee which recommended the expenditure of £76 million over five years to improve defences; nothing came of this till 1935.[11] Nevertheless, public opinion was moving sharply in favour of increased defence expenditure. Taken together with the resumption of work on *No. 534* in April 1934, Clydebank could feel that the worst was over. John Brown had survived the great depression, but only just. Beardmore at Dalmuir was not to be so lucky.

Beardmore

Like John Brown and the other armaments manufacturers, William Beardmore's strategy for adjusting to peacetime production was to build passenger vessels and tankers in his shipyard, to begin to construct locomotives in the howitzer shop at Dalmuir, and to expand production of motor cars and bicycles in other parts of his business empire.[12] In a mood of optimism, he is reputed to have called his managers together and declared, 'Transport is the thing'. Convinced that demand for ships would strengthen, he sanctioned the expenditure of £400,000 on an extension of the Dalmuir engine works to provide capacity for constructing large turbines and £250,000 on the laying out of three new berths and associated plate-working sheds for building tankers and tramp ships. In the boom that followed the peace, this confidence did not seem misplaced. Orders were confirmed in 1918-19 for eight ships, including the *Tyrrhenia* (later renamed *Lancastria*) for Cunard, the *Cameronia* for Henderson Bros. and two vessels for Lloyd Saboud, the *Conte Rosso* and *Conte Verde* — approximately the same volume of orders as was placed with John Brown. The *Cameronia* was launched in 1919 and the *Lancastria* the following year. During 1920 Beardmore, along with John Brown, received an unconfirmed order for a new super-battlecruiser.[13]

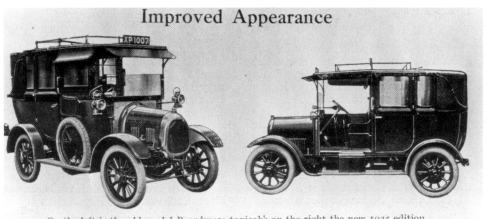

Improved Appearance

On the left is the old model Beardmore taxicab; on the right the new 1925 edition.
The much improved proportions and lines will be appreciated.

Figure 9:3 *In 1919 Beardmore diversified yet again, introducing the production of taxis from their Underwood works in Paisley, the works having been converted from shell manufacture.*

As soon as hostilities were at an end in 1918, work began in converting the howitzer and field gun shops at Dalmuir for locomotive construction. The techniques acquired during the war in manufacturing field ordnance, particularly the inter-changeability of parts, was to be transferred to the building and repairing of locomotives. It was intended that the new locomotive works should act in concert with Vickers and Beyer Peacock & Co., the Manchester locomotive builders. This came to nothing and Vickers abandoned its ambitions to enter this market early in 1920. At Dalmuir an order for 35 standard design locomotives was placed by the East Indian Railway as early as the winter of 1918 and the first deliveries were made during the following year. In 1919 further standard design contracts were placed for 20 locomotives by the Great Eastern Railway Co. and for 19 by the Crown Commissioners for the colonies on behalf of the Nigerian Government Railways. The rapidity of the change from ordnance to locomotive production reflected the management's determination to meet effectively the challenge of new products and customers. This diversification into locomotive building was strongly criticized by Sir Hugh Reid, chairman of the North British Locomotive Co. in Glasgow, on the grounds that there was insufficient work to support any more builders.[14]

Figure 9:4 *The single-engine, two seater biplane fighter, the WBXXVI armed with three Beardmore-Farquhar machine guns. Due to a lack of orders the above prototype aeroplane was not repeated.*

THE HISTORY OF CLYDEBANK

Sir William Beardmore's interest in transport also extended to aircraft. He believed that the prospect for the growth of commercial air routes was promising and wished 'to take such a part in the development of the services on these routes as shall be commensurate with its importance'. Although aircraft design at Dalmuir had not produced a successful design during the war, a price list was published in 1919 advertising no fewer than 13 different types of civil aircraft. These ranged from 'a single seat bi-plane of 21 feet wing span, known as *WB V II*, to a lage cargo and passenger triplane of 120 feet wing span, the *WB V III*. Only two of these designs were ever built at Dalmuir; the single-seater bi-plane *WBIIB* of which two were constructed, and the two-seater bi-plane *WBX* of which only one was constructed. When orders failed to materialise, the company announced on 19 July 1920 the opening of an air route between Glasgow and London 'for the carriage of goods and passengers'. The first flight took four hours, but the service never proceeded beyond the experimental stage.[15]

The sea-plane shed at Dalmuir continued to manufacture airship parts for the *R34* and *R36* which had not been completed by the time the war ended. The Air Ministry hurriedly explored civil uses for airships and in March 1919 accepted an invitation from the Aero Club of America to send *R34* on an experimental flight to America. On 2 July the newly commissioned *R34* left East Fortune aerodrome outside Edinburgh for her historic voyage to America, completing the journey in 108 hours. Despite this achievement, proposals to develop the route commercially were abandoned. The *R36*, fitted out for passenger transport, was not completed until April 1921 and, except for a few publicity flights, was never used successfully. Work on the only remaining contract with Beardmore's *R40* had been halted in August 1919. With the delivery of the *R36*, the aircraft department at Dalmuir was closed through lack of demand.[16]

To finance his postwar plant, Sir William Beardmore raised about £4 million in additional capital. The company's overall results were excellent in 1919 with profits of almost £1 million, but fortunes were reversed the following year when the sudden downturn in the economy resulted in a loss of an equivalent sum. By the end of the year the company was in a vulnerable position and needed sustained profits for several years to meet its commitments. Following the sharp reduction in freight rates, shipowners had ceased to order new tonnage and either cancelled or postponed existing contracts. At first the problems did not affect the Dalmuir yard; five vessels were launched during 1921 of a record 54,547 tons and in the following year four vessels of 33,736 tons.[17] Sir William, recently created Lord Invernairn, was deeply troubled about future prospects. At the launch of the *British Enterprise* on 18 October 1921, when the new East yard was officially opened, he attributed the deteriorating position of the shipbuilding industry to wartime wage rises and called for all round reductions.[18] With the signing in December 1921 of the Washington Naval Treaty, severely limiting naval shipbuilding, Dalmuir's prospects were bleak. The tentative order for the battlecruiser was cancelled after the expenditure of £1,700. Only a trawler, built as a speculative experiment, and two small ferries for the London Midland Scottish Railway, the *Hebble* and the *Rye*, were launched during 1923. The following year in an effort to bring more engineering work to Dalmuir, Beardmore leased the old Allan Line's engine works in Bootle Docks, Liverpool, from the Canadian Pacific Co. and set up a ship repairing works to be supplied with replacement parts by the engine and boiler shops at Dalmuir.[19]

With a slight upturn in the economy, Dalmuir fared better in 1924 and 1925. The vessels launched in 1925 were the passenger liner *Conte Biancomano* for the Lloyd Sabaudo and the ice-breaker *Krisjanis Valdermars* for the Latvian Government. The fortunes of the yard plunged again in 1926, when only the sludge boat *John Perring* for the London County Council and the motor passenger cargo ship *Itope* for the Brazil Companhia Nacional de Navegacas Costeira were launched. Matters improved once more in the next two years, with the award of

116

Admiralty contracts for one cruiser and two submarines under the 1927 programme as a belated attempt to preserve the yard's warship building potential.[20]

With the generalized nature of the depression in shipbuilding in the 1920s several shipbuilding companies began to press for some form of co-operation. Beardmore, through A.J. Campbell, the manager at Dalmuir, took the lead in these discussions in Scotland. On 1 February 1928 a meeting at Edinburgh resolved to form the Shipbuilding Conference, whereby shipbuilders would pool tenders and add sufficient sums to cover the cost of the unsuccessful tenders. Late in 1928 the Conference appointed a sub-committee under the chairmanship of Sir James Lithgow to examine the possibility of setting up a fund to purchase redundant yards.[21]

Throughout the 1920s the locomotive industry, like shipbuilding, was severely depressed and competition for orders was fierce. From 1920 to 1928 Beardmore constructed only 360 locomotives of which 173 were built in 1920-21. Despite this lack-lustre performance, the new Dalmuir locomotive works managed to hold its own against the established private builders without making large losses. In the five and a half years between January 1924 and June 1929 Beardmore won more business than such established firms as Beyer Peacock & Co. and Robert Stephenson & Co. Imaginatively, Beardmore attempted to enlarge the market for locomotives by combining with British-Thomson Houston Ltd. to design prototype diesel-electric railcars and locomotives. The first nine sets, supplied to the Canadian National Railway in 1928 were well received. Attempts to repeat this success in Britain failed because the narrower gauge track required the machinery to be compressed into a smaller space. In the very depressed conditions of the late 1920s scarcely any orders for diesel locomotives were forthcoming, and, as a make-weight, a scaled down version of the engine was developed at Dalmuir for use in commercial road vehicles.[22]

Encouraged by the formation of Imperial Airways Ltd. in 1924 and a resurgence of interest in commercial aviation, Lord Invernairn decided to re-open the airframe department at Dalmuir to manufacture Rhorbach all-metal stressed-skin aircraft. In the autumn of 1924 the company unveiled the *Wee Bee*, a two-seater light monoplane powered by a 30 horsepower engine. Although this aircraft won the Air Ministry trials at Lympne in October, it was quickly superseded by the De Haviland *Moth* and no more were built. Meanwhile, the department at Dalmuir was designing three military aircraft: a two-seater and a single-seater fighter, and a two-seater reconnaissance seaplane. The only one to be built was a prototype two-seater bi-plane fighter in the expectation of an order from the Latvian Government which failed to materialize. During 1924 the Air Ministry ordered two Rhorbach-type flying boats, the *Inverness* and one land plane, the *Inflexible*. The first *Inverness* was built to Beardmore's designs by the Rhorbach company at Copenhagen and trial flights took place at Felixstowe in September 1925. The other *Inverness* and the *Inflexible* were constructed at Dalmuir and delivered in 1928. They were the first all-metal stressed-skin aircraft to be built in Britain and were received with interest. No Government orders were available for further development and the airframe department was closed for a second time early in 1929.[23]

The problems experienced at Dalmuir in the 1920s were mirrored throughout the whole of the company. By 1923 Lord Invernairn was deeply concerned about the finances of his vast enterprise. As a temporary measure an additional half million pounds was borrowed from Lloyd's Bank, but he and his directors could see no prospect of an immediate recovery, blaming their difficulties on the wartime extensions. The company's overdraft ceiling was reached in 1926 and the banks agreed that no further cash would be made available until Lord Invernairn had taken steps to put his house in order. Accordingly, Sir William McLintock, one of the leading accountants of the time who had begun his career in Glasgow, was

Figure 9:5 *A. J. Campbell was a pupil at Mrs Pitblado's Clydebank Adventure School and winner of the first scholarship at Clydebank School in 1879. For many years an employee at the Clydebank Shipyard, he later joined Beardmore, ultimately becoming manager at Dalmuir.*

called in during June to determine what could be done to shore up the business. His report, submitted in October, painted a grim picture and called for drastic action. Neither the banks nor Lord Invernairn were prepared to accept such a radical solution and appealed to the government to postpone the payment of the company's wartime debts. Winston Churchill, the Chancellor of the Exchequer, turned down this request on the grounds that if Lord Invernairn could not come to terms with his predicament, he should accept the consequences of the collapse of the company. The banks, dismayed by this outcome, urged Lord Invernairn to take action. When nothing happened, the banks seized the initiative and appointed a Committee of Investigation on 29 March 1927 with powers to impose a strategy for the company's survival.[24]

It took the Committee of Investigation more than a year to find a way forward and on 13 June 1928 Lewis Craven Ord, a consulting engineer and a director of the armaments firm, Armstrong Whitworth & Co., was appointed joint managing director with Lord Invernairn. He embarked at once on an internal holding operation, closing unprofitable departments and firing staff. In October the company's share capital was massively reduced by writing 95 pence off the value of each £1 share. Further rationalization followed with the closure of the boiler works at Parkhead and a light marine diesel plant at Coatbridge, and the transfer of the work to Dalmuir. By early 1929 Lewis Ord was confident that his policies were taking effect and that 'as soon as the shipbuilders of the country decide to drop their suicidal policy of building ships at a loss, Dalmuir should become a paying asset'. He was also expecting to have considerable success with diesel electric locomotives. This appraisal of the prospects for Dalmuir was not borne out by a surge in orders. On the contrary, within a few weeks the company's accountant was forecasting monthly deficits in the region of £150,000. The general manager of Lloyd's Bank, W.W. Paine, deeply worried about Beardmore's chances of survival, wrote urgently to the Governor of the Bank of England, Montagu Norman, to ask his help saying 'I have for some time past been wanting to have one of my little chats with you'.[25]

Montagu Norman, from his experience in dealing with the recent serious problems of Armstrong Whitworth, the armaments company, was in no doubt that overcapacity was destroying the shipbuilding, heavy engineering and steelmaking industries. After some hesitation and pressure from the Treasury, Montagu Norman agreed to provide funds to keep Beardmore going until a rescue package could be hammered out. His private inquiries suggested that the situation was not completely irretrievable. He insisted that Lord Invernairn was to leave 'lock, stock and barrel', and be replaced as chairman by Frater Taylor, an Aberdonian who had masterminded the reconstruction of Armstrong Whitworth. A small committee was formed to supervise the rescue operation. Known as the Voting Control Committee, it had authority to sell all the company's assets with the exception of the Parkhead forge.[26] There were difficulties in implementing this strategy, largely because Frater Taylor was reluctant to accept the post of chairman. Months dragged by and it was not until September 1929 that he finally took the job. He immediately put pressure on Lewis Ord to 'get a move on with the re-organisation programme'. When his instructions failed to produce any results, Frater Taylor proposed that the board should be strengthened by the appointment of new directors who had the stomach for the job. Frustrated by the lack of progress, both at Beardmore and in the other shipwrecked companies with which the Bank of England was involved, Frater Taylor resigned as chairman in mid-December.[27]

Dismayed, Montagu Norman ordered a further enquiry into the affairs of Beardmore which he had unkindly christened Beardless. It quickly emerged that one of the chief bones of contention was that Lewis Craven Ord hoped to sell the Dalmuir shipyard and locomotive works as going concerns, whereas Frater Taylor wanted to close them at once. Only too aware of the overcapacity of both industries,

Montagu Norman decided that they must be sold as soon as possible. He told the new chairman, H.A. Reincke, to conclude the negotiations that were already under way with Sir James Lithgow and representatives of the Shipbuilding Conference. In April 1929 they had outlined to Montagu Norman a proposal 'for an association charged with the task of securing the closure of uneconomic yards'. Although there had been many discussions in the intervening months, no agreement had been reached by November 1929. During that month Montagu Norman had undertaken to effect the sale of the Dalmuir yard to the proposed association as a means of strengthening Sir James Lithgow's hand. In March the scheme became a reality with the formation of National Shipbuilders Security Ltd. (NSS Ltd.) whose first action was to acquire the Dalmuir shipyard for £200,000 this sum representing its nuisance value.[28]

Few vessels had been completed at the yard since 1927. During 1929 only two ships had been handed over — the 9,000 gross ton *Manunda* for the Adelaide Steamship Co. and the motor yacht *Romany Rye* for Sir Gervase Becket. Four orders were in hand in the spring of 1930 — another motor yacht, the *Virginia* for Major Stephen Courtauld, two tramp steamers, the *Daldorch* and *Dalhanna* for the Glasgow firm J.M. Campbell & Son, and the *Pole Star* for the Commissioners of Northern Lighthouses.[29] To the distress of the people of Clydebank, the closure of the yard was made public on 9 September. The *Glasgow Evening News* carried the banner headline 'BIG BLOW TO THE CLYDE'.[30] A press statement issued by the NSS Ltd. blamed the closure on the post-war depression, the naval disarmament programe, and on the company's lack of 'co-operative arrangements with lines such as other naval shipbuilding yards have had'.[31] The yard shut finally late in 1930 after the completion of the *Pole Star*, with the loss of 500 jobs. The bulk of the plant and machinery had been sold off by 5 April 1933 and in July 1938 the shipyard was purchased by the shipbreakers, Arnot Young & Co.

Since NSS Ltd. had been formed to rationalize shipbuilding capacity, the Dalmuir marine engine works remained open. The company found it almost impossible in the deep recession of the early 1930s to find orders for marine engines of any size or type. Between 1930 and 1934 only four sets of turbine engines were constructed, all for the Admiralty and all built at cut-prices. The machinery contracts for the cruisers *Amphion* and *Apollo* were secured in 1932 and 1933, after Montagu Norman had intervened with the Treasury in the knowledge that without them the company as a whole was in danger of collapse. During the autumn of 1933 and spring of 1934 there were abortive negotiations for the merger of the Dalmuir engine works with the Fairfield Shipbuilding & Engineering Co. which was in an equally parlous state.[32] Meanwhile, the main naval marine engineering contractors were pressing for a scheme to put 'an end to the present suicidal competition with an object of each firm obtaining a fair share of such Admiralty work as is available at a reasonable price'. On 9 February 1934 at a meeting of representatives of fourteen marine engineering companies it was agreed that the Dalmuir engine works would also be purchased by NSS Ltd. for £200,000. While the details of this transaction were being finalized Beardmore agreed to load their tenders to make them non-competitive.[33] Despite protests from the workforce and representations to the Conservative Government by the local MP David Kirkwood, the Dalmuir marine engineering works closed towards the end of the year.[34] Because of the adverse publicity, the engine works was not closed completely. The manufacture of diesel engines for locomotives and road vehicles was centralized at Dalmuir late in 1934. At the same time an order was announced for 30 engines for installation in buses being built by Albion Motors Ltd. in Scotstoun. No further contracts were forthcoming and diesel engine production was abandoned the following year.[35]

When H.A. Reincke was appointed chairman in January 1930, Montagu Norman had told him that the unprofitable locomotive department at Dalmuir should be closed as soon as an order for two diesel electric locomotives for the North Western Railway of India had been completed. He had reached this decision after the failure of lengthy discussions to rationalize the whole of the United Kingdom locomotive building industry, which made it impossible for the Dalmuir locomotive plant to be 'run on an economic basis'.[36] Although the plant was shut down during 1930, parts for locomotives continued to be supplied until diesel engine manufacture ceased in 1935. What was left of the Dalmuir works then remained unused for two years until May 1937 when the rest of the plant and machinery was auctioned off.

The *Daily Herald* commented at the time of the sale, 'The dismantling of the engineering plant at the Dalmuir works of William Beardmore & Co is a sad commentary on capitalist industry . . . Great Britain now needs an establishment such as existed at Dalmuir but it is being reduced to scrap under the agreement with National Shipbuilders Security Ltd . . . Thirteen shipyards have been dismantled on the Clyde since the war, and it is now realised that this was a huge mistake on the part of those responsible for the control of the industry'.[37] Such a simplistic view took no account of the problems that had surrounded the yard from its very beginning and the huge difficulties that faced the shipbuilding and marine engineering industries as a whole in the inter-war years.

CHAPTER TEN

Shipbuilding: Rearmament and Recovery, 1935-1945

John Brown

As John Brown emerged from the worst of the Depression with the launch of the *Queen Mary* in 1935, the company could look back on 15 years of difficult conditions with modest satisfaction and considerable relief. John Brown had not only survived while many other famous shipbuilders had closed, but the company had tried to

Figure 10:1 *On a wet day, the 26th September 1934, thousands gathered in the yard and on both banks of the river to watch the launching, by Queen Mary in the company of King George V, of the Cunard White Star passenger liner RMS* Queen Mary. *Weighing over 80,000 tons, 1,018 feet in length and with a top speed of over 30 knots, she was the largest and fastest passenger liner in the world, twice holder of the coveted 'blue riband' for the fastest crossing of the Atlantic.*

121

make provision for new developments. Even though the shipbuilding industry was in difficulty throughout the world, suffering badly from surplus capacity, weak demand, and fierce competition, individual companies still had to face up to the challenge of technical change, particularly in the development of the diesel engine and in electric welding.[1]

Of these two developments, the motor-ship made most rapid progress between the wars. In 1914 only 0.5 per cent of the world fleet was powered by the diesel engine; by 1920 this had increased to nearly 5 per cent and, between 1920 and 1939, about 36 per cent of all new merchant tonnage launched in the world was of motor-ships. In Britain motor-vessels represented 18 per cent of all tonnage built in the 1920s, but this increased to 46 per cent in the 1930s; even then Britain lagged behind the rest of the world where one quarter of all tonnage built was diesel driven in the 1920s, and nearly two-thirds of the total in the 1930s.[2] In spite of difficult trading conditions, John Brown did make early efforts to add diesel engine expertise to their well established skills in the marine steam engine, and in steam turbines. As early as 1921 John Brown engined the *Loch Katrine* with diesels supplied by Harland & Wolff to gain experience of the new engines. In addition, the company took up a licence from 1920 to build the Cammell Laird Fullager diesel, but did not find this a very successful experiment. In 1923 John Brown acquired another licence to build the Swiss Sulzer engine, and in 1932 took up a Doxford licence, the English diesel by then having required a reputation for reliability. Consequently, as the yard emerged from the Depression it had developed some diesel engine experience and capacity. In fact, Clydebank built five diesel driven merchant ships in the 1920s, and another five in the 1930s; indeed, only the *Queen Mary* and *Queen Elizabeth* were not diesel powered of the merchant vessels built at Clydebank in the period 1930-38.

The other challenge for shipbuilders at this time was the introduction of electric welding. Here it was the Admiralty rather than commercial customers who forced the pace, and by the 1930s John Brown was having to cope with welded sections of up to ten tons for naval vessels.[3] Since most of the cranes in the yard had only a five ton lifting capacity, John Brown modernized the cranes on four of the eight berths to cope with ten ton sections.[4] The major push into welding was in fact undertaken in the middle of the depression in 1933 when the yard was closed. This gave John Brown an opportunity to install equipment without disrupting work, and terms were agreed with the English Electric Company to construct a welding shop, together with the installation of transformers, machines and other equipment. The new facilities were concentrated in the four berths in the East yard where the new cranes were being installed. The cranes, however, were purchased cheaply, second-hand, from McMillan's yard at Dumbarton which had been purchased and closed under the shipbuilding rationalization scheme operated by the NSS Ltd. It is not easy to disentangle the investment directed solely to the diesel and welding facilities at this time, but not less than £100,000 seems to have been allocated to these ends between 1934 and 1939.

All these developments were coming to fruition by 1934 and at the same time other changes contributed to make this a clear turning point in the fortunes of the firm. As work on the *Queen Mary* recommenced, Lord Aberconway stood down from the Chairmanship of the company and died shortly afterward at the age of 83; his son took over his position. At Clydebank Sir Thomas Bell retired as Managing Director in 1935, though remaining on the Board, and his place was taken by the American, Stephen Piggot. He had been an assistant to Charles Curtis in the development of the Curtis turbine, and had first come to Clydebank from the USA in 1908-9 as part of the licensing agreement upon which Clydebank was to develop the Brown-Curtis turbine. Piggot became a Clydebank director in 1920, and now succeeded to the position of Managing Director at the end of the prolonged years of depression. New hands were now at the helm.

Even so, Piggot took over at a difficult time. With the launch of the *Queen Mary* the yard was desperately short of work; in 1935 only the cruiser *Southampton* was under construction on the slipways.[5] The Board at Clydebank was aware that orders for merchant vessels could be obtained, but only at prices that were likely to entail a loss; indeed, the prices being quoted were insufficient to cover labour and materials. Nevertheless, the choice was either to take such an order or to let the nucleus of the skilled workforce disband. To allow that to happen would be dangerous, for there was a prospect of more naval work in the pipeline. Consequently, in order to keep the workforce together Brown took a tanker order for the Anglo-American Oil Co. in June 1935, and two others for the New Zealand Shipping Co. in October. These last two were to be powered by Brown-Doxford opposed piston engines delivering about 13,000 HP.[6]

These orders were fillers, and it was ultimately the renewal of naval construction which transformed the fortunes of the yard. As Sir Thomas Bell was retiring as Managing Director in March 1935 the Government published a White Paper announcing its intention to increase spending on defence. The long awaited response to the recommendations of the Defence Review Committee was at last forthcoming. In 1936 Clydebank succeeded in obtaining orders for two destroyers and a submarine depot ship for the Admiralty, and two further destroyers for the Argentine, the *San Juan* and *San Luis.* The transformation of the order book was completed when, in July 1936, it was announced in the House of Commons that Cunard-White Star would place the contract for the sister ship to the *Queen Mary* at Clydebank. The contract for what was to be the *Queen Elizabeth* was signed on 6 October 1936.

Within a six month period the order book at Clydebank had been marvellously replenished, so much so that at the end of the year Piggot was turning away enquiries from several old customers including the Royal Mail, Shaw-Savill and Albion. The capacity of the yard was now so stretched that Piggot claimed it could not fit a further large vessel into its building programme. This was only partly the case, for the Board knew that further orders for two battleships, the *King George V* and the *Duke of York* were intended for Clydebank, and another merchant order would have made it difficult to take these more lucrative naval contracts. The orders for the two battleships together with another depot ship and two destroyers came into Clydebank in 1937.[7] This rapid build up of activity placed considerable strain on available manpower and materials. Employment in the yard, which had been only 675 men in 1933, climbed to 5,381 in 1935 and reached a weekly average of 6,198 employees in 1937. Wages similarly increased from an average weekly pay of £2 13 11d. in 1935 to £3 0 2d. in 1937.[8]

Building up the labour force, indeed, proved to be easier than ensuring supplies of equipment; steel deliveries were especially difficult giving rise to regular concern from the middle of 1936.[9] The problem of steel supply was partly made worse by the fact that John Brown's main supplier, Colville, was in the middle of a reconstruction programme at Clydebridge. By 1937 the inability of Colville's rolling mill at Motherwell to meet demand for ship's plate meant that Clydebank was receiving only half the steel it needed to keep all its contracts up to schedule. Colville undertook to extend the mill but this was not completed till February 1938.[10] Although the supply of steel plate then improved, John Brown also found increasing problems in obtaining sufficient supplies of armour plate for its naval contracts. The parent company at Sheffield could not meet all of Clydebank's demands, for the long run down of the armaments industry since 1921 had resulted in a much reduced capacity in Britain as a whole. Under pressure to meet Admiralty delivery dates in 1938 John Brown arranged with Stephen's yard to take a delivery of armour plate allocated to Linthouse, on the understanding that Firth-Brown would replace this consignment when Stephen required it. This allowed Clydebank to keep its work on the cruiser *Fiji* on schedule.[11]

Figure 10:2 *Some few years after the launch of the* Queen Mary *a second, and larger Cunarder,* Queen Elizabeth, *was launched by the Clydebank yard, destined after the war to sail with her sister ship across the Atlantic. In the above view, the giant 85,000 ton Cunarder sits on the stocks immediately prior to her launching alongside two destroyers being built for the Argentine Navy.*

While this flurry of activity rejuvenated the yard and brought new hope to Clydebank as a community, no one could be sure how long the bubble of prosperity would last. By mid-1938 Clydebank had sufficient work in hand to carry the yard through to 1940, but in the shipbuilding industry generally the brief surge in placing new merchant orders was receding, and the published naval programmes had been fully placed. Indeed, during 1938, expenditure on the naval programme was being curtailed as defence spending was switched to other and more pressing areas of priority, especially aircraft production. Yet, although there was growing tension in Europe, the peace still prevailed, and in June 1938, with its slipways bristling with warships, Clydebank received official visits from the German Naval Attaché, and two days later entertained a visiting member of the German Bureau of Transport. Both visits had been arranged at the special request of the Admiralty and must have provided much thought and considerable information for the Germans.[12]

As in the years before the First World War, Clydebank found that the renewal of high levels of Admiralty spending on contracts brought with it a return to high levels of profitability in the yard. The losses of 1932 and 1933 were turned into a modest profit of nearly £30,000 in 1935, but in the next five years the trading profit at Clydebank averaged £220,000. Virtually all of this was earned on the naval work.[13] This was clearly a welcome turn of events, but it did not immediately produce any new or large scale policy of investment or development in the yard. While some £180,000 was expended on capital additions between 1935 and 1939, virtually all of this was devoted to refurbishment and maintenance of existing plant, rather than being employed in any great extension of the facilities. Where extra plant was acquired it was mainly purchased second hand from the sales of equipment in yards which had been closed down. This policy of buying plant cautiously, and cheaply, allowed Clydebank to strengthen greatly its cash reserves while the fixed assets of the company were at best maintained rather than extended during the run-in to the Second World War.

The second half of the 1930s also saw some recovery of economic opportunity for the town of Clydebank. The community had been badly hit between 1930 and 1934 with the loss of Beardmore, one of the burgh's three most important employers. The great shipyard at Dalmuir was in some ways the most modern on the Clyde, and had been the first victim of the shipbuilding rationalization scheme when it was purchased and closed by NSS Ltd. in 1930; a restriction of 25 years against shipbuilding was placed upon the site. Four years later the great engine works followed the fate of the shipyard. NSS Ltd. purchased the engine bulding rights in August 1934 and placed a 40 year restriction against any further marine engine building there. Both measures were designed to reduce capacity in the industry, but also eliminated an employer who had provided up to 10,000 jobs in the district. However, when NSS Ltd. acquired Beardmore's engine building rights the company did not purchase the site of the works; it remained available to new tenants. Although there was no immediate customer, three tenants had been found by 1938 under the provisions of the Special Areas Funds, measures intended to bring new employment to areas designated as suffering from heavy unemployment. Part of the site was acquired by Arnot Young & Co. as a shipbreaking establishment; another section was sold to the GPO for storage purposes, and a third portion was given over to an English based company, Turner and Newal. They set up as Turner's Asbestos and Cement Co. to manufacture asbestos sheet and materials. At the same time some modest recovery returned to the other important local employers; Singer, Aitchison Blair, D. & J. Tullis, and Dawson & Downie all experienced improved employment as the pulse of shipbuilding raced faster and more steadily between 1935 and 1939.

With the outbreak of war on 3 September 1939 Clydebank again became an Admiralty controlled establishment. On 4 September 1939 the Clydebank Board papers show that instructions were received from the Admiralty to the effect that all work for foreign governments had to cease immediately, and that a Board of Trade licence would henceforth be necessary before any construction of merchant tonnage could be undertaken. Moreover, the Admiralty was anxious to have the *Queen Elizabeth* moved out of the Clydebank basin so that all the facilities of the yard could be devoted to war work.

Figure 10:3 *The* Queen Elizabeth *in wartime grey. During the Second World War she served, with the* Queen Mary, *as a troopship before, with the cessation of hostilities, reverting to her intended role carrying passengers across the Atlantic.*

Considering that Clydebank had increasingly taken on the look of a naval dockyard since 1936, the transition from peacetime to wartime work might be thought to have been fairly simple. This, however, was not the case, and the changeover was not made easily or smoothly. In spite of long preparation the Admiralty and Government had no clear plan of action, certainly not for individual shipyards. The Admiralty itself was pushed and pulled by shifting priorities dictated by a rolling sequence of emergencies. Although it was desirable to complete the fitting out of the *Queen Elizabeth*, this meant devoting men and materials to merchant work when the Admiralty wanted war work expedited. Consequently, Clydebank did not get a Board of Trade licence to continue with work on the liner till December 1939,[15] and the vessel did not leave the basin for Greenock till 20 February 1940. Even then no one knew what was to become of the great liner; it had been painted Admiralty grey in September on the announcement of war, but no role had been decided upon. Some thought was given to converting the liner for service as an aircraft carrier, while Sir Percy Bates, Chairman of Cunard-White Star proposed it be employed as a troopship. That role was not finally agreed till June 1940, and men were sent from Clydebank to New York to supervise the conversion.

The lack of any clear policy meant that much work in the yard was repeatedly delayed by suspension. Suspensions and re-starts became a regular headache for management as emergency needs switched men and materials to new priorities. A classic illustration of this shifting nightmare was the building of the great battleship *Vanguard*. Laid down in 1939, work was suspended at the outbreak of war, and repeatedly treated in an on-off basis throughout the first 18 months of conflict. Ironically, permission to re-start work came to the yard on 14 March 1941, the second day of the Clydebank Blitz. Even after that, work on the *Vanguard* was erratic and the great vessel was not launched till November 1944; it was only completed in 1946, a year after the end of the war. Too many other priorities had intervened and made the construction of the battleship less and less necessary as the conflict proceeded.[16] This type of episode was repeated many times on a smaller scale with many vessels in all the yards on the Clyde as desperate needs pushed the Admiralty to transfer work and men among the yards to bring particular vessels into service as soon as possible. In January 1941, for example, Fairfield had fallen far behind on progress on a battleship, *Howe*.[17] In order to relieve pressure on the yard the Admiralty transferred two destroyers on its books to Clydebank. Later that year John Brown had to lend 80 engineers to Govan to help complete that much delayed vessel.

After the first six months of hectic confusion John Brown settled down to pour out vessels to meet the demands of war. In 1940 the yard launched eight warships and a number of landing craft; this tally included the battleship, *Duke of York*, a depot ship, four destroyers, and two escort vessels. In 1941 the output was six vessels including a cruiser and three destroyers. The flow of work in 1941 was interrupted by the devastation of the town in the mass aerial bombardment of 13 and 14 March, and the lesser attacks of 6 and 7 May. Clydebank was itself very badly affected. In two nights of sustained bombing the town was continuously ablaze. A later survey reported that only 8 of 12,000 houses had escaped without some damage, and that some 4,300 homes were destroyed or damaged beyond repair.[18] Thousands of injuries were sustained and the deathroll was placed at 496 persons. The devastation of the town meant that virtually the entire population of the burgh, 53,000 of 55,000 inhabitants, had to be evacuated. For the shipyard this meant that the workforce was dispersed, some of it up to 40 miles away, with all the problems that that involved for transport and travel.

Considering the destruction in the town, the Blitz had relatively little effect on the shipyard itself. Gas and water supplies were cut off for three days and provision was made from mobile supplies.[19] The scattering of the workforce by evacuation was the worst problem, and two weeks later only 70 per cent of the labour force had found its way back to work. The later incendiary attacks of 6 and 7 May 1941, indeed, caused greater damage in the yard than the main attacks of 13 and 14 March. In the later raids the mould loft and canteen burned down, and the jetty and its equipment were damaged. Even then the total cost was modest, the estimated replacements being set at about £19,000.[20]

1941 was a year of intense pressure on the shipbuilding industry as Germany and Britain strove for mastery of the sea-lanes in the Atlantic. The yard was working at a high pitch, and in the midst of this the Admiralty approached John Brown to manage and take on more repair work; this was to be undertaken in a floating dry dock which was brought to the Clyde from Devonport in September 1941. The management at Clydebank was not keen to take on this responsibility, partly because repair contracts were not as lucrative as new construction, and partly because providing management for the dry dock would drain scarce personnel away from the yard. In the end, Fairfield at Govan managed this work.[21]

Although John Brown managed to avoid taking on extra Admiralty agency work on this occasion, the same problem reappeared in 1942 when the Admiralty proposed to use the old Beardmore fitting out basin at Dalmuir to fit out and complete 60 corvettes.[22] The Admiralty wished John Brown to manage the work which was part of a larger scheme to build rapidly some 200 corvettes utilising non-warship yards for basic hull and engine construction, leaving the fitting out and completion to tried and tested warshipbuilders. The scheme was first proposed in November 1942 but agreement on terms of managing the business was not concluded till July 1943. The first corvette was not delivered to Dalmuir until October 1943, the hull being constructed by A. & J. Inglis at Pointhouse, the engines being manufactured by Kincaid at Greenock.

Like so many plans in a fast moving war the need for corvettes had diminished before the planned solution could be implemented. By late 1943 the war in the Atlantic had been won and attention was switching to the conflict in the Far East. The corvette programme was first cut back from 60 to 7, and then abandoned entirely at the end of 1943. By then the Admiralty had expended £500,000 on

Figure 10:4 *The floating dry dock on the Clyde brought up from the south by the Admiralty and intended to increase the work capacity of a yard already brimful with war work.*

Dalmuir and wanted some use made of the facilities.[24] The decision made was to use Dalmuir for repairs and alterations under the management of John Brown. Brown managed Dalmuir for the rest of the war and would, in 1945, have liked to retain access to the basin to help cope with the expected flood of postwar construction. However, in December 1945 the Admiralty decided to transfer the Dalmuir basin to Arnot Young & Co. because of an acute need for shipbreaking facilities, and for the need to increase supplies of scrap steel to the hungry furnaces of Scotland's steelworks.[25]

Naval building, in fact, began to slacken appreciably in 1944. By mid-1944 John Brown was able to apply to the Board of Trade for licences to build engines for four merchant vessels, Doxford diesels for two vessels proposed for the New Zealand Shipping Co., and two sets of geared turbines for proposed Cunard vessels. At the same time the company opened negotiations with Cunard-White Star for the reconditioning of the *Queen Elizabeth*, and possibly also the *Queen Mary*, at the end of the war. By the end of 1944 licences had been granted to begin work on one vessel for the Port Line, and another for Cunard-White Star. From then on the commencement of new naval tonnage was severely restricted. Only three destroyers were begun at Clydebank in 1944, and only two, *Barosa* and *Matapan* were completed, the third, *Talavera* being unfinished. The rapid cut-back in naval building also postponed work on the *Diamond*, a destroyer ordered in May 1945 and intended to be John Brown's first all-welded destroyer. Men were sent from Clydebank to Samuel White's yard at Cowes to examine the process involved; the work was, however, much delayed, and the *Diamond* was not launched till 1950.

There were many parallels between the First and Second World Wars in the demands the conflicts made on John Brown. In both wars the yard became a controlled establishment and poured out a huge volume of highly profitable work which pumped a transfusion of cash into the company. John Brown's record of production in the Second World War was impressive. Naval work comprised 53 vessels of 222,440 displacement tons and some two million horse power of engines. The main work comprised 36 warships including two battleships, two aircraft carriers, two cruisers, and 30 destroyers. In addition, the yard launched nine merchant vessels of 196,113 tons, these being taken over for war work. On top of this, Clydebank managed the repair and fitting out as an agent of the Admiralty at Dalmuir basin; 11 merchant vessels were converted there together with repairs and reconditioning to another 116 ships.[26]

By the end of the hostilities John Brown had enjoyed a decade of full employment with the yard order book bulging with profitable work. The memory of the lean years had not been forgotten, and there were indeed fears of a return to the slack work and unemployment of 1921-34. In the event, however, Clydebank was to enjoy a further decade or more of busy work before the fears of contraction and unemployment once more became a reality. That was in the future, and in 1945 John Brown was confident of winning a new prosperity in the postwar period.

CHAPTER ELEVEN

The Clydebank Blitz

'That night both in Glasgow and Clydebank countless deeds were done which belong to the fighting traditions of Scotland, though they were done not by picturesque kilted figures at the charge but by drab, dungareed men and women in "tin hats"'.[1]

In 1954, a Roll of Honour was compiled by the Imperial War Graves Commission listing 'those civilians, citizens of the Commonwealth and Empire, who were killed in the United Kingdom by enemy action during the 1939 — 1945 War, while engaged in household or business activities, or at their posts as members of the Civil Defence Services.' The majority of the 60,000 fatalities that feature in the Roll of Honour can be attributed to the series of evening air-raid attacks carried out by the Luftwaffe between 9 September 1940 and 16 May 1941.[2] These 'blitz' or 'blitzkrieg' attacks were based on a concept of 'total air warfare' — a concept briefly experienced in Britain during the First World War.[3] The belief that 'the bomber will always get through,' produced great apprehension in Government and public alike at the outbreak of the Second World War. These raids were initially conducted in daylight hours but, by October 1940, with increasing losses, Goering switched the Luftwaffe to evening attacks, the planes being guided to their targets by radio navigation beams.

While London remained the primary target throughout the period the offensive was gradually extended to the large industrial centres and ports. The raids on Glasgow Clydeside of 13 and 14 March 1941, 7 April 1941 and 5 and 6 May 1941 were but one 'piece' in the German strategy, but it is commonly accepted that in proportion to its size Clydebank suffered more than most.[4] The 'blitz' offensive had been widely foreseen. The novelist, J. B. Priestley, opined that, 'It so happens that this war, whether those at present in authority like it or not, has to be fought as a citizens' war. There is no way out of that because in order to defend and protect this island, not only against possible invasion but also against all the disasters of aerial bombardment, it has been found necessary to bring into existence a new network of voluntary associations such as the Home Guard, the Observer Corps, all the ARP and fire-fighting services, and the like . . . They are a new type, what might be called the organised militant citizen.'

As early as 1935, air-raid precaution (ARP) measures had been drawn up for implementation by local authorities. Ironically, Clydebank Town Council was among the many local authorities who initially resisted these measures. As late as

Clydebank Civil Defence, Wardens Service
Senior Officers, 1939 - 1945

Front Row: Staff Off. W. McFarlane, Div. Wards. J. Longden (F), Mrs. J. Hyslop (E), R. Turner (A), Controller C.D., H. Kelly, Chief Warden A. J. V. Cameron, Training Officer Inspector A. Macdonald, Div. Wards. C. MacKenzie (B), W. Laurie (D), W. Bowie (D).
Second Row: Sen. Ward. A. Little, Head Wards. E. Connell, H. Brown, Div. Wards. R. Baird (A), T. H. Overend (C), Head Ward. T. Rae, Sen. Ward. S. McLintock, Head Ward. J. Menzies.
Back Row: Sen. Wards. D. Rendall, P. Wallis, W. Ross, R. Caldwell, D. McMillan, E. Brash, A. McKellar, J. Johnston.

Figure 11:1

January 1937, Clydebank Town Council was one of only three Scottish authorities still resisting. This resistance, however, ceased with the passing of the Air Raid Precautions Act in December in that year and thereafter the Town Council made strenuous efforts to prepare itself for air attack. By March 1941 a Central Control Centre had been set up in the basement of the Public Library and ARP Wardens Posts, First Aid Posts and Ambulance Depots had been established. Some 462 ARP Wardens (50 of whom were full-time, paid personnel) had been recruited, supplemented by specialist squads for decontamination and clearance work, etc. Notwithstanding such progress there was still some unease among both officials and the public. Evidence of this dissatisfaction surfaced at a meeting held in the Town Hall on Tuesday, 25 February, 1941, organised by the First and Second Ward Committees and chaired by Provost Low. The meeting, arranged to familiarise the public with fire prevention measures following an air attack, was poorly attended, causing the Provost to remind those present that:

> 'In the early stages of the war they had been warned of the vulnerability of this part of the county, and that it was said by the enemy the *"Queen Elizabeth"* would never leave the basin, the Provost added, well, she had left, and therefore they had never had any bombs since, but that did not mean to say that some night they might not get it'.[5]

This remark was not 'prophetic'; the evidence was already to hand, for, on the evenings of 14 and 15 November, 1940 some 450 bombers led by a pathfinder group had devastated the city of Coventry, leaving over 550 citizens dead. Despite the evidence of the Coventry raid and of later similar raids it is clear that there existed a popular belief that Clydeside would not be too greatly affected by this offensive:

> 'The threat of war from the air did not seem quite so immediate to Clydesiders. A survey carried out at the beginning of March 1941 — just before the mass air raids — by Tom Harrison's mass observation unit (who so accurately observed the reactions of ordinary folk throughout Britain to the war) revealed that only 30% of the people expected heavy raids, 42%

were quite vague or indifferent to the threat and 28% were not expecting any large scale raids at all. This last group advanced an interesting set of theories as to why Clydeside might be spared, ranging from the protection afforded by surrounding mountains, magnetic elements in the hills which would dislocate aero engines, the impossibility of locating the Clyde accurately amongst the myriad of west coast lochs, the region was too far from German bases and the attitude — which was especially popular with the upper and middle class respondents — that the Germans believed that revolution would develop on Clydeside so long as the people weren't stirred up by bombs'.[6]

On Thursday, 13 March 1941, the same pathfinder group as had attacked Coventry led 236 bombers on an attack on Clydeside, returning again the following evening to resume the attack. The story of the Clydebank Blitz has been fully covered elsewhere,[7] but the following contemporary accounts graphically illustrate the horror and devastation that ensued:

'There is one town somewhere on Clydeside the inhabitants of which will remember till the end of their days their experience during the nights of Thursday and Friday, March 13 and 14, 1941, for on those nights a fierce attack raged — two nights of merciless bombing — having the effect of razing tenements, villas, bungalows, churches, schools, etc., and rendering families homeless, many of whom also suffered the ordeal of sudden bereavement. Like many other areas on Clydeside, this particular town had expected that sooner or later it would be singled out for aerial attack, but the deliberate unloosing of incendiary and high explosive bombs at random angered the people of the neighbourhood to the highest degree'.[8]

'On Thursday night 13 March the first air-raid affecting the Burgh of Clydebank occurred. The attack was very severe and prolonged — starting at 21.10 on Thursday and lasting until 06.20 on Friday — a period of over nine hours. During this time there were some very short intervals when no bombs were falling, but there was no respite of any duration. Wave succeeded wave of bombers and for long periods the attack was sustained, all kinds of bombs being used — incendiaries, with high explosives and parachute mines — the last being used in great numbers. Not even an approximation of the numbers that fell in the raid can be given — the whole Burgh being pitted with more than four hundred craters — for the most of the damage was done by the incendiaries which numbered many thousands. Several hundreds of unexploded bombs were later located and rendered harmless. The areas attacked were in every section of the Burgh and very considerable damage to property was effected by fire and blast. The Dalmuir, Radnor Park and Parkhall areas received the brunt of the attack but no part escaped entirely. It was early evident that the resources of the Burgh would not be capable of coping with the situation so recourse was had to re-inforcements.
Night fell on a Burgh which was strangely quiet, after a most exciting day — and at 20.35 the siren sounded and the raiders arrived almost at once. The intensity of the attack was greater than on the previous night — a veritable hail of incendiaries and high explosives falling constantly for almost six hours, till 02.27 when the "All Clear" sounded. Later at 04.10 they returned again for further bombing until the "All Clear" sounded at 05.30.
All parts of the Burgh were involved in the attack and when it was very evident that a heavy raid was in progress, re-inforcements were asked for at an early stage. These, as on the previous night, arrived and were most welcome — fifteen parties augmenting our own eight'.[9]

No written account can fully describe the pain and suffering endured on those evenings but again, as contemporary reports show, stories of courage and fortitude abounded:

'Calmly they viewed in the light of day the wanton destruction wrought on their homely flats in a long night which was probably calculated to strike terror in their hearts, and they faced the future with a quiet bravery that showed that they "can take it".
Their homes, with their windows shattered and in many cases roofless and utterly destroyed, were gaping ruins containing all their worldly possessions. "But", said one man, "this town will rise again, if it takes us years to build these houses again"'.[10]

After the first night's bombardment the population dropped dramatically to 2,000 as those rendered homeless left the area to seek shelter with friends or relatives or at nearby evacuation centres. This phenomenon, known as 'trekking', had first become evident in the spring of 1941 in the provinces and was little reported on, since, in the Government's eyes, it came perilously close to panic:

'The ordinary man in the street did his part nobly and well. The day following the "blitz" was a Saturday, and a tremendous task faced those in authority in evacuating a large proportion of

Figure 11:2 *Among the many headaches resulting from the blitz was the problem of stray animals, especially dogs and cats. On Wednesday 20 March an animal clinic opened in Kilbowie Road. Homeless families waiting to be evacuated was a common sight.*

the citizens who had suffered most. Motors of every description were passing east and west. Anxious looking mothers and fathers with their children were waiting patiently by the roadside to get on buses which were already overcrowded. Many of the children were carrying ordinary pillow-slips packed with all the goods and chattels they possessed.'[11]

The Clydebank Blitz also put paid to the belief that areas such as Clydebank could not 'take it', for it soon became apparent that the civilian population regardless of its background universally reacted with calmness to their predicament:

'A week ago tonight the Nazis made the first of their murderous attacks on Clydeside area. Today a "Times" man visited the district where most of the damage was caused, and one impression he formed was that the life of the community, although seriously disrupted by the two-nights blitz, is gradually beginning to reassert itself.
Some semblance of order has been created out of the chaos which formerly reigned. Buildings considered unsafe are being demolished; others are being repaired.
The cool, unwavering courage of the people is evident, and when the full story of their heroism in the face of Hitler's Luftwaffe is told they will take their place alongside the citizens of London, Coventry and other bombed areas.'[12]

The scars left by the Clydebank Blitz, both physically on the landscape and mentally in the memories of who survived it, are still very apparent today. The greatest loss was suffered by innocent civilians, many of whom lost their families, friends, homes and possessions. Some 47,000 persons were housed in approximately 12,000 houses, many of which were overcrowded tenements. While the precaution of providing Anderson shelters, surface shelters and protecting close mouths with both scaffolding and baffle walls diminished casualties, only approximately seven houses were left unscathed out of the total housing stock. A report issued by the Research and Experiments Department of the Ministry of Home Security on the Clydeside Raids showed that 33 per cent of the houses were so badly damaged that they required to be demolished while another 43 per cent were rendered unfit for habitation. Within seven months 95 per cent of the immediate repair work had been carried out but an average of 800 men were employed for 18 months on rebuilding work. Elsewhere within the community, post-war reconstruction work on, for example, public buildings, schools and churches continued, with inevitable temporary inconvenience, into the 1950s. In many instances blitzed buildings were not replaced.

The effect of the Blitz on industry was less marked. During the war years John Brown was an Admiralty controlled yard receiving preferential treatment in respect of labour and supplies. During the period, the yard was busy launching battleships, cruisers and destroyers to aid the war effort. Likewise, Singer converted and re-equipped entire departments for wartime production work.[13] As a Report from the Glasgow Emergency Reconstruction Panel of 1 April 1941 showed, the damage suffered by local industry was surprisingly superficial. The yard suffered little damage and although the Singer factory lost some 390,000 square feet of floor space, partial resumption of work was possible by Monday 17 March 1941. In less than six weeks the factory was back to pre-Blitz production levels. The evidence from the affected areas was clearly that if the intention had been to disrupt industry by disrupting community life that strategy had signally failed to produce the desired effect. On Clydeside work was quickly resumed as the workforce either travelled distances of up to 30 miles daily to their place of work or sought temporary accommodation close at hand.

Mentally, memories of the events of the Clydebank Blitz remain, sometimes vividly, in the minds of those who suffered personal loss. The number of casualties has been open to question since 1941. Initially, the imposition of censorship which meant, for example, that Clydebank was not immediately identified gave great offence, but the more lasting controversy related to the number of fatalities. As was normal practice, actual figures were not given but an early communique from the Air Ministry and Ministry of Home Security carried in the *Evening Times* of 15 March 1941 seemingly played down the enormity of the event, stating that:

'Damage was done to business premises and to houses, some people were killed and a large number injured when a block of flats was destroyed, but apart from this incident, casualties are not expected to be heavy'.[14]

Figure 11:3 *Scene of devastation on Dumbarton Road immediately east of the Glasgow Corporation tramway terminus at Dalmuir West. Communications and rescue work was severely hindered until the main routes through the burgh were cleared of blitz debris.*

THE HISTORY OF CLYDEBANK

These figures were instantly greeted with disbelief and on March 18 the Ministry of Home Security was obliged to further report a figure of 500 deaths. On that same day, however, a Department of Health report suggested that 527 plus another 200 from Clydebank's first raid was a more accurate figure. In April, due to persistent questioning by J. McGovern, MP for Shettleston, Herbert Morrison, the Home Secretary, was forced to report to the House of Commons that although it was not normal practice to issue precise figures they would do so in this instance — the figure being approximately 1,000 dead and 1,000 seriously injured. He defended the revised figures, indicating that reports had previously suggested lighter casualties:

'He explained that in view of the nature of the attacks it was impossible in the early stages to obtain definite figures, and the first reports indicated that, although the attacks had been heavy, the casualties, though serious, were not expected to be numerous.
As soon as it appeared that the casualties were heavier than at first anticipated the communiqué was issued giving the latest figures as reported by the Scottish authorities, though it would be appreciated that any figures given soon after a raid could not be final and complete'.[15]

Figure 11:4 *On Monday 17 March 1941, in the presence of Sir Iain Colquhoun (Lord Lieutenant), David Kirkwood (Member of Parliament), Tom Johnston (Secretary of State) and Sir Steven Bilsland (District Commissioner), a mass burial of unclaimed Blitz victims was carried out at Dalnottar Cemetery.*

While it is impossible to simplify or sum up the lasting effect of the Clydebank Blitz, local artist Tom McKendrick has expressed the opinion that:

'There can be no doubt that Blitzkrieg in Clydebank succeeded in causing massive dislocation and hardship to the population. But Clydebank people were no strangers to hardship, as those acquainted with the town's history will know. More importantly, the psychological effect was the exact opposite of what was intended. Rather than divide the community and throw it into frenzied panic, it strengthened and immeasurably hardened people's resolve to survive and resist. There was however a lingering anger, tinged with sadness. The once close-knit communities passionately desired to be reunited. This never happened. The ties severed, many thousands drifted; time passed and people began to make new lives elsewhere. Many still bear the mental and physical scars; all have vivid recollections. The Blitzing of Clydebank was as far-reaching in time as it was in effect'.[16]

134

Part Three

The Town in Transition, 1945 - 1980

CHAPTER TWELVE

Shipbuilding in Decline

The Industrial Structure of the Town

In the period from the end of the Second World War to 1980 the industrial structure of Clydebank changed dramatically. It is no exaggeration to say that in 35 years a heavy industrial town, dominated by shipbuilding and engineering, shrank to a service centre with a few local-serving manufacturing industries and one vulnerable shipyard. Table 12:1 shows how total employment shrank from over 35,000 jobs around 1950 to under 15,000 in 1981. In the 1950s there were about 27,000 workers in the town engaged in manufacturing, compared with about 8,000 in services, and of these 24,000 were employed in shipbuilding and engineering. By the early 1970s service employment had risen to 12,000 but with the loss of population from the town it too has since declined.

Table 12:1   *Clydebank: Employment change, 1952-81*

	Total employment	Manuf.	Ship + eng.	% in all jobs in ship./eng.	Services	% in all jobs in services
1952	35,020	27,181	23,841	68.1	7,793	22.3
1963	37,120	26,949	24,255	65.3	10,134	27.3
1968	35,028	24,214	19,635	56.1	10,746	30.7
1973	28,919	17,141	12,998	44.9	11,778	40.7
1978	23,023	11,699	8,816	38.3	11,324	49.2
1981	14,881	4,321	3,126	21.0	10,560	68.9

Source: Department of Employment. Annual Census.

The change in the structure of employment in the town has inevitably altered the social character of the town. Unemployment has risen sharply as Table 12:2

Table 12:2   *Clydebank: The growth in unemployment, 1951-81*

	Male	% rate	Female	% rate	Total	% rate
1951	325	2.2	131	2.0	456	2.1
1961	540	3.4	200	2.6	740	3.2
1971	1600	9.5	360	4.4	1960	8.6
1981	3023	20.8	930	9.7	3953	18.2

Source: Census of Population.

shows. In the post-war boom in Clydebank there was work for virtually everybody who wanted it. Compared with the 35,000 people in work in the late 1940s there were a mere 300 — 400 registered as unemployed and only half of these would be adult males. By the late 1950s an inexorable and steepening rate of increase in unemployment had begun. Perhaps significantly, after 1959 the Ministry of Labour had ceased to count the unemployed of Clydebank separately, preferring to merge Clydebank into the Glasgow 'travel-to-work' area as the Clydebank unemployed faced the reality of the prospect of fewer and fewer jobs locally and were forced to travel into the conurbation at large to look for work. The really dramatic leaps in unemployment occurred in the 1960s when the overall rate rose from 3.2% to 8.6%, and the 1970s when it rose further to 18.2%, with the rate of unemployment for males at over 20.0%. The rise in unemployment shows the operation in Clydebank of a cyclical process. By this, when major manufacturing firms close or contract, their demand for local products as inputs, raw materials or components also ends or contracts, thereby creating further decline. At the same time the growth of unemployment means that local people have less money in their pockets to spend on local services, reducing demand in Clydebank's shops, pubs and other services, and in turn making the position of the Burgh Council with a declining rate base more difficult. Of those who did have jobs in Clydebank, an increasing proportion were female. As Table 12:3 shows, the decline in heavy industries and the growth of service jobs has meant that the proportion of the workforce made up of females has risen from only a quarter in 1952 and little more in 1968 to almost a half in 1981. The stereotype of the Clydebank family with father

Table 12:3   *The sex composition of Clydebank's workforce*

	Total	Male	Female	% Female
1952	35,020	25,926	9,094	26.0
1963	37,120	26,447	10,673	28.8
1968	35,028	25,422	9,606	27.4
1973	28,919	18,863	10,056	34.8
1978	23,023	14,519	8,504	36.9
1981	14,881	8,156	6,724	45.2

Source: Department of Employment.

at work, bringing in the weekly wage packet to a house maintained by his wife is breaking down. The pram is now as likely to be pushed along the streets of Clydebank by a man as by a woman. Significantly, however, the absolute number of women in work in the town has also declined since the mid-1970s.

With the collapse of the major employers in the town, inevitably more people living in Clydebank have been forced to look for work elsewhere, commuting daily. Table 12:4 shows that in the 1950s less than one in five of workers living in Clydebank daily travelled to work in Glasgow but by 1981 the proportion was more than two workers in every five. At the same time Clydebank went from being a major provider of employment for workers from outside the town to a net exporter of labour, as comparisons of Tables 12:3 and 12:4 will show. This shift from being a town with high employment levels attracting workers from surrounding areas to one which daily exports part of its workforce has further economic effects as workers take some of their spending power with them.

Table 12:4   *Looking for work further afield*

	Workers resident in Clydebank	Workers travelling to Glasgow	Percentage
1951	21,188	4,078	19.2
1961	22,330	5,250	23.5
1971	20,670	6,450	31.2
1981	20,380	8,420	41.3

Source: Censuses of Population.

Table 12:5 gives the most detailed breakdown of employment which official figures permit. In the early postwar years the engineering and shipbuilding sectors stand out, dominating the employment structure of the town. The collapse of employment in the mechanical engineering industry between 1963 and 1981 is the most dramatic feature of the table, with the loss of 15,000 jobs, or almost 45% of the

Table 12:5 *Employment change by sector, 1952-81*

	1952	1963	1968	1973	1978	1981
Agric., forest., fish	46	32	66	0	0	0
Mining, quarry.	0	5	2	0	0	0
Food, drink, tob.	1,172	1,735	1,897	1,826	1,280	794
Chemicals	1	11	4	28	154	35
Metal manuf.	0	322	153	410	231	13
Mechanical eng.	15,344	16,155	11,185	6,225	5,598	466
Instrument eng.	9	5	17	7	0	0
Electrical eng.	54	88	119	92	0	0
Shipbuilding	8,443	7,007	8,314	4,688	3,218	2,660
Vehicles	469	16	476	123	5	9
Metal goods	656	24	128	214	167	70
Textiles	57	50	9	23	0	0
Leather	1	5	3	1	0	5
Clothing, footwear	36	468	395	319	120	124
Bricks, pottery	691	444	530	114	3	3
Timber, furniture	206	217	186	137	104	28
Paper, printing	0	18	14	16	17	88
Other manuf.	42	384	784	899	783	7
Construction	1,394	1,128	1,680	1,208	1,112	829
Gas, elec., water	641	692	571	283	190	201
Transport	1,445	1,418	1,094	1084	794	404
Distribution	1,831	2,803	2,687	2,606	2,697	2,481
Insurance, banking	175	279	253	260	206	326
Professional services	643	1,177	1,843	3,164	3,285	3,186
Misc. person. serv.	797	1,305	1,099	1,716	1,771	1,751
Government	861	1,048	1,177	1,490	1,288	1,385
Total*	35,020	37,120	35,028	28,919	23,023	14,881

Source: Department of Employment.
*includes some unclassified workers.

total employment in the town in 1951. Apart from the core industries in manufacturing, the food industry, especially bakery and confectionery products, has continued to provide a significant number of jobs, despite the closure of the UCBS bakery, but other sectors such as vehicles, metal goods, clothing and non-ferrous mineral products (eg. asbestos, cement manufacture), all once significant employers, had largely disappeared by 1981.

Within the service sector, too, there were major job losses in public utilities (mainly gas and water) and transport. However, the growing service sector in Clydebank provided additional jobs in retailing (although this reached a peak in the mid-1960s) in banking and insurance, in professional services (health, education, etc.), in personal services (including leisure activities) and local government. It is clear though that these new jobs, welcome as they were to the sorely pressed economy of Clydebank, were unlikely, given the white collar clerical and professional skills which they demand to be adequate or effective replacements for the jobs lost in the historical core of the town's economy.

Shipbuilding in Clydebank: John Brown's yard, 1945-81

The story of the shipbuilding industry in Clydebank in the post-war period can be reviewed at three levels. Firstly, it is possible to examine the changing pattern of

Figure 12:1 *On Thursday 30 October 1946 the second Cunarder to bear the name* Caronia *was launched from the Clydebank yard by Princess Elizabeth on her third appearance in Clydebank. The elaborate preparations visible for the launching ceremony were once typical of most of the major launches from the yard.*

products and the changes in ownership of the Clydebank yard itself; secondly, the Clydebank yard's history can be explained, particularly from the mid-1960s onwards, as one of a group of yards on the Upper Clyde whose fortunes and management became increasingly linked; thirdly, the patterns of change can only be fully understood when the Clydebank yard is viewed in terms of changes at the global scale as demand for ships of different types fluctuated and as international competition for orders intensified from the mid-1950s onwards.

The immediate postwar period saw the Scottish shipyards, including the Clydebank yard of John Brown, adjusting to the changing pattern of demand for shipping. In 1945 there remained seven Admiralty orders on the stocks including four destroyers and a submarine, all of which were launched in that year. The yard was also involved in reconverting civilian ships which had been adapted to wartime use, and the world market in cargo vessels was buoyant with the need to replace the tonnage sunk during the war. The Shipbuilding Advisory Committee set up in 1946 was concerned not with problems of demand but with problems of a lack of labour for the yards and a shortage of materials, particularly coal and steel.

There was in this period an acute need for yards such as John Brown to modernise. New production techniques, including the use of welding (to replace riveting) and prefabrication were introduced. These techniques produced lighter ships but, more importantly, prefabricated units could be assembled indoors and then fitted together, making the building of ships cheaper. The shipbuilding industry became more capital intensive, and there was a remarkable shift in the types of labour required. For example, in 1939 the Upper Clyde shipyards employed 1,600 riveters but only 830 electric welders; by 1955 the figures were only 700 riveters but 2,300 welders!

Figure 12:2 *Until the advent of electric welding, the riveter and his team were an important component of the many workers involved in a ship's construction and were, by tradition, highly skilled and adept at their work.*

Major shipbuilding competitors such as Japan and West Germany had been more severely hit by the Second World War, and in 1947 the UK share of the world market for shipping was 50.2%, of which the Clyde produced 38.0%. By 1950, however, there were signs that this period of prosperity on the Clyde would not be sustained. Competitor nations were re-emerging from their post-war collapse. The British mercantile marine was back up to its pre-war level. Britain's share of world tonnage was falling (by 1951 it was down to 37.7%) and the nature of demand for ships was changing. Larger ships were required and non-deep water yards such as John Brown would be at an increasing disadvantage. The most rapidly expanding market for ships was for tankers of ever-increasing size, and the types of ships requiring the old craft-based labour skills assembled at Clydebank would form a smaller proportion of total demand.

The pattern of buoyant demand continued into the early 1950s boosted, just when it looked like flagging, by the Korean War. The general trends of the immediate postwar period are picked out in Table 12:6. After the 1945 boom, Admiralty orders faded away to be replaced by a growth in demand for oil tankers and cargo ships. The concept of the mixed cargo-passenger ship was replaced by more specialist ships. The passenger liner market was a combination of new build (including the *Arcadia,* the *Saxonia,* the *Carinithia,* the *Ivernia* and the *Sylvania* for Cunard) and a number of refits to pre-war vessels. In addition, John Brown

Table 12:6 *John Brown's yard: launchings 1945-57*

	Passenger liner	Cargo/liner	Cargo	Tanker	Admiralty	Other	Total
1945					7		7
1946		1	2			Cross-channel	4
1947	1	2	1(2)			Train ferry	5(2)
1948		2	1				3
1949		1	2	2			5
1950	(1)	2	1		1	Cross-channel	5(1)
1951	(2)	1		3		Train ferry	5(2)
1952	(1)	1	2	2			5(1)
1953	1		1			Royal yacht	3
1954	2		1				3
1955	1		4	1	1		7
1956	1(1)		2	1		Train ferry	5(1)
1957			1	2	1	Cadet ship	5

Source: Shipbuilding records.

Figures in brackets refer to refits.

launched a number of specialist ships including cross-channel ferries and train ferries, and in Coronation Year the Royal Yacht *Britannia*. By June 1952 John Brown's order books stood at a record level[2], but all was not well. Yards in Europe and the Far East were re-equipping rapidly with massive financial assistance from Government in countries such as West Germany and Japan,[3] whilst at home expansion was limited by low levels of capital investment, a shortage of materials such as steel, and there was still a lack of certain types of labour, particularly welders.[4] In consequence, orders piled up and yards such as John Brown found themselves quoting longer delivery times than their competitors abroad.

During the 1950s, the Clyde yards such as John Brown found themselves handicapped by four factors. In addition to the long delivery times which they were

Figure 12:3 *General view of the Clydebank shipyard from the Renfrew side of the river in the 1950s.*

offering, they were handicapped by the traditional practice of quotations with fixed prices which, as costs mounted due to delays in delivery, incurred increasing losses, whereas competitors were insuring themselves by tendering on a cost plus profit basis. In addition, the credit terms which yards were able to offer were inferior those of foreign yards with higher levels of government support, and yards such as John Brown were suffering from their older capital vintage compared to foreign yards. The changing types of shipping being ordered were a further problem. In the decade 1956-66 'the demand for new ships seems to depend primarily on the transport of oil'[5] but the Clyde yards were not well placed to tender for the new larger oil tankers. Thus, by 1956, the UK's share of the world market had fallen to 23.7%, and by 1963 it was 12.1%, and the Clyde's share of UK ship production was also falling.[6] In the late 1950s and the early 1960s, the roll of closed shipyards on the Clyde grew longer and longer with the demise of Denny at Dumbarton, Harland and Wolf in Govan, Simons and Lobnitz at Blythswood, and Hamilton. Although nowhere near to closure, John Brown felt the wind of change, particularly in 1956-57 when four orders were cancelled and the Government intervened by placing Admiralty contracts which Moss and Hume argue were inappropriate, when what the yard needed was a steady flow of merchant ship contracts to encourage new capital investment.[7]

Recoveries such as that of 1959-60 were brief, and the yard entered the 1960s with little optimism. By 1961 it was possible to point not only to low order books, heavy over-capacity in both shipbuilding and related marine engineering, and the lack of new investment, but also to the 'inefficient practices (and) deplorable labour relation's[18] within the yards. By 1962 the managing director announced, 'there is no indication of a revival in shipbuilding which could keep an engineering works employed to capacity' and John Brown Engineering began to separate from the shipyard, seeking non-marine work. Demand for warships was falling, and the growth of transatlantic and other long distance air travel was reducing demand for passenger liners which increasingly would be used for cruising holidays. The new markets for bulk carriers would have required the total reconstruction of the John Brown's yard, for which capital was unlikely to be forthcoming, and even though the yard had substantial tanker-building experience, it could not finance this development to match foreign competition.[9]

By the early 1960s it was clear that shipbuilding on the Clyde would have to be restructured to meet foreign competition and that this would require Government intervention. From this point the destiny of the John Brown's yard became inextricably linked with the fortunes of the other yards on the Upper Clyde. The incoming Labour Government in October 1964 faced the situation in which

Table 12:7 *John Brown's yard: launchings 1958-70*

	Passenger liner	Cargo/liner	Cargo	Tanker	Admiralty	Other	Total
1958				3			3
1959		1		1	1		3
1960				2			2
1961	1	1			1		3
1962			1	1	1		3
1963	(1)		1	1			2(1)
1964	(2)				1		1(2)
1965	1		1	1		2 Oil rigs	5
1966	1(1)		1			Oil rig	3(1)
1967	1(a)					Oil rig	2
1968			1				1
1969			2			Oil rig	3
1970	1						1

(a) Queen Elizabeth II.

Britain's share of world shipbuilding had fallen to 8.3%, and in February 1965 the Geddes Committee was set up. Even whilst waiting for the Geddes Report, the Fairfield's yard in Govan called in the receiver, only for a rescue package to be announced. Fairfield, with 5,000 workers, modern technology and £32 million of orders, had to be helped with Government support. Significantly, a new company was formed with an experimental venture in social and industrial democracy with greater worker participation and shareholding, and higher wages, in exchange for more flexible working patterns.

The Geddes Report when published in March 1966 indicated that Britain's share of world shipbuilding should be raised from 7.0% to 12.5% and a £68 million package of Government aid (£5 million grants, £33 million loans, and £30 million credit for buyers) would be made available. Most significantly for John Brown, regional groupings of shipyards were to be established. Merger talks began in June 1966, linking John Brown with Stephen of Linthouse, Connell, Yarrow, Fairfield and Barclay Curle. The Shipbuilding Industries Bill was passed in 1967 and the working party report in July of that year concluded that the five remaining yards, other than Barclay Curle, of which Yarrow was the only consistently profitable yard, should merge, after which Stephen and Connell should be phased out. The total number of jobs in the consortium would fall from 13,000 to 7,500 of which John Brown's share would be about 3,000.

The resultant body, Upper Clyde Shipbuilders, was formally registered in September 1967 and began trading in February 1968. However, the trade unions had rejected the idea of job loss and the full 13,000 jobs were guaranteed for two years.

The company had an issued capital of £4 million plus a £1 million rights issue, and John Brown's share was to be 30%. Much of the finance made available by the Shipbuilding Industries Board was used to pay off shareholders in the constituent companies who did not wish to be associated with UCS and to make provision against operating losses. By August 1968 there were provisions for losses of £4.8

Figure 12:4 *On 20 September 1967 Clydebank's 'hat-trick' of 'Queens' was completed with the launch of the* Queen Elizabeth II. *The smallest of the three 'Queens', the QE2 was, nevertheless, an impressive 963 feet long. In May 1969 she left Southampton for her maiden voyage to New York and in 1982 she sailed for the Falklands as a troopship thus emulating her two larger sisters.*

million and by February 1969 UCS hit its first liquidity crisis as Cunard refused to make the final £1.5 million payment on the *Queen Elizabeth II* then at John Brown's yard.[10]

The *QEII*, possibly the most prestigious ship ordered from John Brown's yard in the post-war period, had been refused by Cunard in December 1968. On trials in the Clyde estuary, oil had seeped into the ship's water feed system to the boilers, a charity cruise was cancelled and on the shakedown cruise the *QEII* sailed with 250 workmen still on board. Turbine damage delayed new trials until March 1969, and eventually the maiden voyage took place in May 1969. Not all the problems and delays could be blamed on the yard. The Cunard technical directors changed the specifications and even altered the engine room very late in the construction of the ship. Nevertheless, in the final accounting, Cunard claimed to have lost £3.5 million in the delays, and John Brown lost £1.3 million on the contract.[11]

UCS, including John Brown, encountered rapidly worsening financial problems. By February 1969 a further £6 million was needed to keep the yards in business, of which central Government reluctantly provided £3 million. By mid-1969 UCS was predicted to lose £8 million in the year, and by August this estimate was raised to £10 million. In this context the jobs guarantee could not be sustained, and 1,300 jobs were to be lost at once, and a further 1,300 would be lost in the next twelve months.[12] Under these strains UCS was in danger of breaking up. In a surprise move in June 1969, Lord Aberconway, the chairman of John Brown, offered his company's share of UCS to the Government for a nominal sum if the Government would help the workforce by guaranteeing the completion of the ships on the stocks and helping to find new work. The Government refused the offer.

There was a further threat of closure to UCS in December 1969. A further Government grant of £7 million and the loss of 3,500 jobs in March 1970 and August 1970 kept the consortium afloat although Yarrow left the group in February 1971. Table 12:7 shows how the struggle for orders affected John Brown during this period. No further Admiralty orders were placed after 1964 and the last tanker was

Figure 12:5 *The launching of the* QE2 *was yet again an opportunity to celebrate, and thousands took to the street to see both the Royal party approach the yard and also the launching of the vessel into the river.*

launched the following year. The passenger liner market continued with launchings of the *Kungsholm* in 1965, the *QEII* in 1967 and the *Blenheim* in 1970, all three produced at substantial losses. The only growth sector in the period was that of oil rig production, introduced in 1965 with two rigs, the *North Star* and the *Constellation,* for the International Drilling Company, followed by three further orders.

How much longer UCS would have operated on this basis is open to question, but the election of a Conservative Government in June 1970 changed the political environment for John Brown and the other yards. The new government's position was broadly one of non-intervention, summed up in October 1970 by Nicholas Ridley, junior minister at the Department of Trade and Industry, when he said, 'We entered the election with a conviction that the Labour Government were wrong to bale out lame ducks'. In the later months of 1970 the Conservative Government were made increasingly aware of UCS's difficult financial position and decided not to authorise guarantees on ships to be built. Despite assurances from UCS's board that the company had reasonable prospects of success and should continue to trade, the Department of Trade and Industry was not reassured, and refused to resume issuing guarantees until after Yarrow had been allowed to leave the consortium in February 1971.

By June 1971, UCS was assuring the Government that it could be saved by an immediate injection of above £5 million and that at that point the company had money only to pay wages up to 18 June. On 14 June it was announced in Parliament that the Government would allow UCS to go into liquidation and shortly afterwards the UCS liquidator announced that UCS's deficit of liabilities over assets was £28 million. In response to the announcement of liquidation a campaign to save John Brown and the other yards was quickly mounted. A sequence of meetings involving the Scottish TUC, the local authorities, Glasgow's Lord Provost, the workers and their shop stewards occurred, culminating in a mass demonstration in George Square and Glasgow Green on 23 June in Glasgow. The entire Clydebank Town Council were present and Clydebank itself was deserted. The Government chose to await the recommendations of the Advisory Group, known as the 'Four Wise Men'.

By 28 July 1971, rumours of the closure of the Clydebank yard were rife. Production would be limited to Govan and Linthouse; Clydebank and Scotstoun would be closed or sold off, with the loss of 6,000 jobs. When the announcement came on July 30 1971 the *Glasgow Herald* described Clydebank as 'a town in mourning . . . groups discussed the decision in hushed tones . . . the atmosphere was that normally found at the scene of a disaster'. In response to the Government's acceptance of the Advisory Group's report, the shipyard workers took effective control of the entrance gates. The shop stewards indicated to the media that management had refused to let them make statements to the press and in consequence they had taken over the yard. Jimmy Reid, the co-ordinating committee's chief spokesman said, 'We are not going on strike, we are not even having a sit-in. We do not recognise that there should be any redundancies and we are going to "work-in"'.[13]

Views of the effects of the Upper Clyde work-in at the Clydebank yard and elsewhere differ widely. To some, the work-in represents a major challenge by the workforce to uncaring monopoly capitalism in the West of Scotland and elsewhere. Alex Murray, the Scottish Secretary of the Communist Party, for example, said on 18 August 1971, 'It is the action of the UCS workers that has been a catalyst, that has galvanized millions of people to united action in their support. Their action, their struggle has become the focal point of the common struggle of millions of workers throughout Britain'.[14] Conversely, commentators like Hogwood[15] described the work-in as 'a myth' pointing out that only small numbers of workers were involved, for a short period of time, with little actual work being done. Sykes pointed out that

Figure 12:6 *UCS shop stewards and demonstrators marching down Renfield Street in Glasgow.*

the workers never actually ran the yard, the liquidator and management fulfilling this role.[16] Lastly, Broadway concluded that nothing was achieved by the work-in that would not have happened anyway.[17] All told, the Government paid out £35 million to UCS, unsecured creditors (suppliers, etc.) lost £7.5 million, and a further £12 million had to be provided to make the Clydebank yard saleable. In total, some £90 million was spent without creating a viable shipbuilding industry on the Upper Clyde, with little capital investment, and with a halving of the 12,000 workforce in the five yards.

However, the work-in did achieve several things. As far as the yards themselves were concerned, the strength of opposition characterised by the work-in had an important influence on the Government's willingness to make payments to the liquidator and these kept the yards functioning. Secondly, the Government reappraised the Advisory Group's report and decided to include Scotstoun in the successor grouping to UCS, which would comprise Scotstoun, Govan and Linthouse, with a major capital injection into Govan Shipbuilders. However, the effect on Clydebank was largely unchanged — it was to be sold off. The last achievement of the work-in was its effect on worker attitudes to large-scale capital. In a sense, the UCS work-in became the model for a significant number of worker rejections of factory closures. Workforces thereafter engaged in more determined resistance to closures decided by often remote managements of multiplant and multinational companies.[18]

Of the UCS yards, then, Clydebank came out of the work-in with the poorest prospects. Yarrow had left UCS before its final stages, and the other three yards, Govan, Scotstoun and Linthouse, were to form a new company, Govan Shipbuilders, with heavy Government backing. Clydebank was to be sold off if a buyer could be found. Early in 1972 there were discussions with Breaksea Tankships of Houston, to determine whether the company was interested in acquiring the Clydebank yard for the production of oil rigs. These discussions came to nothing. Later in January 1972, Wayne Harbin, president of Marathon Manufacturing, came to Clydebank to talk to the Department of Trade and Industry, the workers and the unions. Marathon were known to have heavy order books for oilrigs and were looking for capacity in Europe. The take-over was dependent upon central government's financial help and satisfactory agreements on wage rates and working practices. The deal was likely to cost Marathon about £15 million, but of this £6 million was met by a loan repayable over seven years from the Department of Trade and Industry, and a similar sum was to be forthcoming in the form of financial aid under the new 1972 Industry Act. The real cost of the acquisition to Marathon was of the order of £2 million.[19]

By April 1972, the deal was signed in London, but there were delays as unions negotiated wage rates, numbers of redundancies, and completion bonuses.[20]

By October 1972, the deal was complete and the work-in technically ended. Marathon Manufacturing started work in December 1972 with about 1,200 workers; John Brown's shipyard had ceased to exist in Clydebank. It was truly the end of an era.

Other Shipbuilding, Marine Engineering and Other Industry

The employment structure, and indeed the character, of Clydebank in the postwar period was so dominated by John Brown's shipbuilding and Singer's sewing machines that it is easy to overlook the other elements in the picture, but for comprehensivity they should be included.

Alongside John Brown's shipbuilding yard was the related company of John Brown Engineering, which for many years supplied the marine engineering needs of the ships built and refitted in John Brown's yard. Indeed, it has been argued that the link between the yard and the engineering works prevented the growth of an independent marine engineering industry in Clydebank.[21] John Brown Engineering, however, always had wider interests than merely serving the adjacent shipyard. In 1947 it designed and built the first effective gas turbine, and continued to work on the project until 1960 when work was stopped. However, a new agreement with GEC in the United States caused the company to restart work on heavy industrial gas turbines in 1965. In that year the Geddes Report, in addition to recommending the formation of Upper Clyde Shipbuilders, recommended the separation of the engineering and shipbuilding divisions of John Brown, and accordingly John Brown Engineering became a separate independent company in 1966. In 1967 the first contracts for industrial turbines came in and JBE effectively ended the production of marine diesel engines. The period 1966-71 was one of great success for JBE, although after 1971 the initial growth slowed and through the 1970s employment hovered around the 1,400 mark.

The history of John Brown Engineering was, as its name implies, closely linked with that of John Brown's shipyard until they were organisationally separated in 1966. Many other firms in Clydebank and the West of Scotland were also strongly tied to John Brown's shipyard although never formally or organisationally linked to it. Some, such as Aitchison Blair, Clydeblowers, and Dawson and Downie supplied component parts to the shipyards directly, including pumps, ventilating equipment, engine components, insulation, wiring and tubework. Other companies were equally dependent upon the yards through the wage expenditure of the shipyard workers, and these would include retail firms, food manufacturers, personal services and even local government itself. When the whole of the Upper Clyde Shipbuilders was threatened in 1971 it was estimated that a loss of 6,000 jobs in the shipyards would lead to a loss of a further 15,000 jobs through the so-called direct and indirect multiplier effects.[22] This 1:25 ratio reflects the interrelations within the whole of the West of Scotland, and would not be representative of

Clydebank alone. Nevertheless, it seems safe to assume that for every job in shipbuilding in Clydebank, another job in the burgh would be dependent upon shipbuilding until the mid-1970s.

The remainder of the story of shipbuilding in post-war Clydebank lies in the hands of the successive owners of the John Brown yard. Marathon Manufacturing set up a company, Marathon Shipbuilding Co. (UK) Ltd., to manage the Clydebank yard to produce 'self-elevating drilling platforms, semisubmersible drilling platforms, drill ships, barges and other off-shore exploration vessels'. A specialisation of this type, however, did not solve the yard's problems for long.[23]

By December 1976, 1,000 of the 1,400 workforce were suspended due to lack of orders and the Government had to be persuaded to place a speculative order for a rig on behalf of the British National Oil Corporation, but ultimately sold to Penrod of Texas, which also ordered a second rig from the yard. The future of the yard was made more uncertain in mid-1976 by the failure of the Bill to nationalise shipbuilding. However, this only proved to be a stop-gap, and by September 1978 Marathon again was laying off 900 of its 1,000 workforce. There had been difficulties is servicing rigs in the Gulf of Mexico; the Government had proved reluctant to place another speculative order; productivity was lower than in completing yards; and Marathon could not meet the £11 million price of a possible oil rig for BNOC-British Gas. By April 1979 the Government had agreed to cover Marathon's losses on the BNOC-British Gas rig tender, and *Penrod 81,* the ninth rig to be launched by Marathon in seven years, slid into the Clyde. In July 1979, Marathon failed to gain a contract to convert a supertanker owned by Shell Petroleum to a storage vessel, and the yard was threatened with closure. A number of potential buyers were canvassed late in 1979 including Penn-Central, but eventually the Union Industriel d'Enterprise of Cherbourg took over the yard in February 1980. The conditions of the take-over included a guarantee of £1 million of capital investment, a starting workforce of 750 and a guaranteed share of £15 million of a £40 million contract for a rig for the North Sea placed by Marathon Oil.

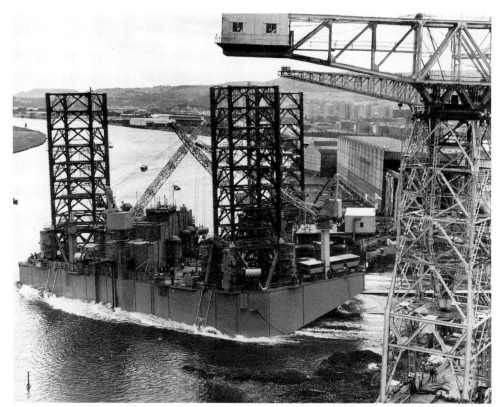

Figure 12:7 *Launch of the oil rig* Penrod 64 *from the Clydebank yard in 1973. The transition from ships to oil rigs was made without fuss and ensured, in recent years, a steady stream of launches of rigs firstly from Marathon and latterly from UIE, culminating in 1986 with the launching of* Mr Mac, *one of the largest jack-up rigs built in Europe.*

Table 12:8 shows how employment at the yard declined throughout the postwar period from almost 10,000 in the days of peak demand immediately after

Table 12:8   *Employment in the John Brown shipyard, and after*

	1954	1964	1970	1972	1981
John Brown + JBE*	9,200	6,799	5,400		
John Brown			4,011		
Marathon Mfr.				1,250	
UIE					891

*Separated in 1966.

the Second World War to under a thousand by the early 1980s. Not only had the numbers employed declined drastically but the types of vessel constructed, and hence the types of labour required, had changed almost as radically. In 1950 it would have been inconceivable that by 1976 there would have been a debate in the House of Commons as to whether what went into the Clyde from the yard could actually be described as a 'ship', but such a debate took place in May 1976.[24]

CHAPTER THIRTEEN

Singer: Competition and Closure

Post-war Competition

By 1946 Singer was no longer enjoying a monopoly of the sewing machine market and competition was intense. The company was exposed as having failed to move with the times. Singer had been lulled into a false sense of security, and during the 1950s it continued to market machines of nineteenth-century design, manufactured with ninteenth-century tools, in similarly outdated buildings. In 1957, sewing machines accounted for 94% of the Company's total sales, with virtually all domestic machines being sold in Singer's own retail outlets. Singer was therefore highly dependent on a single product, and one which it had failed to develop, for the modern consumer. This alone made Singer very vulnerable to the competition which was emerging in the *domestic* sewing machine market, especially as virtually all of the production facilities were located in high-wage countries, with almost half of its machines being produced in Clydebank.

To make matters worse, the cost of maintaining sales-service centres was as high as 50% of retail prices, and these were a luxury the firm could not afford. When the sewing machine was first launched on the market, and no-one knew how to operate it, Singer needed trained staff to demonstrate the unknown to confused customers. Once established, the brand name 'Singer' sold the machine, and operating instructions were readily obtained from friends or neighbours if the manual was found too complicated. In the early days Singer's other advantage in having its own shops was that it could offer credit, but hire purchase was now universal. In short, after the war there was nothing to suggest that Singer sold more machines because it had its own shops, than it could have done had independent retailers sold them. On the contrary, they would have sold them more cheaply, and there would have been a consequent increase in demand.

Competition came first from Pfaff of Germany, Necchi and Vigorelli of Italy, and Elna of Switzerland. Eventually, in 1954, Singer responded to this threat and launched a new range of advanced and lightweight domestic models in pastel colours. This retaliatory measure dealt a significant blow to these European producers, but in the meantime the Japanese had stormed world markets with low-cost domestic machines making substantial inroads into Singer's markets. Before the war, Japan had produced virtually no sewing machines and Singer had a 90% share of the Japanese market, but in 1945 US General Douglas McArthur, responsible for rebuilding the war-torn Japanese economy, decided that the vanquished Japanese should produce sewing machines instead of munitions. Singer was forbidden to re-enter the Japanese market. The irony was that Singer patents and plans were provided along with US capital investment to establish the industry in Japan. By the 1950s Japan had made great progress, and by 1957 over 300 companies were producing over two million machines. The Japanese firms succeeded where their European counterparts failed. Singer's US market share for domestic machines plummeted from 66% in 1950 to 33% in 1957, and to make matters worse the latter year saw a sharp decline in the US market. Singer's market share fell to approximately 35% in most foreign markets.

The decline of Singer in the domestic sewing machine market was in marked contrast with the company's continued dominance of the *industrial* sewing machine market. In 1957 the world's industrial sewing machine output worldwide was 400,000 units, of which Singer produced 175,000 units (44%). The company still dominated the US market with a 35% share. Its main rivals were six major American companies, but the largest of these had only a 14% share. It was, therefore, the poor performance in the domestic sewing machine markets that accounted for Singer's 25% drop in profits between 1951 and 1957.

Figure 13:1 *Among the many recreational activities enjoyed by the Singer workers and the community, the annual Sports Galas were especially welcomed, providing an evening of games, sports and entertainment. In 1950 the Sports Gala was enhanced by the visit of Hollywood's 'South Seas' queen, actress Dorothy Lamour who came to Clydebank to attend the Gala and crown the Singer Gala Queen, Frances Black.*

Company and Plant, 1958 - 1975

It was against this background that a new president was appointed on January 1 1958. Donald Kircher took over 'the stumbling sewing machines giant . . . at the time of its greatest crisis'. He correctly recognised that the root cause of Singer's difficulties was its management, not competition 'per se'. Kircher's priority was not diversification, but the revitalisation of the sewing machine industry. This demanded major changes at Clydebank. Singer's difficulties were due largely to its poor performance in the market for domestic machines. Between 1948 and 1952, 79% of Clydebank's total production was of domestic machines. Apparently Singer's oldest factory outside the US partly contributed to the Company's problems.

Kircher was aware that the Scottish factory as it stood was a monument to Singer's period of masterly inactivity — a relic of the nineteenth century. Machine tools, bought for opening the factory at Love Loan in 1867, were still in use at Clydebank during the 1960s. In 1867 feudalism prevailed in Japan, yet by the 1960s low-cost Japanese sewing machines, and a host of other manufactured goods, produced by cheap labour, often with the most advanced technology, had erupted onto the market. Japan had become one of the world's most advanced economies. Major changes were necessary if Singer and its Clydebank factory were to compete successfully against such a rival. The plant was to be reorganised and revitalised.

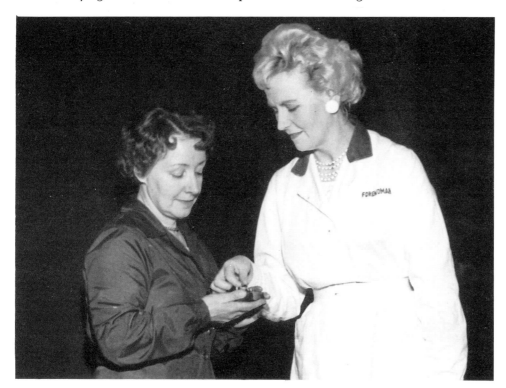

Figure 13:2 *Agnes Stewart (right) who became the first woman executive in the factory in January 1963. Formerly chargehand, quality and inspection control, Miss Stewart became directly responsible for production, quality, cost control, safety and discipline in 8 Department.*

It was felt that new faces were needed to implement the proposed changes. In the period between 1912 and 1962 there had been only four Managing Directors at Clydebank; all but one were local to the area. Managerial positions were filled by men who had worked their way up through the factory's ranks. This pattern was now to change. In the period 1962-70, there were four Managing Directors and all but one were American.

In 1961 a Forward Planning Unit (FPU) was established and staffed by Americans from the parent company. Its task was to pinpoint and remedy the defects within the factory, and devise a campaign of modernisation which would reduce costs and increase productivity. It immediately announced that substantial investment would be forthcoming, and that the main five-storey building upon which stood that famous Clydeside landmark, Singer's clock, would be demolished. A new single-storey 'factory' would be built on the site.

On November 23 1964, the new building, measuring 650 feet long and 175 feet wide, was formally opened by Lord Polwarth, the then Chairman of the Scottish Council (Development and Industry). The actual building cost £350,000, and its plant and machinery another £4m. In this new building, the High Volume Domestic Building, nearly all domestic sewing machine parts would be produced and assembled. The building incorporated all the most modern methods of production, and was fitted with advanced equipment, such as a deburring machine

Figure 13:3 *'Years later . . . I cried when they pulled down Singer's Clock . . . you could see it from anywhere in Clydebank . . . I thought . . . Oh, God! It was the only thing left . . . it came through the Blitz untouched . . . it was a symbol of survival and meant so much to the people of Clydebank . . . I hate them for that.'*

and an electrostatic paint spraying shop. It was described at the time as 'undoubtedly the finest domestic sewing machine factory in the world'. The new building was tangible evidence of Singer's commitment to its Scottish plant, and with domestic machines accounting for 66% of the factory's total output, this investment was a boon to Clydebank.

Figure 13:4 *Lord Polwarth, Chairman, Scottish Council (Development and Industry) with, seated alongside, the Rev. Stewart Borthwick, factory chaplain, at the opening of the new main factory occupying the site on which had previously stood the Clock Tower. The opening of the new factory marked the completion of the first phase of a modernisation plan.*

The FPU decided to decentralise the plant and introduce Divisional control, in a bid to improve communications and to develop cost-conscious need and authority among middle and lower management. Previously there had existed more than 50 departments, all centrally controlled, but now six independent divisions were introduced: Cabinet, Needle, Electric Motors, Process, Domestic and Industrial Machines. Under this set-up, while the Company had a clear picture of each division's performance, it did not know exactly how much it cost to produce one complete sewing machine. Accordingly, in July 1964 the Divisional structure was replaced, and the factory was basically divided into two Groups, the Consumer Products Group (CPG) and the Industrial Products Group (IPG). The CPG manufactured only domestic machines, the IPG only industrial models. As a result, Singer could better assess the efficiency of the Clydebank plant.

Kircher had also recognised the dangers involved in Singer's excessive reliance on its nineteenth-century Scottish plant. He decided that this should change:

'We are scaling down Clydebank somewhat by transferring one line to Bonnieres. Clydebank will still be our largest factory, but the other will be much closer in size than in the past'.

Clydebank and Bonnieres were to produce 'middle-of-the-line' domestic sewing machines, but demand in Europe and the US was increasingly either for the best, or the cheapest models produced at Karlsrube and Monza respectively. Therefore the Scottish and French plants produced domestic machines with the least market potential. Bonnieres had a great advantage over Clydebank, however, as it was closely integrated with Monza, Karlsruhe, and Wurselen, in Germany. The closure of any one of these plants would have upset production in at least two of the others. Clydebank, being a 'serious anomaly' in its singular self-sufficiency, was more vulnerable to closure.

Between 1961 and 1965, £7.8 million was invested in Clydebank, most of it in the CPG which continued to produce models designed for the European and American markets. Singer's return on its investment was determined by the level

Figure 13:5 *HRH Queen Elizabeth talking to Singer employees during the occasion of the visit of the Queen, accompanied by HRH Duke of Edinburgh, in June 1965.*

and nature of demand in these markets. During the same period, investment in the IPG was almost negligible. This appeared very ominous to the local workforce who had been informed that a new factory was being built at Blankenloch in Germany, which would produce only industrial machines; it opened in 1967. The IPG at Clydebank remained housed in a six-storey Edwardian building which was unsuitable for manufacturing any sewing machines, never mind heavy cumbersome models. From 1964 on, the IPG was trapped in a 'Catch-22' situation. Unless a profitable position was reached there would be no investment; unless there was investment, a profitable position could not be reached. As early as May 1965, employees were warned that the IPG's future was uncertain. By the 1960s it was evident that Clydebank was no longer consistently profitable. During the period, 1962-71, it made a profit of only £4.6 million, and there was considerable fluctuation in profits from year to year, as Table 13:1 shows.[3]

Table 13:1 *Performance data on the Singer Manufacturing Company Limited* (i.e. the Clydebank factory), 1962-71

Year	Sales	Pre-Tax Profits	Post-Tax Profits	% Return on Investment
1962	n.a.	74.5	52.7	0.9
1963	n.a.	246.8	246.8	2.9
1964	n.a.	58.1	58.1	0.7
1965	n.a.	(889.0)	(889.0)	negative
1966	n.a.	(117.0)	13.0	negative
1967	11,826	(183.0)	(294.0)	negative
1968	15,478	1,388.0	1,388.0	13.5
1969	19,463	2,516.0	2,516.0	20.0
1970	17,219	1,110.0	766.0	8.3
1971	18,445	1,312.0	738.0	7.7

Source: Company Accounts, Extel Statistical Services.

In 1972 the US market peaked, and two years later the European market stopped growing. As demand from these depressed markets dropped, the closure of Clydebank grew nearer. The growing Third World markets were now being served by new plants which Singer had opened in the developing countries. The Company was clearly reducing the strategic importance of its European operations and of Clydebank in particular. This was indicated by the drastic reduction in the Scottish plant's labour force from 15,866 to 6,400 during the decade 1960 to 1970. This was mainly due to Kircher's decision to reduce Clydebank's production capacity, and therefore its level of output. Table 13:2 below reveals the scale of the contraction.

Table 13:2 *Numbers employed in last week of the year, 1960-75*

1960	15,866	1964	9,905	1968	7,843	1972	6,107
1961	13,021	1965	9,107	1969	7,856	1973	6,095
1962	10,307	1966	8,170	1970	6,400	1974	5,111
1963	10,135	1967	6,249	1971	5,986	1975	4,902

Sources: Dorman, A., *A History of the Singer Company (UK) Ltd Clydebank Factory;* AUEW Minute Books; Mr. T. Craigie, Manager in Personnel Department.

Prior to 1963 Singer did not include in their figures on the factory's labour force those employees earning above a certain sum, but in 1963 changes in National Insurance legislation resulted in all employees being counted. So, in 1960, the factory employed not 15,866 people but 16,055 — its all-time record. It is significant that in 1913, the year of record output, 14,000 employees produced 1.3m machines, yet in 1960, 16,055 workers (2,000 more than in 1913) could not break the output record. This would suggest that the modernisation programme was long overdue.

Figure 13:6 *Mass rally at the Singer factory as stewards and workers fought to save their jobs and prevent the closure of one of Clydebank's largest employers.*

Shedding of labour had evoked tension and insecurity from the workers, but the innovations introduced in 1965 made for a further deterioration in industrial relations. Whereas in 1964 the factory's Managing Director commented on the workers 'praiseworthy restraint,' in the first six months of 1965 there were 75 separate work stoppages! Although 1965 was a particularly bad year for industrial relations, reporters state that the factory was always 'labour troubled'. One author even suggests that 'the impact of labour disputes' was one of Kircher's reasons for 'scaling down' Clydebank. However, the facts of the matter are, that during the 1960s, industrial relations, if measured by the number of stoppages, were excellent. For instance, between July 1965 and July 1966 there was only one stoppage, and even then it did not disrupt production. Consequently, in 1966 the Managing Director described 'employee-management' relations as 'exceedingly good', and the actual relationship between management and worker is a much better yardstick of labour relations than the number of disputes. Labour relations remained good until the late 1970s. In 1976 the Managing Director, John Wotherspoon, described them as 'very good' and indicated that in Singer's factories in the US, Canada and Italy 'there are up to three hours per man lost in industrial disputes each year', whereas 'the figure for Clydebank is 15 minutes'. However, by the late 1970s the workforce was to become completely disenchanted with Singer.

In 1975, the IPG at Clydebank was still producing machines in conditions which rendered profit-making well-nigh impossible, and indeed it had not known a single profitable year in the 1970s. The closure of the IPG seemed imminent, but instead, in 1975, Singer announced that Blankenloch would be closed and production transferred to Clydebank, thereby creating 500 jobs! There was sound logic behind this apparently surprise decision; closing Clydebank's IPG would have involved considerable losses in write-offs, whereas the modern German plant could be sold. The transfer of plant was completed within a year and was fraught with difficulties. Management later described it as 'a mistake before we even started'.

Meanwhile the Company's troubles were not confined to Clydebank. By 1975, Singer's total debt exceeded £1.25 billion, its diversification policy was in tatters and the Company's banks were by now disillusioned. The resignation of the autocratic Kircher created yet another problem. He had not identified his successor and the banks demanded that the next Chief Executive be experienced in finance. None of Singer's Vice-Presidents were thus experienced.

In September 1975 Joseph Flavin, the Chief Executive Vice-President of Xerox, was first approached, and in December he was appointed President. He did not have any experience of the sewing machine industry but in other respects he was exceedingly well-qualified to tackle Singer's problems. An accountant by training, he had spent most of his life in finance with IBM and Xerox. Singer was highly dependent on its sewing related products, and ironically the Company's domestic sewing machine operations proved highly profitable in 1975. The CPG at Clydebank had not contributed to this success while the IPG at Clydebank had been largely responsible for the Corporation's worldwide industrial sewing machine operations reporting a loss of $10 million. The Clydebank factory was a massive drain on corporate resources. Its role in the Corporation's strategy had been greatly reduced during Kircher's reign, and the Company was no longer dependent upon it. The question was whether Flavin would prefer closure to trying to return Clydebank to a profit.

Clydebank: the Final Years

During the Blankenloch transfer, Flavin came to Clydebank on a fact-finding mission. He realised that the sewing machine business had to be rationalised. Clydebank management attached great importance to Flavin's first visit on St Andrew's Day, 1976, and prepared a comprehensive report on the factory. Ian MacGregor, a former Director of the Company, and former Chairman of the National Coal Board informed the author that:

> '. . . due to low productivity and high costs the plant (Clydebank) was very vulnerable. So when Singer's set out to rationalise, it was very high on the list'[4]

However, the report prepared for Flavin shows that, despite a lack of investment, there had been significant increase in productivity since 1967. Given the age of the plant's capital equipment this was quite an achievement. In November 1976, the total number of machines in the factory was 7,512, of which 862 were over 50 years old.

In 1976, the Singer Organisation made a profit of $74.2 million, and in 1977 the profits rose to $94.2 million. It appeared to some commentators that Flavin had saved the Company. The Scottish plant, however, remained the thorn in Singer's flesh. Clydebank lost £2.6 million in 1975 (the IPG alone lost £2.2 million) and £680,000 in 1976. The following year Larry Neely, an American, replaced John Wotherspoon as Managing Director, Wotherspoon being made Chairman of Singer UK. In that year, Clydebank's loss was $2.8 million and this could be directly attributed to IPG which reported a staggering loss of $8 million. The CPG, on the other hand, which had received some investment, made a profit of $5.2 million.

The US and European markets were of vital importance to the Clydebank factory for together they had accounted for 80% of its production. Between 1972 and 1979, the American market for domestic machines fell by 50% and the European market began to show a significant drop in the late 1970s. As a result of this slump in domestic sewing machine sales, the Singer Company had 'serious overcapacity' in Europe and the US. The *Singer Shareholder News Letter* produced in the third quarter of 1979, suggested that the first step of a 'restructing programme' to solve this problem was the closure of Clydebank. The CPG of the company's oldest factory in Europe had the lowest productivity of Singer's 28 plants, and unlike the others in Europe it could be closed without disrupting production elsewhere. Clydebank was an anachronism. Its productivity in the late 1950s was lower than in 1913.

The result of lack of investment was clearly illustrated in the IPG at Clydebank. Management recognised that productivity was low and costs high, but instead of providing investment, it expected the workers to find a solution. In 1977, the year Queen Elizabeth celebrated her Silver Jubilee, the IPG, operating Victorian tools, and functioning in an Edwardian building, reported a loss of $8 million. Even the CPG which had received almost all of the £10 million invested at Clydebank did not get sufficient resources — 50% of the CPG's tools which had been in use during the 1950s were still in use in 1976. This lack of investment and a demoralised workforce explains the CPG's low productivity. During the late 1960s, Singer management constantly broke its promise not to introduce compulsory redundancies. As the labour force contracted, many of the remaining workers believed that the company had already decided to close the Clydebank factory, although, by doing so, they credited management with a long-term strategy it did not possess.

Figure 13:7 *In this view of workers leaving by the Kilbowie Road entrance the importance of the factory in terms of employment can still be sensed. Although the workforce had contracted greatly since the boom years the factory remained important to the wellbeing of the community.*

However, by the end of 1977, it was hard to believe that the Clydebank factory had once been the hub of the Singer empire. Its ancient buildings served as a powerful symbol of a by-gone age, and dwarfed the smaller, newer factory unit which housed the CPG. This indeed was tangible proof of the Company's failure to invest in Clydebank. Such an ill-equipped and inappropriate facility was no match for modern Japanese producers. The town had viewed with dismay the workforce dwindling from over 16,000 to under 5,000. Redundancies had been the order of the day for almost 20 years, and morale fell. Closure seemed inevitable, but the shop stewards were determined to fight for the plant's survival.

The Fight Against Closure

On March 13 1978, John McFadyen, the factory convenor, and his deputy, Hugh Swan, travelled to London to meet national union officers, including Gavin Laird of AUEW. Two days later, these officials discussed the factory's future with Mr Bruce Millan, the then Secretary of State for Scotland, and he indicated that Government money was available, but that so far Singer had not approached the Government. A few days later, the Labour Party in Scotland held its annual conference. A lobby of shop stewards from the Clydebank factory attended to convey the gravity of the situation at the factory. They discussed the matter with the then Prime Minister, Mr Callaghan, who promised to raise the matter with President Carter during their forthcoming meeting in America.

On March 22 1978 trades union representatives met Mr Ed Keehn, President of Singer's European Division, Sewing Products Group. According to the press release issued by the unions after the meeting, Mr Keehn had agreed to the stewards request:

'. . . that prior to any decisions being made relative to the future of the Clydebank factory and its total workforce, and in light of the fact that Management is currently conducting a World Wide Survey of its product's manufacturing base and selling outlets, the Trade Unions should be given an opportunity to —

a) examine the draft proposals arising from this report.

b) be given the opportunity to view the alternatives contained within the report, as these alternatives may affect the Clydebank plant, and

c) be given a commitment that no decision will be taken by Singer Corporate Management on the results of this survey prior to the foregoing procedures being carried out'.

The statement does not reveal, however, that during this meeting, Keehn assured the union delegation that the Clydebank plant would not be closed. In the first six months of 1978, Singer had reported a loss of $3.4 million on industrial sewing machines. Clydebank's IPG, which produced half of all Singer industrial machines, was 'mainly to blame'. In early April, a union delegation met Mr Keehn who had discussed the Clydebank factory with Flavin during their recent meeting at Company Headquarters in Connecticut. Keehn informed the stewards that Flavin had agreed to visit Britain in June to discuss the factory's future with Government Ministers and the TUC.

On June 22 1978 Flavin announced his plans for the Clydebank factory. These are outlined in his letter, to its employees, which is reprinted below.

'Dear Fellow Employees:

I am sure that you are aware of my visit this week to Scotland and London in order to discuss the future of the Clydebank Factory with senior government ministers, civic leaders, trade union officials and local management. I would like to share with you some of the facts and conclusions of these conversations.

For a number of years demand for all sewing machines in the US and Europe, Clydebank's principal markets, has gone down. As a result we face a serious problem of excess capacity. The future, unfortunately, shows no sign of change. Thus, we have spent many months exploring ways to remain viable in Clydebank, to protect as many jobs as possible as we can under the circumstances, and to remain the leader in sewing worldwide.

With the help and co-operation of our unions and managers, we can accomplish all of this. As we see it, the mission for Clydebank's future must be one which permits most cost efficient manufacture based on fewer products, with high volume and streamlined methods. We are prepared to spend about £8 million in updating operations, restructuring of work force and tooling for a new household sewing machine — one that will give Clydebank a vital new role in developed markets. However, to accomplish these goals will require a streamlining of consumer sewing operations, phase out of industrial sewing machine and needle manufacturing with concentration on household needle production only.

This program will take some five years, after which time, by a continuing and evenly spread programme of natural attrition, early retirement and minimal redundancies the factory will be operating with a labour force of around 2,000 people. It is our belief that this course of action and no other can ensure the continuation of the Clydebank Factory.

I do not expect the loss of jobs to be welcomed and I do not enjoy having to carry this news. The main point which I wish to leave with you is that we believe this program can succeed, and it will, as long as we can count on the co-operation and understanding of the Clydebank workforce which has contributed so well to our history'.

According to newspaper reports, the whole factory had faced closure, and it was only the personal intervention of the then Prime Minister, Mr Callaghan, in talks with President Carter, that saved the CPG and 2,000 jobs. Mr Gregor MacKenzie, MP for Rutherglen, who was Minister of State for Scotland, and Mr Callaghan's Parliamentary Private Secretary, states that one cannot be sure whether Singer did plan to close the entire factory, but what is certain is that there was considerable pressure on the company to retain its manufacturing facility at Clydebank.

However, Flavin's plan involved reducing the labour force of 4,800 to 2,000. This was unacceptable to the unions and even though Flavin had stated that 'this course of action and no other can ensure continuation of the Clydebank factory', they demanded time to review the company's proposals. Having promised not to take any action until the unions had considered its policy, management was forced to concede. The company agreed to delay implementing its plan until the autumn to allow the unions time to produce, if possible, a viable alternative. In June, Flavin had declared that the viability of Clydebank must be a prerequisite of any alternative solution and this would be the only background against which the company would consider an alternative solution. He said that:

'Key conditions required from the unions to make Clydebank a cost effective operation were:
1. Subcontracting of parts and services.
2. Labour flexibility to move to areas where openings exist, when their own areas did not have enough work.
3. A new pay plan to generate more productivity, reduce incentive anomalies, and to reduce administration costs'.

On June 27, John McFadyen, the factory Convenor, addressed the workers, and asked them to support the following resolution:

'This meeting of Singer workers totally rejects the company's proposals to run down Industrial Sewing Machine Products, and calls for the reversal of the present company Policy by immediate cash investment to achieve:
(a) Continuation of all Industrial Products.
(b) Maximum job opportunity in the short term and the long term at Singer, Clydebank'.

Only 'about ten' workers voted against the resolution.

Two days later, the unions agreed that the services of professionals should be called upon to advise on a viable alternative for the factory. It was decided at a Factory Committee Meeting on July 24 that PA Management Consultants should get the contract. The unions hoped that the Government would completely finance the project. By early August, McFadyen was able to report that he had received a letter from Gregor MacKenzie, which stated that if the unions put up £25,000 the Scottish Development Agency would provide the other £50,000. The Factory Committee unanimously decided to accept this offer. The unions would raise their share by a levy of 50p per worker, per week, for a period of ten weeks.

According to the minutes of the union meeting held on September 12 1978, documentary evidence was produced which indicated that the Company was already in the process of phasing out the IPG — this to be completed by 1980, and not 1981 as had appeared in Flavin's Plan. When confronted, Management denied that they were breaking the agreement not to implement the phasing out plan until the unions had some time to consider a viable alternative.

While PA carried on preparing the report in order to save jobs, the workers themselves were apathetic and the minutes of the Special Factory Committee Meeting on October 3 1978 record that one shop steward stated that only 30% of his members wanted to fight for their jobs. The other 70% wanted to collect redundancy money and go. During the first week of October, McFadyen informed the Factory Committee that Mr Jack, Director of the Scottish Development Agency (SDA) had been informed that if quick decisions were not made, then there was a danger the Company would possibly close down the whole factory. Later that month it was revealed that all Singer's European plants, with the exception of Clydebank, had obtained an increase in orders for domestic machines in 1979. Clydebank had fewer orders than in 1978.

Early in November, the union-commissioned consultants report was submitted to Singer management. This comprehensive 120 page report outlined the alternative strategy which retained a reduced Industrial Products facility at Clydebank, provided employment for 3,000 people (compared with Singer proposals for 2,250) and envisaged development, over the next two years, of an enhanced Industrial Products range to secure the future and possibly generate further employment. At the end of November, Singer replied to the factory trade union leaders on PA Consultants' alternative strategy. It agreed to continue manufacturing two industrial models and thus save 335 jobs. This would involve a further investment of between £1-2 million beyond the estimated £8 million. The unions were 'bitterly disappointed' that the Corporation had not accepted the alternative strategy in full, and 'at this juncture are rejecting the company's proposals'. Neely remained convinced that 'if all the parties co-operate to the fullest. . . there can be a future at Clydebank'. He did warn, however, that the plant had 15 months to prove itself or it faced closure.

On December 8 1978 Singer revised its offer and stated that 'subject to external finance of the estimated order of £2 to £4 million becoming available on terms acceptable to Singer', production of another two industrial machine models and related spares would continue, thereby supporting 165 jobs in addition to the 335 previously offered. Three days later, Keehn told the factory's 130 shop stewards that Singer had reluctantly agreed to accept the Government's offer to provide the finance necessary to retain a reduced IPG, only because the Company wanted to continue producing domestic machines at Clydebank. He also warned them that if the workers rejected this latest proposal, Singer would close down the whole factory. Swan, the factory's Deputy Convenor, then called on the shop stewards to accept, in principal, the company's proposals, and to advise the workers to do the same. Seventy four Shop Stewards agreed with Swan's recommendation. Fifty four voted against his motion.

On December 13, the workers rejected 'by about 2-1', the shop stewards' recommendation 'to accept in principal the company's proposals'. The factory Deputy Convenor, Hugh Swan, warned that rejection would lead to closure; he was booed by the workers whose attitude was typified by the one who said, 'Singer Management have held a pistol to our heads, let them pull the trigger'.[5]

A company statement from the US New York headquarters was issued saying that the Singer company was 'extremely disappointed and apprehensive about the implications of the vote taken today by manual workers in Clydebank, Scotland to reject the proposal of union leadership to implement a plan designed to save its sewing products factory there.'[6] Mr Keehn explained that:

'This was hoped to have become a solution to benefit everyone concerned, including the Clydebank community as a whole. It is unfortunate that the workforce has chosen to be so cavalier in its first reaction.

Without the endorsement by the total workforce the plan to save Clydebank cannot be successful. And without the plan the Company can see no practical way to continue operations there much less invest one penny more in the plant.

Although the financial impact on the total Company of the plant being closed would be significant, it is a step the Company will take if the membership causes it.

We are hopeful that more responsible consideration will be given to the leadership's call for support of the plan. It would be tragic to force the closing of the plant on the eve of such an enlightened solution to the situation there; a solution developed in an atmosphere of almost unprecedented co-operation between management, labour leaders and government.'[7]

The shop stewards realised that closure was likely unless the manual workers accepted the company's plan. Saving the factory was not uppermost in many workers' minds. The majority were apparently urging their representatives to restrict negotiations to securing favourable redundancy payments.[8]

On December 15, a detailed study was published which forecast that the closure of the Clydebank factory would have significant impact on the local, regional and national economy. It outlined its consequences in terms of job losses, income, emigration and fiscal costs. The following Sunday, a 'Joint Clergy Statement on the crisis at Singer' was read out in every Church in Clydebank and the surrounding areas. It said that the clergy were 'distressed' to find that the workers had rejected the company's amended proposals, and appealed 'to the workforce of Singer's to think again and to act responsibly in the best interest of their families and the community'.

Early in the New Year at the meeting held in London at the request of Singer, Mr Keehn informed a trade union delegation which included national officers of the AUEW and the GMWU, that Mr Flavin's original plan would be implemented immediately. The trades unionists asked Mr Keehn for a seven day extension before implementing the original plan proposed by Flavin. They argued that the manual workers were now ready to approve the modified plan which would save an extra 500 jobs. Their argument proved persuasive and the company agreed to give the manual workers a second chance. There was to be another vote a week later when, once again, the workers would be asked to accept the same motion which they had rejected in December.[9] On January 12 1979 the acting factory Convenor, Mr Swan, instructed the stewards 'to go back to their members and impress upon them that this is their last chance to save the factory'.[10]

Five days later, employees voted, this time two to one in favour of the motion. Shortly afterwards, the *Financial Times* observed that the future of Singer's Clydebank factory looked 'reasonably sure, if not secure'. By May, however, a threatening cloud once again hung over the factory's future. On May 4, it was learned that the Conservatives, led by Mrs Thatcher, had won the General Election. On the same day, Keehn announced that the Clydebank factory faced closure unless the unions agreed to accept the new Pay Plan which Flavin had described as one of the three 'key conditions . . . to make Clydebank a cost effective operation'.

A settlement was reached on 14 May 1979 but the factory's financial problems remained. In the first six months of 1979, Clydebank made a loss of £6 million and the order books were very low. The company indicated that it intended introducing a four-day week in several areas of the factory, and that 598 people would be made redundant by September. The alternative was to continue with a five-day week in all areas, but the workforce of 3,703 would be reduced to 2,466. On June 27 the shop stewards agreed unanimously to accept a four-day week. In the meantime the factory's losses had continued to mount, and in August Hugh Swan informed his fellow shop stewards that losses for the current financial year had reached $14.25 million. The £8 million of investment promised by the company had still not materialised, although all the conditions laid down by Flavin had been met. It was rumoured that the company had decided to withdraw from Clydebank and that machinery was already being sold. Labour had lost the General Election in May and the company felt it was no longer constrained to honour the promises, made to Labour MPs, to remain in Clydebank.

Figure 13:8 *A stark reminder of the dying throes of the one time Singer giant.*

The Closure Announcement

On October 12 Flavin confirmed the worst fears of the 3,000 employees. The US Board had decided that the Clydebank factory should be closed by June 1980. A copy of his letter to employees is printed below:

'Dear Clydebank Employees,

It is with the deepest regret that we announce that Singer will be unable to continue sewing manufacturing operations at the Clydebank plant beyond June of 1980. This conclusion was reached after exhaustive studies of all options available to help us to arrest the persistent and growing losses being experienced by our sewing machine operations in the markets of the developed world.

We are announcing our conclusion fully eight months early, in order to provide more time for more people to make adjustments in their personal and vocational lives. This timing will also give us a chance to pursue a very intensive effort to find a buyer for the factory and new jobs for its workforce. I'm sure you appreciate that this effort will be enhanced by the continued support of everyone in the manufacture of sewing machines according to schedule.

The closing of Clydebank is only a part of a sweeping program to restructure, consolidate and streamline Singer manufacturing and marketing operations throughout North America and

Europe. It is a program that will take years but is essential if we are going to arrest the crippling losses mentioned earlier.

We will do everything in our power to minimize the effects on our Scottish employees and we will co-operate with government, unions and civic groups to assist in an orderly transition.

But, in the final analysis, it is your continued support that we must have to keep Clydebank, operating as effectively as possible through those next several months during which we will be trying to make the facility as appealing as possible to a prospective buyer and bring new work to Clydebank'.

Lay-offs would begin after the New Year. At the time, Larry Mihlan broke the news at a press conference in the Central Hotel, Glasgow. The promise of 'a fight to the death' was the first reaction of the union leaders, but their members did not support this line of action and encouraged the unions to channel their energy into negotiating as satisfactory a severance settlement as possible. The reaction of some politicians was not so docile. Mr Bruce Millan, who had been Secretary of State for Scotland until May 1979, accused the company of breaking its word. He said that Singer had told him 'it would maintain a substantial operation in Clydebank'. In contrast, the new Secretary of State for Scotland, Mr George Younger, adopted an attitude of 'don't cry over spilt milk' and urged the workers 'to do everything they could to bring a new industrial concern to Clydebank'. The factory finally closed in late June 1980.

Epilogue

The design and condition of the Singer factory building precluded the possibility of their being sold to a private concern, and anyway, other areas, such as the new towns, had more to offer than Clydebank. The SDA bought the site at a cost of £850,000 in June 1980, the machinery which had not been transferred to other Singer establishments having been sold by public auction.

The SDA realised that virtually all the buildings on the site would have to be demolished and replaced by new, modern premises that would attract firms. These in turn would provide jobs. The Government, aware of the town's problems and poor prospects, decided that Clydebank should be Scotland's 'Enterprise Zone'. As such the town could offer special conditions to any business prepared to set up in the zone — 100% de-rating for Industrial and Commercial Companies, and very low, or rent free premises being just two of the financial inducements the zone offers. Ironically, the Singer Company availed itself of the 'no rates' offer and opened an office where six engineers designed machines for manufacture overseas.

In retrospect, Singer management had been completely out of touch with the market. As one Singer executive concluded on his firm's decline in the November 1979 edition of *Fortune:*

'What happened is not at all mysterious.
— We neglected product development
— We neglected manufacturing facilities
— We neglected our retail stores
It's a classic case that will be studied for a long time to come!

Since Clydebank closed, Singer has finally realised that it sold machines in spite of, not because of, its retail outlets, and has continued its rationalisation of manufacturing facilities. The shops have been sold and Monza is now the only plant producing sewing machines in Europe. Its two large US plants have also been closed. Virtually all sewing machine production has been concentrated in distant Brazil and Taiwan. By 1986 Singer had finally diversified successfully. In February 1986 it made the anticipated announcement that its sewing machine division would be spun off as an independent, separately-quoted enterprise. The stock market's reaction was unequivocal; Singer's share price showed an almost immediate gain of 20%.

CHAPTER FOURTEEN

Social Trends, 1945-1980

The immediate task before Clydebank at the end of the Second World War in 1945 was one of reconstruction. The Clydebank Blitz had inflicted crippling damage on the town's housing stock, and while the main industries had escaped the greatest damage, virtually every other aspect of Clydebank's community life was affected by Blitz damage and the need for reconstruction. That reconstruction took place within the framework of social and economic legislation passed by the post-war Attlee Labour Government. The Attlee Government was to have a profound impact in shaping post-war social and welfare provision, perhaps especially in the creation of the National Health Service. The period has generally seen a significant improvement in the standard of living in the town, although severe social and economic problems remain. For Clydebank, the post-war period has not only been one of reconstruction but one of transition as its main employers, John Brown and Singer, went into decline. Reconstruction and economic decline have had their impact upon social trends in Clydebank as the following sections on redevelopment, health, education, religion, and leisure and recreation show.

The Redevelopment of the Town

In terms of more than a century of urban growth, the period from 1945 to 1980 makes up only a small proportion of the lifetime of Clydebank, but at the same time encompasses changes in its structure and fabric on a huge scale. These 35 years represent a story of urban renewal of massive proportions, of decades of innovative and energetic striving, often in the face of severe economic pressures, to create a new Clydebank. Perhaps Clydebank may be regarded as a town with no choice but to make large efforts to renew itself after wartime devastation, but such a view would be unfortunate, since it would exclude the firm conception, insight, concern for the future and effective implementation of those who guided the building of a better Clydebank. Their efforts took place within a framework of, and were in a range of ways partly responsible for, changes in the number, structure and distribution of the burgh's and later the district's population. These changes in turn were directly related to the provision of housing, its type and location, the development of shopping and other services, the zoning of new sites for industry, and the upgrading of old ones, a transport infrastructure serving both the internal needs of burgh and district, and providing a network of external connections with the rest of the Clydeside conurbation and beyond. What was involved was nothing less than a complete and complex restructuring of Clydebank.

The Road to Recovery: Basic Needs

After the interminable depression of the Thirties and the wartime material and personnel shortages of the early Forties, all Scottish towns and cities faced up to the requirements of recovery in the post-war period. More than any other town, in proportion to its size, Clydebank had suffered crippling damage from air attacks, and the level of response required was staggering. Of its 12,000 houses, only seven remained intact after the German bombing raids of 13 and 14 March 1941. 4,500 houses had been completely destroyed and a further 4,000 seriously damaged. Destruction and serious damage also spread to schools, churches, shops, factories and shipyards and a host of other structures within the burgh. 48,000 people had become refugees, and of a small population, a reputed 528 were dead and over 1,000 injured.[1] The dead were buried and the debris cleared, and emergency programmes of rebuilding concentrated on vital industrial production and the replacement of housing on a temporary basis. Work continued, albeit at a low level, through the war years, and the Burgh Council *minutes* of the time record the competing demands for skilled tradesmen and the shortages of labourers, the source of requests for greater use of German prisoners of war.[2]

Figure 14:1 *W. R. Milligan, town planning consultants and local officials touring the blitzed areas in preparation for the massive rebuilding and replanning developments.*

Planning for the post-war period began immediately. At the instigation of the War Damage Commission a complete redevelopment plan of the town was prepared, and permission obtained to erect 500 houses in two schemes at Whitecrook. The Clyde Valley Regional Plan of 1946 drew attention to the difficult site of Clydebank, and to the way in which the town was badly cut by roads and railways, making redevelopment in normal circumstances very difficult. However, as a result of the Blitz, the scale of destruction had presented the town with an opportunity for comprehensive replanning not available elsewhere in the region.[3] The perceived future for Clydebank was similar to that of other industrial units, large and small, within the Clydeside conurbation. Basic to the Plan were the twin aims of decentralisation of industry and population from the clotted cores of older industrial areas, and the creation of new poles of growth in the rural hinterland of the conurbation. Around these nuclei an 'overspill' of excess population and industry would be located, while the existing patterns of older areas would undergo restructuring.

For Clydebank, the Plan proposed the creation of a 70-acre site, fronting the river Clyde between the Glasgow Corporation Outfall Works and Old Kilpatrick. Pessimistic about the long-term future of shipbuilding, the authors of the Plan saw this flat site with its long river frontage and good rail links as being potentially attractive to firms of the heavier variety requiring a waterfrontage. It would serve the Duntocher — Clydebank — Dalmuir — Yoker area where considerable unemployment was anticipated once the shipbuilding boom was over. Together with blitzed sites in the central area to be developed as an industrial estate, clearance for industrial use would produce a big overspill population, and the Plan proposed the creation of a 'quasi-satellite', north of the Great Western Boulevard near Duntocher, to meet the burgh's requirements.[4]

The old villages of Duntocher and Hardgate, more or less connected by building developments, were almost entirely residential in character since their pre-war industrial activities of furniture-making and hosiery production had been discontinued during the war and never resumed. The proposed new development at Faifley was perceived by the authors of the Plan as a substantial new town. A well-planned community would stand on one of the finest sites in the region, with its southern aspect, magnificent views and recreational hinterland. Integrating the proposed development with the old industrial housing and uncoordinated inter-war housing groups of the existing villages was perceived as a potential problem.[5] By the Boundary Extension Act of 1947, which provided for extensive rebuilding, Clydebank took in 633 acres of hill-land between 250 and 400 feet in altitude, attached to the burgh by a narrow neck about one-third of a mile wide, avoiding the old villages of Hardgate and Duntocher. When the Act came into force in 1949, there were only 70 people in the new district of Faifley.[6]

The First Step

Clydebank Burgh Council reacted vigorously to the situation as soon as legislation gave them the power to do so. By the end of 1948, 403 temporary houses had been erected, and a planned target of just over 2,000 permanent houses was well on its way to completion. The two Whitecrook schemes, comprising 532 houses for which permission had been obtained during the war, were completed and a third development was well under way, while construction at North and South Drumry Road, Overtoun Road and Boquhanran brought the total of completions to 1,068. With another 932 under construction, the housing programme was off to a flying start. In addition to Council building, the Scottish Special Housing Association Limited (later SSHA), as it was entitled then, had completed 20 houses in Riddell Street, and 240 of a projected programme of 660 houses in the Livingstone Street

Figure 14:2 *In February 1948 the Dunbarton County Council's Public Health Committee, on the chairman's casting vote, rejected a proposal to increase rents by 33 per cent. This move followed months of agitation throughout the County with meetings of ratepayers being held and petitions organised. In the above picture tenants from Duntocher and Hardgate converge on the County Buildings armed with 'ricketies', bells and whistles to lobby the monthly meeting of the Council to guard against a change of mind. In the event, the Council delayed the proposed rent increase for a period of one year.*

area. At the same time the Burgh Council was revealing large-scale plans for central area redevelopment, using powers of compulsory purchase provided by the Town and Country Planning (Scotland) Act of 1945. In February 1948 they applied for an Order covering about 70 acres of Radnor Park and Boquhanran districts which had suffered the most severe damage during the 1941 air raids. Council proposals for the area, to be known as the Central Redevelopment Area, involved the construction of multi-storey housing blocks, community and shopping centres, new administrative offices and ample facilities for educational, cultural and recreational purposes.[7] The focus of activity was thus firmly fixed on the central area, while the newly acquired land at Faifley was still subject to forward planning and the early stages of site preparation.

The 1951 Census revealed considerable progress in the battle to create decent housing conditions for Clydebank's population. Admittedly there had been a 5.1 per cent decrease in the burgh's population between 1931 and 1951, with a natural increase of over 6,600 more than offset by a migration loss of 8,100.[8] Also, many thousands of sub-standard houses had been destroyed by bombing. However, it was principally the effectiveness of Clydebank's response to its housing needs which made the statistics so interesting. As the 11th largest town in Scotland in 1951, and 5th largest in the Clydeside conurbation, Clydebank was bound to exhibit some of the grosser legacy of shoddy nineteenth-century housebuilding. However, in comparison with other Scottish urban areas, Clydebank ranked very highly. Of the existing 12,049 houses only 36 per cent were of one or two rooms, compared to 48 per cent in Glasgow and Paisley, 45 per cent in Coatbridge and 43 per cent in Rutherglen and Motherwell. 61.4 per cent had exclusive use of all conveniences compared with the Scottish average of only 50.5 per cent, while only 21.8 per cent shared a WC compared with the higher Scottish average of 28.9 per cent. From a level of 1.83 persons per room in 1931, densities had fallen to 1.24 persons per room in 1951.[9] An enormous effort of construction between 1945 and

Table 14:1 *House building in Clydebank by Local Authority and SSHA, 1941-1981*

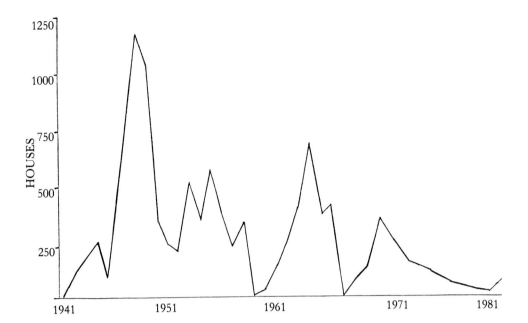

1950, at the highest rate in Britain for the size of its population, had not sacrificed quality for quantity, but had combined the two to provide vastly improved living standards for thousands of families.

The graph of housing completions for Clydebank in the immediate post-war decades is an interesting one in that it differs considerably from that of its neighbour Glasgow, and indeed from that of Scotland as a whole. In the latter two cases, the graph lines, while reflecting vastly different completion totals, are roughly parallel, with their first major peaks between 1953 and 1955, a relatively steady level of completions throughout the 1950s and thereafter a slight falling off until a major resurgence in the 1960s. Clydebank's total peaked in the late 1940s, especially 1948-49, then dropped steeply for the next few years, achieving lower and intermittent peaks in the early 1950s, then dropping off steeply before surging once again in the late 1960s.[10] This profile reflects the swiftness of Clydebank's post-war response to housing need, and thereafter a slower and steadier process of land acquisition and site preparation in advance of central area redevelopment. Early beginnings gave Clydebank a head start in gaining experience of the problems and pitfalls of large-scale area building, but on the other side of the coin produced a sector of housing stock destined to reach replacement or at least refurbishment age just at a time when public funds were being drastically reduced.

By 1954 the earlier post-war schemes at Whitecrook and Drumry were largely complete and work was under way on new areas, as well as on new types of housing. North Mountblow now had 324 new houses, and in Faifley the combined efforts of the Council and the SSHA had produced 589 dwellings, with a further 982 under construction. In common with the majority of peripheral public housing schemes in Scottish cities, the Faifley houses were overwhelmingly of the three or four apartment family house type, built in flatted accommodation to locally high densities. In an era of intensive housing need, this type of accommodation was exactly what was required to take the maximum number of families off the Council waiting list, thereby clearing substandard properties in the burgh centre, and throughout the 1950s this type of build-up continued in Faifley. In the burgh centre on cleared sites, a wider range of housing types was under construction including 112 houses for the elderly and 18 for single women. By 1956 a prototype eight-storey

Figure 14:3 *Housing at Whitecrook.*

block of high-flats had been built at Mountblow; 32 houses of three apartments with central heating, lifts and a communal laundry, proved extremely popular at first, but because of high building costs involved the Council decided that it was unlikely that further houses of this type would be constructed.[11] This decision was to be overturned all too soon, with unfortunate consequences.

Another early initiative was the acquisition of tenement blocks for improvement. Compulsory purchase powers permitted local councils to acquire sub-standard tenements, but throughout urban Scotland the majority of councils used this mechanism in advance of demolition. Clydebank certainly exercised the latter option, as in the case of part of Buchanan Street, where the Town Planning Consultant recommended the site, together with ground at Boquhanran Road, as suitable for 226 new houses. However, the Council also gave active consideration to other options, such as rehabilitation, a decision which was to be prophetic for the future, but at the time flew in the face of accepted wisdom. As early as the formulation stage of the Clyde Valley Regional Plan, from 1944 to 1946, political pressure on planning officers dissuaded them from advocating tenement renovation. Politicians at all levels believed that revitalisation of older neighbourhoods was not desirable, as it would leave residents in the hands of private landlords, in poor local environments. The clean new strands of public housing on the peripheral estates were an easier and more attractive, not to say vote-catching package to deliver.[12]

In this light it is interesting to examine a joint report by the Sanitary Inspector and the Burgh Engineer to the Housing Committee, on properties with the potential for rehabilitation, not least because of the insight into tenemental housing conditions in 1956.[13] The tenement stump at Dumbarton Road and Buchanan Street had been left standing after adjoining properties had been destroyed by bombing, and the exposed part walls, now acting as gables, permitted dampness to seep into the houses. There were 50 houses in the grey sandstone block, with one apartment and two apartment ground floor flats in Dumbarton Road unfit for human habitation and recommended for closure. Above them, the three apartment flats had small bathrooms, with a WC, bath and cold water, and no wash-basin. The Buchanan Street flats were poorer, all of two apartments, with a kitchen sink and cold water supply and common WC serving three households, or in some cases four. The slated roofs were leaking in places, dampness had discoloured ceilings of top flats, masonry was worn and open jointed, and eaves, gutters and down-pipes needed repairs. Broken plaster in common passages and stairs, and defective windows and woodwork, completed a list of defects which the observers felt was redeemable. They proposed a modernisation scheme on the Buchanan Street site whereby 36 modernised houses would result from the existing 48, and the two ground floor flats would be incorporated into business premises. The shelving of schemes of this type in many Scottish urban areas condemned to demolition many tenemental properties which could have been retained as viable parts of housing stock, and in many cases, only the accidents of the pattern of demolition saved a residue.

By the time of writing of the Dunbartonshire volume of the *Third Statistical Account of Scotland* in 1959, Clydebank's housing programme was well under way.[14] Of around 14,000 houses in the burgh, 6,400 were owned by the Council (including inter-war houses), and 1,580 owned by the SSHA, initiating the rise to dominance of public ownership and management of Clydebank's housing. The peripheral scheme of Faifley now totalled around 1,800 houses, entirely in public ownership, and large districts of the inner burgh were dominated by public tenure. The estates were constructed as neighbourhood units with their own shops, and street layouts were designed to deter through traffic. Identity was conferred through associated street names. Faifley names were based on local history, while the area north of Drumry station took the names of great ships, including the *Hood, Vanguard* and *Queen Mary*. Livingstone Street scheme, renamed Linnvale by its tenants, enshrined for posterity the names of ministers in the post-war Labour Government which had provided the subsidies upon which the houses were built. Attlee, Bevin, Shinwell, Morrison, Kirkwood and many others live on in the streets which mark the achievements of their time.

Towards the Seventies: The Comprehensive Approach

Until 1956 Clydebank had acted as a reception area for population, partly because of wartime refugees returning. After 1956 there began a steady drift outwards, becoming more pronounced during the 1960s and rising sharply between the

Figure 14:4 *Faifley housing scene — a post war development.*

sample census of 1966 and the decennial census of 1971. However, overall population loss from the burgh was only one part of a complex picture of migration patterns, motivated on the one hand by lack of available employment, and on the other by new housing opportunities in both the public and private sectors. By looking at the broader migration field of Clydebank, in effect the area which was to become Clydebank District, these detailed patterns may be analysed.

Table 14:2 *Clydebank: Population and Household change: 1961 to 71*

		Persons			Households		
		1961	1971	% change	1961	1971	% change
Clydebank Ward 1 Whitecrook		7804	6095	−21.90	2192	1930	−21.96
,, ,, 2 Clydebank Central		5674	3635	−35.94	1885	1285	−31.84
,, ,, 3 Dalmuir		6399	7450	+16.42	2092	2610	+24.76
,, ,, 4 Parkhall-Mountblow		6449	6830	+15.90	2126	2375	+11.71
,, ,, 5 Linnvale-Drumry		8290	6445	−22.26	2403	1870	−22.19
,, ,, 6 Kilbowie		5831	8750	+50.06	1668	2565	+53.77
,, ,, 7 Faifley		9204	8935	−2.93	2414	2365	−2.03
Total		49651	48155	−3.02	14780	15000	+1.48
Duntocher		3032	3525	+16.25	849	1050	+23.67
Hardgate		1904	3870	+103.25	576	1175	+103.99
Old Kilpatrick East		1479	1425	−3.66	437	445	+1.83
Old Kilpatrick West		1756	1790	+1.93	594	660	+11.11
Old Kilpatrick District		9393	11820	+25.83	2827	3740	+32.29

Source: Census of Scotland: Enumeration Abstracts 1961, 1971.

Table 14:2 shows population and household change in the seven wards of Clydebank burgh, and in the suburban villages of Old Kilpatrick Registration District between 1961 and 1971. The most obvious changes are the overall loss to Clydebank of around 3 per cent and the gain to its hinterland of over 25 per cent, and the great internal variation in population loss and gain within the seven burgh wards. Looking at Clydebank itself it is obvious that the dominant process was one of redistribution rather than of massive loss. The heaviest loss was from the central area where large-scale displacement in advance of comprehensive redevelopment was a herald of greater losses to come. In Whitecrook, Linnvale and Drumry, developed in the 1940s and 1950s, second generation children were forming their own households and moving out largely to newer public sector housing areas beyond the core. Faifley's minor loss was below the burgh average, and the scheme was expected to accommodate further displaced families from the older tenement areas. On the positive side, the huge increase in Kilbowie ward was a result of the completion of a large area of public sector housing of mixed types during the 1960s, in the Radnor Park area, and to a lesser extent in Dalmuir Road. Parkhall and Mountblow showed a small increase largely due to the availability of new housing in Mountblow, while Parkhall retained its remarkably stable character.[15] The most remarkable feature of population change in Clydebank's hinterland was the contrast between the relative stability of Old Kilpatrick, experiencing only minor building activity, and the dramatic increases in Duntocher and especially Hardgate, feeling the full effects of the 1960s private sector building boom. During this decade the general affluence of a rising middle class was reflected in the proliferation of suburban, owner-occupied housing estates. Discrimination against private housing by city councils forced builders to seek sites beyond the urban cores, and the huge levels of population gains in Hardgate and Duntocher may be seen as a reflection of neighbouring Glasgow's policies, since Clydebank's population loss could only account for a fraction of the villages' gain.[16]

Figure 14:5 *Multi-storey development west of Mountblow Road sandwiched pleasantly between the public park and the golf course.*

Table 14:3 gives an indication of the general levels of improvement in housing facilities between 1951 and 1971, and shows the great strides made by large-scale public sector housebuilding. By 1971 over 88 per cent of the burgh's household enjoyed exclusive use of a fixed bath or shower, toilet facilities, and a hot water supply, compared with only just over 64 per cent at the time of the post-war census. As Table 14:1 shows, house completion levels varied during the 1960s with an early peak in the first half of the decade falling away later, to give by 1970 a total of post-war completions of 5,556 by the Council, and 2,885 by the SSHA.[17] In contrast with the 1940s and 1950s, house type was much more varied. The 1959 and 1962 Housing Acts reduced the generous general needs subsidies and introduced an extra subsidy for houses in blocks of flats of more than six storeys. Local authorities with urgent housing needs and large-scale planned programmes were encouraged by the Scottish Office to adopt system building techniques to house their working classes, and with no real possibility of cutting back, many local authorities were forced to attempt economies, false in the long run, by opting for high-rise building. Clydebank was no exception, and by 1967 a large number of multi-storey blocks were either complete or under construction. In Dalmuir, six 15-storey blocks each contained 28 two-apartment and 60 three-apartment flats, while in North Drumry and the Central area, six 12-storey blocks each provided 46 three-apartment flats.

Table 14:3 *Improvement in housing facilities, 1951-1971*
(figs. for facilities in %s)

	Households	hot water shared	hot water none	bath/shower shared	bath/shower none	WC shared	WC none	Exclusive use of all facilities
1951	12,370	*n.a.	n.a.	3.8	31.4	21.3	0.1	64.7
1961	14,543	1.4	17.7	1.3	23.0	12.5	0.4	75.3
1971	15,000	0.1	6.7	0.1	11.0	2.7	0.1	88.6

Source: Census of Scotland: Abstract 1951, 1961, 1971.
*n.a. = not available.

In the East End a further three 15-storey blocks were almost ready for occupation, and would each provide 30 two-apartment and 61 three-apartment units.

A policy of letting the two-apartment flats to single persons only was designed not only to avoid overcrowding but to encourage them to vacate much larger houses which could be re-let to families.

The provision of over 1,000 flats in high-rise structures, making intensive use of cleared or vacant sites close to the public facilities, and using rapid methods of assembly of prefabricated components, appealed to Council and consumers alike, and at first these structures were extremely popular. It was only after a period of experience of the inevitable congestion and claustrophobia of multi-storey living, and the rapid decay, malfunction and breakdown of its systems, that doubts began to creep in concerning the wisdom of the strategy. It was at this time also, in the early 1970s that ageing of the public sector housing stock was producing sharp variations in housing quality and socio-economic structure within council stocks. Contrasts were becoming apparent between areas of high-quality housing often inhabited by relatively high-income tenants paying modest rents, and areas of social and environmental deprivation, often on the outer edges of town, where large low-income families were overcrowded.

Table 14:4   *Age of Housing Stock 1970*

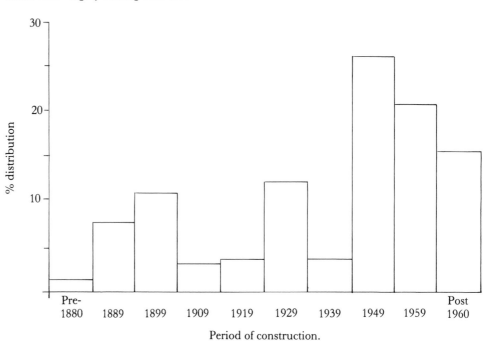

On a conservatively estimated basis, Clydebank had 3,400 houses due for replacement at January 1968, while the repair and maintenance needs of the large element of 1940s and 1950s houses were beginning to cause problems. At the same time, 4,160 houses were deemed to be sub-standard because of their sanitary condition. Thus, on paper at least, 26 per cent of the burgh's 12,800 houses were substandard, quite apart from the problem of age.[18] The bulk of these poorer dwellings consisted of 4,182 occupied tenement flats, housing 11,674 people, and concentrated largely in three areas which came to be known as the Kilbowie, Eastern and Dalmuir Comprehensive Development Areas.

The idea of Comprehensive Development Areas was not new. Elsewhere in Scotland, in Glasgow in particular, they had been seen as the best solution to the

Figure 14:6 *Throughout its history the burgh suffered from a shortage of land, a situation worsened by the effects of driving major roads, rail links and the canal through its heart. This scene at Dalmuir is typical of the congestion, with tenements bunched together between road and rail.*

clearing of decayed central area buildings once new homes had been built for their inhabitants. The idea of abandoning piecemeal replacement for a clean sweep treatment was extremely attractive, not least in the opportunities which it afforded for large-scale integrated replanning. As early as 1957, Glasgow had outlined no fewer than 29 CDAs, covering one-twelfth of the city area. Clearance in these areas was to focus mainly on areas of working-class housing and obsolete industrial premises, and throughout the 1960s demolition proceeded rapidly, involving in the end over 100,000 tenement flats. Clydebank began its programme much later, and on a vastly smaller scale, but its roots went equally far back in time. The rapid industrially-based growth of the later nineteenth century had created a congested waterfront town, badly cut up by canals and railway lines, consisting largely of high-density tenements erected on flat land alongside the highly industrialised foreshore. Over 90 per cent of the tenemental housing was to be found south of the canal, mainly along the Dumbarton-Glasgow road. Together with areas of disused railway sidings north of the canal, these areas could be developed on a comprehensive basis without prejudice to the overall replanning of the town.

The Central Redevelopment Area had been outlined as early as the immediate post-war years, and in 1963 two areas were proposed for CDA treatment along Dumbarton Road and Glasgow Road between Canal and Miller Streets, and Livingstone Street between Victoria Street and Kilbowie Road. These were later merged to form the Kilbowie CDA.[19] Obsolescence and constriction were its main problems, with a hopelessly inadequate road system, causing severe congestion, especially at peak times, but also during shopping hours. Of the shops in this principal service area of the burgh, a higher than average proportion were devoted to foodstuffs, with extremely poor provision of consumer durable goods. At one shop for every 156 persons, Clydebank compared badly with, for instance, Ayr, which had one shop for every 87 persons, and in fact within the Clydeside conurbation only Coatbridge was as poorly provided. The 1,400 occupied houses held almost 4,000 and overcrowding affected over 36 per cent of households, while in many tenement blocks, such as Bannerman Street and Livingstone Street, exceptionally

Table 14:5   *Kilbowie CDA Structural and Sanitary Conditions of Housing, 1969*

Sanitary condition	Class 1	Class 2	Class 3	Class 4	Total	
A acceptable	—	2	180	—	182	12.99
B capable of improvement to A	6	—	105	208	319	22.76
C incapable of improvement to A	—	—	14	153	167	11.92
D unacceptable	—	—	15	107	122	8.71
E completely unacceptable	—	—	69	542	611	43.62
Total	6	2	383	1010	1401	
%	0.42	0.14	27.34	72.1	100	

high densities of 200-300 persons per acre occurred. Table 14:5 shows the extremely poor quality of the tenement stock, with less than 1 per cent being in structural class 1, and 53 per cent unacceptable for human habitation. All but four of the area's houses were tenemental, 78 per cent of them of only one or two rooms.[20]

A carefully zoned and integrated development plan for this key core area of the town was essential, and an £18.5 million scheme was announced by the Council in 1970. 24.5 acres were to be devoted to residential use for a future population of around 2,000, in 800 houses built around a footpath system apart from major traffic routes. Almost 20 acres were zoned for commercial use, allocating 350,000 square feet of retail sales and storage space to meet the future needs of the burgh. Other land uses such as public and community buildings, social uses and offices were to be encouraged, and the general strategy was to contain central commercial users in a manageable complex with a pedestrian walkway linking the blue train stations of Singer and Clydebank Central. The whole central business district would be contained within a complex of new road works, and the focal point of the development would be a large landscaped square enclosed by the civic offices, theatre, entertainment and community centre, with a town park leading off the square, and access both by foot and from extensive car parks. Beyond this core, major industrial units were not to be relocated, but provision for improved access and new development would be made.[21] Phase One, taking 5 years, covered

Figure 14:7   *Signing of Phase 3 of the Clyde Shopping Centre development, one of the largest shopping centre developments in Scotland.*

around 39 acres of residential development and the first stage of the commercial centre, with part of the car parking and new service roads, while Phase Two took the development to 1980, with 67 acres of residence and commerce, the civic square and offices, town park and Expressway, with a further 5-year phase to come.

On the south-eastern edge of Clydebank, lying between Whitecrook Street and Yoker Burn, was one of the oldest parts of the town, with many of its buildings dating from the 1870s. Physically separated from the rest of the town by railway lines and industry, substandard tenements housed shipyard-workers in a close-knit community. In this Eastern CDA, the two main priorities were firstly the clearance of substandard tenements, especially around Union Street, and secondly, the pressing need to upgrade the Glasgow Road as part of an ambitious and large-scale transportation plan, of which the proposed Clydeside Expressway was a crucial component.[22] After this first five-year phase, the next task would be the clearance of better residential property on the south side of Glasgow Road to permit road upgrading, and in a third phase, the clearance of Dunedin Terrace for new housing, while the area between the Expressway and the River Clyde would be devoted largely to industry. The third CDA, proposed in outline in 1970,[23] consisted of an area of Dalmuir which had suffered severe bomb damage, leaving a patchwork of derelict gap sites, a number of which had been developed under the pressure of post-war needs without much thought to overall planning implications. United in their housing characteristics and in their advanced state of decay, the three CDAs ran along the River Clyde, and their proposed developments, apart from housing, were seen as functionally complementary, with the Eastern CDA being principally industrial, Kilbowie CDA principally commercial-administrative, and Dalmuir outline CDA largely social.

Table 14:6 *Comprehensive Development Areas and house occupancy rates 1970* (figures show % net shift from burgh average, by enumeration districts.)

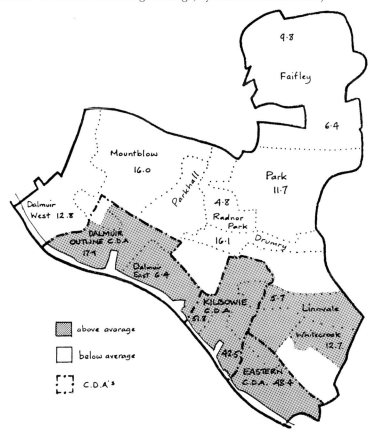

Restructuring Clydebank's Transport

Central to the development of a new Clydebank was the restructuring of its transport system. The early 1960s saw the demise of two familiar parts, with the last ceremonial run of the Dalmuir to Auchenshuggle tramcar in September 1962 prompting Clydebank Burgh Council to mount their own farewell ceremony after that of Glasgow.[24] Shortly afterwards, in January 1963, the Forth and Clyde canal was closed to shipping, and shorn of any useful purpose it simply posed a problem to the town, firstly as a danger to children, then as a major constraint to integrated town planning.[25] In 1969, a major plan for the burgh's roads was prepared, laying out a scheme of improvements which would serve the town's needs for the foreseeable future. Attention was concentrated on the road system, since it was thought that existing bus and rail networks adequately met demands for public transport. The Kilbowie line had been closed to passenger traffic and the Singer and Yoker lines electrified to give an efficient service. One minor recommended improvement was the addition of feeder bus services to the railway stations.[26]

Figure 14:8 *On 6 September 1962, a Coronation Mark I No. 9 tram made its final ceremonial run marking the cessation of the Glasgow Corporation tramway operations. Initially the Commissioners had applied for powers to operate their own tram network but finally accepted a proposal from the Corporation that they would administer the tramway system through the burgh to Dalmuir West and north to Duntocher.*

Attention focussed on the problems of congestion in the centre, at the Kilbowie Road, Dumbarton-Glasgow Road junction, and on the need for adequate connections with west-central Scotland beyond the burgh. A three-phase development was proposed. The first phase included the Erskine Bridge and the northern approach road from Great Western Road, already under way as links in the broader network. The Great Western Road Expressway and the Clydeside Expressway were also to be completed as far as the burgh boundary. Phase two included the continuation of the Clydeside Expressway up Kilbowie Road to the planned Lomond Motorway, never completed, and phase three involved an expressway extension north-east from Kilbowie Road, following the line of the disused Forth and Clyde canal, to the Goodyear factory on Great Western Road. In those elements of the plan which were completed, great attention was paid to separating traffic from housing precincts, retaining suitable 'expressway-side' land uses such as churches, football grounds, steel stockyards and filling stations, and exercising strict control on all other uses.[27] Beyond the burgh proper, local government reorganisation in the wake of the Wheatley Report created a new Clydebank District, including the villages of Old Kilpatrick, Hardgate and Duntocher, and bringing responsibility for a broader pattern of traffic circulation and a wider network of roads. The jewel in the crown of this network was the Erskine Bridge, opened in July 1971. There had been a ferry at this point for centuries, but by the 1950s continued increases in road traffic volumes and the redevelopment of Clydeside stressed its growing inadequacy. Indeed, dissatisfaction had been expressed as early as 1934, and in 1955 the local authorities concerned began a series of planning meetings, culminating in the formation of the Erskine Bridge Joint Committee in 1963. The Scottish Development Department assumed the responsibility for the work in 1965, and in 1967 construction began on a steel-box stayed-girder bridge with a 1,000 feet main span. Between 1966 and 1970, the Erskine Ferry carried an annual total of well over half a million vehicles, and when it made its last run in 1971, this traffic shifted to the bridge, whose approach roads on its northern side connected Clydebank firmly with a new hinterland.[28]

The Later 1970s: Fraying at the Edges

In 1976, in a major review of its social and economic strategy, Strathclyde Regional Council focused attention on a large number of areas which suffered from severe social or fabric problems or both. In its review of Clydebank, classed as one of 114 Areas for Priority Treatment (APTs), it identified the central area as still possessing some outworn property and derelict sites, but directed attention towards the main areas of social problems, principally local authority schemes in Faifley, Drumry and Hardgate.[29] The most severe problems were in the Faifley area, where the early popularity and community identity of the scheme had been quickly eroded, and by the 1960s it had become clearly defined as a problem area, suffering from poor amenities and services, drabness and remoteness, with high population densities

Figure 14:9 *Scene at Dalmuir West looking west, with 30s and 60s housing, the latter replacing 'prefabs' erected after the Blitz and a familiar scene for many years. In the background is the Erskine Bridge. On 2 July 1971 the 4334 foot long bridge was opened by HRH Princess Anne at which time the centuries old ferry operation ceased.*

Figure 14:10 *On 7 February 1958 the* Clydebank Press *carried an article, 'the Faifley story' alleging that not only were the SSHA rents greater than for comparable housing elsewhere within the district but that the quality of the housing was inferior. Wrangling ensued between the Burgh and the Faifley Tenants Association which culminated in one of the principals of the FTA, Finlay Hart, accompanying a deputation of tenants to Edinburgh to lobby Scottish Office.*

and overcrowding in its mainly tenemental housing stock.[30] Severe unemployment exacerbated by the loss of Clydebank's main industries in the later 1970s added a further strain. The SSHA began improvements at a basic level, providing drying greens, and bin storage areas, but the chronic unemployment, lack of schools, no health provision and unreliable public transport continued to contribute to the overall isolation and misery past 1980.

The Town and Country Planning (Scotland) Act 1972, and the Local Government (Scotland) Act 1973 required District Councils to prepare Local Plans for all parts of their Districts, and together with the setting up of a Faifley-Duntocher-Hardgate Initiative, this more sensitive, localised approach to planning began to have some beneficial effects. Apart from environmental improvements, the creation of a single waiting list in October 1979 improved mobility in the public housing sector. Prior to this there had been separate lists for housing areas in which waiting time varied from three-six months in Faifley to three years in Hardgate and up to 16 years for houses in favoured inner areas like Mountblow and Parkhall.[31] Survey Reports for Local Plans for Old Kilpatrick and for Duntocher-Hardgate were published in 1977, and by 1980 that for Clydebank itself was well under way.[32]

In many ways the decade of the Seventies was one of mixed blessings for Clydebank. It had opened with large scale reorganisation of local authority responsibilities, the drawing-up of new boundaries, the demise of the old Burgh Council and the creation of a new District Council. It had seen the continuation of a quarter century's effort in rehousing the population, and the completion of the first phases of commercial developments and a new transport network. It was to close with massive redundancies at Singer, Marathon and Goodyear, and the precipitation of a crisis which threatened the future wellbeing of Clydebank, and cast a pall of doubt over the continuation of its development plans. What could not be called into doubt was the physical evidence of 35 years of post-war striving.

Figure 14:11 *First statutory meeting of the new Clydebank District Council in May 1974 with (standing, left-right), Councillors Ian Smith, John Taylor, Stuart Divers and (seated, left-right) Councillors John Hamilton, William Johnston, Hugh Duffy, Robert Calder, John McPherson, Andrew Veitch and Robert Fleming.*

However disillusioned and threatened the people of Clydebank felt, at least they now enjoyed modern shopping and, for the majority, homes of a size and quality far in advance of those of previous generations, and from the security of which they might face the impending battles of the 1980s.

Health and Welfare, 1948-80

As early as 1918, the Scottish National Health Insurance Committees recommended at their annual conference that the Minister of Health should have powers to deal with preventive and curative medicine for everyone. Under Aneuran Bevan, Minister of Health, the Labour Government enacted this concept, introducing the National Health Service (Scotland) Act of 1947. The Act established a comprehensive health service, bringing sweeping changes to local health administration, in that it then fell to the Secretary of State for Scotland to provide hospital accommodation, medical and nursing facilities within the hospitals and specialist services wherever appropriate. To carry out these and other functions, a framework of regional hospital boards and executive councils was established.

The Dunbartonshire Executive Council of the new NHS held its first meeting in Glasgow on 7 February 1948 with William Jardine as chairman, and Dr William Gibson, Old Kilpatrick, as vice-chairman.[33] Jardine was followed as chairman in 1954 by John Carson, and he, in turn, by Dr John M. Fleming in 1972. The first Clydebank representatives on the Council were Councillors Alexander Braes and Isabella Lappin and Doctors Gibson and Crombie. The Clerks and Finance Officers of the Executive Council were T.H. Souter (until 1952) and John M. Dow (1953-74). From 5 July 1948, the Executive Council was in administrative charge of all the general medical, dental, pharmaceutical and ophthalmic services in Dunbartonshire. Local preventive and public health services including visitations, district nursing, midwives and welfare services were the responsibility of

Figure 14:12 *David Kirkwood, MP for Dumbarton Burghs, at a Day Nursery in Clydebank in 1951 with children receiving welfare food. After the war expectant mothers and children under five received milk, orange juice and cod liver oil. Much of the foodstuffs came from America under the Marshall Aid scheme.*

the Town Council through the MOH (Thomas M. Hunter followed, in 1965, by John B. Morris) and the Burgh Sanitary Inspector (successively, William Cunningham and William Webster).

In 1948 few Clydebank GPs worked in partnership, ten being single-handed with one group of four and two pairs. Each practice had its own consulting room The majority were converted shops or attached to the doctor's residence and only one was purpose built. When the NHS was introduced the following 18 GPs were practising in Clydebank:

Lawrence Crombie (1921), John E. Jeffrey (1924), James A.M. Robertson (1945), John M. Fleming (1948), Hugh Young (1909), H. Boyd Young (1946), William D. Allan (1921), George G. Allan (1948), W. Stanley L. McLeish (1922), William Gibson (1924), Nathan Meiland (1928), Charles S. Garrett (1930), William Anderson (1932), John Hilferty (1939), Alistair H. Millar (1943), Henry L. Hart (1946), Alistair A. Clark (1946), John T. Cunningham (1947). The date of arrival in Clydebank is shown in brackets.

On 11 October 1948, Dr John E. Jeffrey, the Secretary of the old Panel Committee, arranged a meeting of the local GPs and on his suggestion, a Clydebank Medical Society was formed. Its functions included organising medical cover for patients during the Wednesday half-day which had been in existence since the First World War, and arranging social and professional meetings for the doctors, out of which arose the concepts of the GP Maternity Unit at Duntocher Hospital and eventually the Clydebank Health Centre.

At a meeting of the Clydebank Medical Society held on Friday 13 March 1958, at 299 Glasgow Road, the future of medicine in Clydebank was discussed. It was decided to approach the Western Regional Hospital Board to suggest that there should be a GP maternity unit at Duntocher Hospital. Six years later the Board agreed to build a 24 bedded GP maternity unit at Duntocher. The unit was opened in January 1966 at a cost of £117,000.[34] Before this GPs had used Overtoun Hospital at Milton, and the specialist obstetric unit at Braeholm Hospital in Helensburgh. Clydebank, Bearsden and Milngavie doctors used the maternity unit at

Duntocher, but unfortunately the anticipated flow of patients from Drumchapel and Knightswood never took place. The anticipated monthly confinement rate was 75-100[35] but it seldom rose above 50 per cent of that figure. The Western Regional Hospital Board was considering a change of use when the roof blew off the building. It was repaired in 1974 under the new administration of the Greater Glasgow Health Board and its function was then changed to contain 12 GP medical beds and 12 beds for young chronic sick.[36] In 1986 the former maternity unit building contained 24 beds for young chronic sick, and there are presently 12 GP beds in one of the original buildings.

Before the establishment of the NHS only those insured received treatment under the Panel System, and the very poor under the Poor Law Act. Hospital treatment was supplied by the voluntary hospitals supported by flag days, charity days, donations or endowment. Clydebank's main links lay with the Western Infirmary, Sick Children's Hospital and Rottenrow. Children and the uninsured had to pay their family doctor for services. In 1947 the charges were 1/6d. for a consultation in the surgery and 3/6d. for a house call. Money was usually found for children, but after 1948 the number of female patients who came to see their GPs with chronic illness from which they had suffered for many months or even years was quite remarkable. At the inception of the NHS, streptomycin, sulphonamides, and penicillin became available, giving specific cures for many infectious diseases including tuberculosis, pneumonia, meningitis and puerperal fever. By the use of antibiotics in infection of the kidneys and tonsils, the secondary diseases of nephritis and rheumatic fever were almost eradicated. Smallpox and diphtheria had disappeared from the burgh by the late 1940s due to widespread vaccinations and immunisation.

In 1948 a few sisters of the Catholic Order of the Sisters of Charity founded a convent in Millbrae Crescent, visiting the sick and the poor in the burgh. In 1950 the Sisters modernised two adjacent houses in Millbrae Crescent to form St. Margaret's Hospice. This was possibly the first hospice in Scotland. In 1971, they opened a purpose-built building in East Barns Street, administered by the Western Regional Hospital Board with 31 geriatric beds and 29 beds for terminal care.[37] In 1971 a consultant geriatrician was attached to the Hospice. The Queen's visitors, district nurses and midwives, with a superintendent nurse, were then administered by the Town Council. The Nurses' Home and other assets were sold to the Town

Figure 14:13 *Mount Pleasant Home, Old Kilpatrick, opened by Councillor John Gray in June 1969.*

185

Council at a nominal sum of £1,000 and their Eye Clinic to the Western Regional Health Board for a few hundred pounds. The proceeds were divided between a new benevolent body, the Clydebank District Nursing Auxiliary, the British Red Cross Society and the nurses comfort fund administered by the MOH, but with the largest share going to the Queen's Nurses Pension Fund.[38]

Before 1948 the Poor Law Act supplied the only official welfare services for the very poor. People unable to look after themselves at home due to age or handicap were admitted to the Poor Law Hospital at Townend, Dumbarton. From 1948 welfare services financed and controlled by the Town Council were led by specialist officers in charge of probation, care of children, mental health, physically handicapped, geriatrics and home help services. The home help service began in 1948 to help the aged, handicapped and newly delivered mothers.

Over the last 40 years the services for the aged have grown considerably and now there are three old folks homes in the district — Boquhanran with 37 beds, Mount Pleasant in Old Kirkpatrick with 36 beds (both opened in 1969), and Frank Downie House opened in 1974 with 35 beds. Frank Downie House has also 21 sheltered housing apartments and a day centre for 25 persons. There are presently seven groups of sheltered housing complexes jointly administered by the Regional Social Work and the District Housing Departments with two groups run by the Scottish Special Housing Association, each group with a caretaker in charge and totalling 158 houses. There are many other services for senior citizens including four Day Centres, nine Lunch Clubs and 29 Senior Citizen Clubs.[39]

In the District there are three Children's Homes, namely, 'Craigellachie' in Whitecrook, 'Ramsay House' in Dalmuir and 'Hillpark House' in Hardgate. At Auchentoshan, there is a day care nursery for mentally handicapped children up to seven years, a day school for mildly handicapped children from 7-17 years and Mountblow School for severely handicapped 7-17 year olds. The Regional Social Work Department has a training centre at Mountblow for about 70 adult handicapped and also runs 'Marellen', a home for 9 mentally handicapped in Drumry Road.[40]

Like other areas of Scotland, Clydebank has a large alcoholic problem. In the 1950s William Blaney founded the Clydebank Council on Alcoholism with Dr. Peter Kershaw, consultant psychiatrist, as its medical advisor. The Council now runs two male hostels, 'Southill' in Cochno Road, Hardgate, with 8-12 beds, and in the old Eye Clinic at 1 Cochno Street, Whitecrook, with three beds. The Council on Alcoholism's office and female hostel with ten beds at Stirling House, Yokermill Road, opened in 1979. AA run meetings every evening of the week in different venues in Clydebank, and there are also 'Al-anon' meetings to help spouses of alcoholics and an ODATT Centre in Hall Street for social activities for alcoholics run on AA lines.

In 1973, with the coming of the National Health Re-organisation Act, further administrative change took place and the old Western Regional Hospital Board was replaced by the Greater Glasgow Health Board. With this reorganisation the post of MOH disappeared to be replaced by that of Community Physician. Similar sweeping change had occurred within the office of Burgh Sanitary Inspector. After the Blitz sterling work was performed by the Sanitary Inspector and his staff in the field of housing improvement, and slum clearance and vigorous campaigns were mounted to improve the quality of food and milk. With the reorganisation of local government in 1975, the post of Burgh Sanitary Inspector was replaced by that of Chief Environmental Health Officer. Two of the most taxing problems to occupy the Department in recent years were the measures adopted to meet the requirements of the 1956 Clean Air Act and the problem of asbestosis. The former problem was quickly and effectively dealt with, ensuring that the District is now entirely smoke-controlled.

A further development of the NHS was the establishment of clinics. Within the

Figure 14:14 *Whitecrook School and Clinic. The school was constructed at the time of the First World War for wartime use but thereafter was offered to the Education authority for use as a school. During the Second World War it was requisitioned as a workmen's hostel before reverting to educational use. After the war part of the school housed the Whitecrook Clinic.*

burgh, health clinics were established within the Municipal Building and at Whitecrook, the latter also dealing with teeth, tonsils and adenoids. In the landward area, clinics were established at Old Kilpatrick and Goldenhill. However, the key development in health care in Clydebank during the period was the establishment of the Clydebank Health Centre on Kilbowie Road at West Thomson Street. At a meeting of the Clydebank Medical Society in 1961, Dr Malcolm M. Herbert raised the possibility of establishing just such a centre. In 1966-67 central government accepted the GP charter which gave reimbursement of rates and rents and partial reimbursement of ancillary staffs' salaries, thus making the concept of a centralised Health Centre financially more viable. While not all favoured centralised Health Centre practice, doubters accepted the concept on account of demolition of their consulting rooms under town planning redevelopment. While it was then generally agreed that a major Health Centre should contain all three constituent parts of the NHS — general practice, public health and specialist consultant services with, in addition, dentistry and pharmacy — the latter two bodies declined to become involved owing to the high rents envisaged for accommodation in the Centre. By 1968 agreement in principle was reached and an unofficial committee was set up to investigate the detailed working of a Health Centre, thus ensuring that those persons later involved in the official investigations were knowledgeable in such matters and of the problems that might be encountered. Involved in the planning stages were six representatives from the Department of Health led by Neil S. McIntyre, 11 local GPs including the MOH, Dr John B. Morris, Charles Kirk, Director of Social Work, the Dunbarton County MOH (one of 2 representatives from the County Council), 1 representative from the Western Regional Hospital Board, Miss Dow, Clydebank Nursing Officer, and the project architect. On 18 April 1972 this Planning Committee became the Interim Committee of Management of the Health Centre under the chairmanship of Dr Alistair A. Clark. The £400,000 Centre, built in the CLASP system in twelve months, was officially opened on 5 May 1973 by HRH Princess Alexandra.

When opened, the Centre, attending to 65,000 patients, was the largest such complex in Britain staffed by: 34 family doctors, 11 health visitors, 22 district and other nurses, 2 radiographers, 2 oculists, 2 social workers, 17 public health personnel, 1 audiometrician, 70 receptionists, clerkesses, typists and telephonists

Figure 14:15 *Exterior of Clydebank Health Centre.*

and 5 porters. Currently the Centre houses four GP wings, a consultant wing and a community medicine wing. The consultant wing has the following clinics: gynaecological, skin, psychiatric, paediatric, geriatric, chest and cardiac, (physiotherapy, ear, nose and throat, surgical and medical clinics were previously provided). The GP wings contain a waiting room, consulting rooms and interview room used by health visitors, social workers and district nurses. Most practices run

Figure 14:16 *Opening of the Clydebank Health Centre by HRH Princess Alexandra on 5 May 1973. Also present are Sir Simpson Stevenson, Chairman of the Western Regional Hospital Board, Sir John Brotherston, Chief Medical Officer for Scotland, Provost Robert Fleming, the Lord Lieutenant of the County and Dr Alastair Clark, Chairman of the Management Committee of the Clydebank Health Centre.*

child assessment and immunisation, ante-and post-natal sessions and sometimes hypertension and diabetic clinics. The community medicine services include the schools health service with an oculist, audiometrician, physiotherapist and speech therapist. Also in the wing are ante-natal and post-natal clinics, staffed from the Vale of Leven Hospital, family planning and cervical cytology. Other features include three treatment rooms with electroencephalograph, health education rooms for schools, physiotherapy, relaxation, mothercraft and slimming classes, chiropodists' room, a radiology department and the physiotherapy department giving active and passive treatment.

The establishment of the Centre has provided a unique opportunity to monitor and investigate the use of many drugs within a typical community setting. A research unit was established in 1977 by Dr Alan Wade and now employs, along with medical staff, eight full-time nurses and research assistants. The work of the research team includes the organisation of clinics, assistance in patient management and the recording of the effectiveness and side effects of drugs as diverse as creams for dermatitis, tablets for heart failure and interferon for the treatment of viral infection. The help and reliability of the patients in Clydebank has been a major factor in permitting the project to achieve considerable expertise in the long-term use of many standard medications, and consequently the Centre is presently recognised as a world leader in the long term treatment and management of patients suffering from duodenal ulcer disease. In conclusion, the diagnostic and treatment facilities available within the Centre have given a much greater service to the patients than was previously available.

Education

The post-war period ushered in new challenges in education. With the peace, evacuated children flooded back into the burgh, and with Blitz damage to schools still to be made good, the town faced an immediate accommodation problem. Several of Clydebank's schools had been hit during the Clydebank Blitz including St Stephen's, Boquhanran, Radnor Park and Clydebank Schools. Although a temporary respite to the shortage of accommodation was gained by the use of

Figure 14:17 *One of the casualties of the Blitz was the former Clydebank School building opened in 1868 by Sir John Neilson Cuthbertson, Chairman of the Glasgow School Board. Situated on the same site as its predecessor the pupils were temporarily accommodated in the Public Hall in Douglas Street until the new school was complete.*

hutments it was many years before the effect of the Blitz was cancelled. A minor re-organisation occurred when the new Clydebank High School at Janetta Street was finally completed. The new senior secondary school was opened on 1 September 1947, and on that date, secondary pupils attending Dumbarton Academy and the former Higher Grade School in Miller Street transferred to the new school. Infants who up till then had attended Janetta Street were, with the exception of those living furthest away, transferred to the recently completed hutments erected on the site of the blitzed Radnor Park School. On 25 August 1949 three infant and one primary classroom were available in the new West Thomson Street School (re-opened on 24 August 1950 as Kilbowie Primary) and 350 pupils transferred from the Radnor Park hutments. Clydebank Technical College was later constructed on the site of the former Radnor Park School.

With the opening of the new High School, secondary pupils from Old Kilpatrick attended either the Dalmuir Junior Secondary or the High School. In 1947 children living north of Bannerman Street and east of Singer Street were sent to the Radnor Park hutments, as were children within the central area then in hutments in the Clydebank Junior Secondary School together with children transferred to Elgin Street when Whitecrook was requisitioned. Not all of the blitzed schools were rebuilt after the war and some replacement schools such as Goldenhill and Gavinburn Primaries were not opened until the 1950s. Many Clydebank children of the immediate post-war years received their early education in temporary huts and played in bomb-scarred playgrounds.

By the 1950s the redevelopment of the town and the building of new housing schemes created fresh demands on the town's education facilities. The new housing schemes emerged as a great challenge, requiring not only the relocation of schools but the improvement of facilities and teachers to keep up with the pace of advance of British education. As the 'migration' to the new houses gathered speed during the decade, old problems came back to haunt education administrators: schools serving the schemes became grossly overcrowded; there was a shortage of accommodation; schools were badly maintained often with poor heating; and teachers were in short supply.

The worst affected seems to have been Faifley Primary School, and the long-serving chairman of the local education committee, Mathew Bissett, came under sustained attack from local politicans and parents about conditions there. In 1957, there were allegedly three pupils to every seat in Faifley School, with children being taught part-time in shifts. The want of accommodation was perhaps less of a

Figure 14:18 *Built to replace the blitzed Duntocher Public School, Goldenhill Primary School was opened in September 1955 by Matthew Bissett, Chairman of the Dunbartonshire Education Committee. Until its opening, Duntocher pupils were accommodated in temporary huts on the site of their blitzed school.*

problem than shortage of skilled teachers. A short-term solution was the employment of non-certificated teachers, but in the long-term a massive recruitment drive was undertaken by the Scottish Education Department. Leaflets were handed out to Clydebank school leavers trying to persuade them to train for the teaching profession:

> 'Most men with ordinary or third-class honours degrees become principal teachers at junior secondary schools or head teachers or deputy heads in primary schools.'[42]

By today's standards, these are exceptionally low qualifications. Indeed, it became one of the main problems of the state educational system that poorly-qualified and often poorly-motivated teachers were recruited during the expansionary period of the 1950s and 1960s. Parents were justifiably up in arms about the state of affairs in some of the burgh's schools. The problems lay not just in staffing, but in the provision of resources in general. Advance planning for the education needs of the housing schemes were poor; houses were erected and people moved in before schools (or for that matter shops or churches) were provided. The situation was made worse by the raising of the school leaving age to 15 in 1947, thus creating extra pressure upon facilities.

In addition, the school system was constantly being changed. In the years after 1945, the pre-war trend towards junior and senior secondary schools was maintained, with the former providing mainly 'vocational' training whilst the latter trained those pupils who would seek entry to the professions and to higher education. The results of the qualifying examination, widely known as 'the Qualy' or the 'Eleven plus', determined whether a child would have the opportunity of an academic or a vocational education. This left great bitterness amongst parents whose children had been assessed at the age of eleven or twelve years as to their lifetime abilities. By the mid 1950s there were demands from radical politicians and many parents in Clydebank for the establishment of a comprehensive school in which educational opportunity would be widened. Yet the local economy continued to demand large numbers of manual workers. School leavers in the burgh during the session 1955-56 went predominantly into local industry or commerce. Of 3,434 boys and girls, 687, of whom only two were girls, started apprenticeships, 1,425, mostly girls, went into factory work without apprenticeships, 780 found office, shop or messenger jobs, 431 found miscellaneous posts as oilers, usherettes, waitresses and hammer boys, and 111 became vanboys.

The 1960s and 1970s brought more changes. The ideal of comprehensive education came to the fore, promoting the removal of distinctions between secondary schools. The advance of science, technology and skills in general increased the costs of equipping schools, and raised the necessity for creating larger centres where well-qualified teachers and apparatus could be fully employed. The school-leaving age was raised again — to sixteen years — and the birth rate started to fall rapidly. On top of this, the number of people living in the old centre of Clydebank fell away as redevelopment and the provision of new housing shifted population out from the southern district. Some schools were poorly located, old fashioned in layout, and of the wrong size. As a result, older schools closed. The site of Clydebank School at the foot of Kilbowie Road was cleared, leaving only the statue of an early twentieth-century School Board chairman as a reminder. Another School Board foundation, Elgin Street School, was also closed. New sites and schools were established to rationalise and replace older property. By the mid 1980s the burgh contained four high schools: Clydebank, Braidfield, St Columba's and St Andrew's. Further Education, started modestly in the early years of the burgh as evening classes in the elementary schools, was concentrated in Clydebank College.

Clydebank College was officially opened at the present site in Kilbowie Road on

Figure 14:19 *Memorial sundial erected to James Stevenson, and inscribed 'Erected by friends in memory of James Stevenson MB CH FFPS Glasg; Medical Officer of the Burgh of Clydebank 1897-1909 and of the Parish of Old Kilpatrick 1895-1909; Chairman of Old Kilpatrick School Board 1900-1903'.*

15 September 1965. The first purpose-built further education college in the county of Dunbarton, it replaced the former Lennox Technical Centre. At the time of writing in 1987, the college takes in around 2,500 full-time equivalent students and has over 200 lecturers in eight departments, offering a wide range of subjects at non-advanced and advanced levels. Inevitably, the work of the college has changed over the years as the industries which it originally served have disappeared from the town. Students in the 1980s are less likely to be apprentices and more likely to be

Figure 14:20 *Clydebank College. Officially opened in September 1965 by Bailie James Malcolm, Dunbartonshire Education Committee, Clydebank Technical College was built to fill a long felt gap in further education provision in the west Dunbartonshire area.*

full-time students or YTS trainees, or adults undergoing re-training for different types of employment, especially new technologies. The college also has a wide range of community contacts, offering courses for school pupils, the unemployed, the disabled and various minority groups. Links with industry have been developed through membership of local business clubs and increasingly the college offers specialised short courses for industry and commerce, often on employers' premises. It is impossible accurately to predict future developments, but, given further education's ability to adapt to change, it seems safe to predict that the college will survive well into the next millenium.

Since the first school board was formed in 1873, the quality of education has improved very markedly in Clydebank. In 1873, and for many years thereafter, there was not a single graduate amongst the teachers in the district; today, secondary teachers are almost entirely graduates, and a rising number of primary school teachers are also university trained. The objective of schooling in the 1870s was to inculcate the four 'rs' — reading, writing, arithmetic and religion. The task then was to get reluctant children and parents to accept that full-time education until 13 years was a good idea, and the work of the school attendance officer dominated much of the business of the school board. Though the problem of attendance is still there in the 1980s, it is principally the problem of truancy — of children 'skiving' rather than of families denying the benefits that education can bring.

Until the First World War, the facilities for education in Clydebank were amongst the worst in Scotland. The town presented a particular problem, growing from virtually nothing to a medium-sized industrial centre in under two generations. Still, the managers of the school system were noted for their parsimony or, as they would have it, their 'economy'. Schools were left with privies unconnected to any drain, too few cleaners were employed to satisfy the inspectors, and teachers were left unsupervised — in some cases for years — in what they taught to their pupils. Money was lavished on ornaments, on the extravagant design and decoration of the Clydebank Public School of the 1880s, and on the carving of busts of each member of the school board.

Figure 14:21 *The Headmaster's office, or as it was also known, 'pagoda', in the second Clydebank School with its commanding view of the stairs. This was part of the elaborate decorative features of the school which so incensed ratepayers.*

Today, local control of education has been conceded, as with everything else, to a higher authority: to the Regional Council and to the Scottish Education Department. Yet, the resources are more plentiful, if still the subject of dispute. The curriculum and the teaching methods are better; a Clydebank mother played her part in recent years in the legal campaign for the abolition of corporal punishment in Scotland. But some things do not change. In 1891, the teachers were complaining about the low level of their salaries, and the local board established an increased scale. And in the 1880s, the Board had to compensate the Masonic Lodge for damage and broken windows caused by pupils attending a temporary school in the lodge hall. These problems are all too familiar in 1987.

Religion[43]

After the war, the churches were once again confronted with change in the dimensions of the community. The Catholic population of the burgh rose 16-fold between 1900 and 1960, and over the century the number of chapels has increased from three to eight. The most intense activity occurred after the Second World War, with the replacement of the blitzed St Mary's (1954) and St Stephen's (1958), and an extensive creation of new parishes in the housing schemes: St Eunan's (1951), Our Lady of Loretto, Dalmuir (1954), St Mary's, Duntocher (1954), St Joseph's, Faifley (1963), and St Margaret's, Whitecrook (1972). The post-war schemes had higher concentrations of Catholics than the inter-war schemes, with Faifley, Whitecrook and Linnvale accounting for nearly half of the total in the burgh.

The Church of Scotland also had to respond to Blitz changes and to the rehousing of its members and adherents. In one instance, the two tasks were combined; the replacement for Ross Memorial was located, in 1952, in the Mountblow scheme. Church reconstruction proceeded fairly fast, with Radnor Park Parish Church restored in 1948, and the new Duntocher Trinity opened in 1952. New churches for the schemes were rather slow to follow. By 1949, the Presbytery of Dumbarton had only raised £8,000 of its eight-year target of £30,000 for church extension in the schemes, and acknowledged that it was not coping with the rehousing migrations. It was in the next decade that church extension charges were established in Linnvale (1954) and Faifley (1956) from Duntocher East.

As with most of Britain's post-war housing estates, community facilities — ranging from shops to public houses — were in short supply, and it was difficult to

Figure 14:22 *St. Mary's Church, Duntocher. The first St. Mary's, established in 1841, was replaced nine years later by a larger church which served the community until it was destroyed in the Blitz. This third church was opened in 1954 by The Very Rev. Archbishop D. Campbell of Glasgow.*

Figure 14:23 *Started as a kitchen Sunday School in 1886 Radnor Park Parish Church has had a very chequered life. The congregation was founded in 1891 with the Rev. William Orr Brown as its first minister. In 1895 the new church was opened but was badly damaged by fire in 1909. Fully restored in 1910 it was once again badly damaged during the Blitz, but restored again in 1948. In January 1968, during the great storm, a second fire managed to succeed where the Blitz and first fire had failed, and destroyed the church. This view shows the resulting damage of that fire. The remaining shell had to be demolished and a new church was built and opened in 1970.*

promote community activity. By the late 1950s, some tenants' associations were 'caught in the stranglehold of apathy' and threatened with closure. In the same way, church organisations found the whole period from the early 1950s through to the late 1960s 'a difficult time', with rehousing creating 'a floating population' flitting from parish to parish, leaving clergy unsure as to which particular congregation a family was attached. Church members could slip from view and be 'lost'. In practical terms, there was a tendency for the churches to look upon the schemes as missionary fields. Teams of church visitors, Sunday-school teachers and youth leaders 'went in', trying to sustain church connection. In 1957, the Clydebank and District Sunday School Union reported difficulty in coping with the challenge of the schemes. In the following year, the Chief Constable of Dunbartonshire made impolitic remarks regarding the decanting of Glasgow folk to Drumchapel, Knightswood and Yoker. Clydebank, he said, was yet to feel 'the full impact of having these criminal elements on its borders'.[44]

But this comment revealed the widespread sentiment that the schemes were difficult and alien terrain. The churches, once established, could become of special significance when other community facilities were wanting. For Catholics particularly, the Church attained a heightened importance. The building of the schemes presented the opportunity to site chapel, hall and presbytery next to Catholic schools, creating a very important (and perhaps unique) 'community centre' catering for the religious, educational and leisure needs of all age groups. At St Joseph's in Faifley, for example, organisations like the Boys' Guild and youth clubs for boys and girls provided healthy recreation in a wholesome atmosphere.[45] Churches of other denominations, too, developed into important focuses of community activity in the schemes.

The churches have also found a new function in the burgh. The successive industrial crises of the 1970s seemed to local clergy to threaten to make Clydebank a ghost town. This brought ministers and priests into economic and community matters in a manner and to an extent rarely seen before. They worked behind the scenes, trying to maintain contact between management and unions, and more

Figure 14:24 *Aktion Suhnezeichen (Action Reconciliation), a German organisation with the object of promoting international friendship and co-operation, approached Clydebank Town Council in 1965 with a proposal that it help towards the cost of a new leisure centre for the community. Money had been raised in Germany with a view to donating part of the cost for new buildings in countries which had suffered damage during the war and, using this plus money raised by a local Trust, Faifley Leisure Centre (now Faifley Community Education Centre) was built and opened in April 1970.*

visibly giving supportive counselling and speeches to workers and the community. Church activity developed initially in 1972 with the Clydebank and District Christian Action Group which conducted prayer and services connected with the UCS work-in and the Singer dispute. By 1978, however, the clergy were active in a succession of organisations: the Singer Fighting Fund, The Marathon Action Committee of Clergy and, by December of that year, the Clydebank Clergy/ Community Liaison Committee. In the autumn of 1979 the clergy joined trades unionists, councillors, the local MP and traders in the broader Clydebank Campaign on Employment. The redevelopment of disused factory land became a priority, and by the summer of 1980 the Campaign's lobbying of government was crowned by success with agreement to set up the SDA Task Force.

During the hard times of the early 1930s, the churches had been cautious about appearing to endorse the views of the 'Red Clydesiders', even of MPs like David Kirkwood. Even in the 1980s, there was some antipathy in the Clydebank churches to industrial action:

> 'Men say they want a better deal,
>   and on strike they go
> But what a deal we've given God,
>   for everything we owe.
> We don't care whom we hurt or harm
>   to gain the things we like
> But what a mess we'd all be in
>   if GOD WOULD GO ON STRIKE.'[46]

But Clydebank's recent decay has transcended party politics, resuscitating an Edwardian, Christian-Socialist awareness of the ethical implications of economic hardship. As Jimmy McShane said at the launching ceremony for the Enterprise Zone in February 1981:

'Religion is an integration of life and worship. It concerns God and man — man in his human condition. And that in Clydebank includes many who are unemployed or whose jobs are at risk. This is why the churches must become involved, must minister to the needs of the community.'[47]

With the contraction of employment in the shipyards and at Singer, the focus of the community shifted during the 1970s and 1980s away from the axis of Dumbarton Road and Glasgow Road. The planned extension of the Clydeside Expressway and the clearance of industrial property, shops and tenements threatened many churches also — including Our Holy Redeemer's which, despite the loss of many of its parishioners as a result of rehousing, survived the closure crisis of the early 1970s. But the local Church of Scotland, overburdened with excess churches, was urged by its central administration to use the renewal of the burgh as the occasion for cutting the number of congregations and shedding underused property. St James' and Clydebank West churches were both closed, and the congregations united in the new Abbotsford Church in the precincts of the Clyde Shopping Centre. The Union Church became a cold food store. The Hamilton Memorial Church now resembles a frontier fort with barbed wire atop the ramparts of its courtyard entrance — its Boys' Brigade Company noticeboard proclaiming the 'military' garrison holding out against the tribes of graffiti artists and beer-can grenadiers in the desolation of Glasgow Road.

The closure of churches was not merely a product of shifting population. The post-war period has witnessed dramatic changes in popular taste and pastimes which have reduced the social role of religion. The football pools, television, cinema and sport had all but displaced temperance activity in the burgh by the mid 1950s, and church attendances fell dramatically along with church membership. The media might be used to reach the unchurched, but it rarely moved them. The minister at Duntocher Trinity wrote in the early 1970s:

'The great majority who listen to the most popular religious broadcasts on radio and television are non-churchgoers. A great body of people in Britain today is sympathetic towards Christianity and all its good works. But most are unwilling to commit themselves openly.'[48]

Youth culture of the 1960s and after has been difficult to accommodate in the churches. Youth clubs were formed, but they have caused persistent problems of disorder and vandalism; as recently as 1985, the Abbotsford Church had to disband their club. Experiments in worship — in 'strumming and clap-your-hands' worship, as one present Clydebank minister has dubbed it — have created small groups of enthusiastic and committed Christian congregations. But even amidst the widespread experimentation of the 1960s, there was widespread doubt. The priest at St Columba's Episcopal Church wrote:

'We in 1966 live in an age "more curious than devout". The uneasy affluence of today is matched in theology by those who are certain only of their doubts . . . But what ought our attitude to be at a time when the Church appears to show more affinity to the changeable Simon than the rock-like Peter . . .?'[49]

Though congregations of the larger denominations have become increasingly composed of the elderly, new religious movements have appeared, attracting committed and often youthful followers by an appeal to religious isolationism in a hostile secular world. In April 1960, a 'Revival and Divine Healing Crusade', dedicated to the 'Great Covenanters', attracted sufficient numbers in the Masonic Hall that an Elim Church was formed. Other new churches have gathered followers in the district: the Apostolic Church, the Mormons and the Jehovah's Witnesses. The traditional churches tried to use revivalist occasions as well. In 1955, Billy Graham came to Clydebank during his spectacular Scottish Easter Mission, attracting a lunch-time crowd of over 2,000 yard and factory workers in the open air in Bruce Street. Similarly, the Scottish visit of Pope John Paul II in 1982 created great enthusiasm. But the lasting effects of these spectacular events seems to have been limited. For Protestants, church membership started to decline from the late 1950s, whilst some priests reported that the preparations for the Papal visit had more effect than the visit itself, culminating in no great conversion impact.

The churches are in many ways less relevant to the social and cultural life of 'Bankies' now than 50 or 100 years ago. Popular participation has fallen, and culture and morality are now defined in secular rather than religious ways; the temperance issue , for example, is all but dead. Yet the clergy themselves remain important, and Clydebank has had its fair share of characters. Perhaps best remembered amongst Catholic priests was Father John Brotherhood who, like so many others, came from Calton in Glasgow to Dalmuir where he served with 'truly inexhaustible activity', much liked and loved by Catholics and Protestants alike, between 1907 and 1936. Amongst the many Presbyterian ministers, perhaps best remembered will be the Rev Stewart Borthwick, now retired but for 31 years the incumbent at Clydebank West and more recently Abbotsford. The position of the churches is presently in the midst of great change, but the clergy retain a significance that transcends their congregations.

Figure 14:25 *Father John Brotherhood, first parish priest of St Stephen's and a legend in the area with his unfailing generosity and striking personality.*

Leisure and Recreation

The ending of hostilities and the gradual lifting of wartime restrictions breathed new life into those organisations that had survived. As previously, the Town Council played a major role in providing recreational facilities. New public bowling greens, for example, were opened at Dalmuir and Whitecrook in 1950[50] but, undoubtedly, the most 'popular' municipal enterprise was the annual 'illuminations' in Dalmuir Park. The 'illuminations', which included concerts and competitions, continued until the sixties, turning the Park into a veritable fairyland. Major employers similarly played their part, most notably Singer, with their annual Galas.

Figure 14:26 *Started in 1940 as part of the VE Day celebrations, the Dalmuir Park illuminations became an annual event supported by local firms. In the above photograph, models of the* Sylvania, Ivernia, Carinthia, Saxonia *and* Arcadia *can be seen in the pond in the late 1950s.*

Figure 14:27 *Members of the Clydebank Camera Club in the Lecture Room of the Clydebank Public Library in 1953. Several well known clubs have been active locally and include the Singer Camera Club formed in 1926 by Messrs. J. Heggie (first President) and J. Simpson (first Secretary). An excellent start was disrupted by the Blitz and it was not until 1959 that the club was re-constituted meeting, briefly, at 91 Kilbowie Road until the opening of the new Singer Hall.*

From 1913 the expanding Public Libraries facility played a significant and growing role in the community. In the 1950s the Libraries Department played host to an increasing number of groups. The newly formed Gramophone Society (afterwards Clydebank Recorded Music Society),[51] the Dalmuir and Clydebank Burns Club and the Clydebank Public Library Literary and Philosophical Society, all met in the Lecture Room of the Central Library. The Gramophone Society, instigated by the Chief Librarian, John Purdie, was reputedly, when formed, the second largest such society in Scotland. A further organisation, the Clydebank Camera Club (a development from the Clydebank East Community Centre Camera Class) held their first meeting in the Lecture Room on 2 September 1953, continuing to meet there until 1967.[52] Thereafter the Club briefly met in the Agamemnon Street premises of the Repertory Theatre, until Provost Malcolm Turner opened new premises at 35 Dumbarton Road on 5 February 1969.[53]

Until 1939, the Youth Service had been the preserve of voluntary organisations such as the Clydebank Mutual Service Association or the ever expanding Dalmuir Former Pupils but, with the outbreak of war, central government began to take an interest. Statutory recognition came in the shape of the Education (Scotland) Act 1945 and the 1947 SED document, *'Planning for Community Centres'*.[54] In 1949 Cuthbert Douse was appointed County Youth Organiser. Part-time Community Centres were developed in schools, followed in 1967 by purpose built Youth Centres on Kilbowie Road and Duntiglennan Road. On 11 April 1970 a further Youth Centre was opened at Faifley by Pastor Hans Richard Neuermann. Neuermann represented Aktion Suhnezeichen (Action Reconciliation) who had approached the Town Council in 1965. In the late 1960s the Service became the Youth and Community Service and later, at reorganisation, the Community Education Service.

The post-war years held mixed fortunes for the musical and dramatic societies. In 1945 the Duntocher Band re-emerged without ever attaining their former high standards. In contrast, the Clydebank Burgh Band continued on their winning ways and had the distinction of undertaking the first radio broadcast by a Scottish band. In 1953 they won the Glasgow Charities Band Association

Championships for the tenth time. The Clydebank Male Voice Choir's post-war years were highlighted by appearances at festivals at Greenock and Glasgow and, in August 1950, they were joined by the newly formed Clydebank Lyric Choir (a development from the Dalmuir Former Pupils Choir). In 1961, Willie Gough instigated the re-forming of the Singer Pipe Band. Until its demise in 1979 the Band were regular performers at the many Singer functions — Galas, Caledonian and Tartan Balls. During this last great period, many honours were won, including the World Championships at Aberdeen in 1970. The Clydebank Repertory Theatre was particularly successful and, following the move from their Glasgow Road premises, they established themselves in the Dalmuir Former Pupils premises in Agamemnon Street, performing regularly to full houses. In the 1970s and 1980s problems — particularly with the condition of their premises — resulted in the 'Rep' going into decline.

The cinema was also in decline, succumbing to the twin attractions of television and bingo. By the late 1940s the Co-op Cinema, Municipal Cinema and the New Kinema had all gone, although the latter (renamed The Clyde) re-appeared briefly on 6 October 1947. On Sunday 21 June 1959 the Empire was destroyed in a fire and two years later, on Saturday 30 September 1961, the ABC Bank Cinema closed with Richard Todd in *Don't Bother To Knock*. On 1 October 1966 the Dalmuir Regal also closed. On 31 July 1969, Clydebank's last cinema, the La Scala, re-opened following renovations, as, reputedly, Scotland's first twin auditorium film-cum-bingo playhouse. This development, however, only delayed the inevitable and on Saturday, 19 February 1983, Clydebank's only remaining cinema closed.[55]

Outdoors, senior football briefly returned to New Kilbowie Park in 1964-65 when Jack and Charles Steedman unveiled a radical plan to 'transplant' their struggling East Stirling team to Clydebank. This proposed merger with Clydebank Juniors to form ES Clydebank FC failed when the East Stirling Shareholders Protection Association successfully fought a legal battle. Nevertheless, in June 1965, the fourth team to play as Clydebank FC appeared in the Combined Reserve League. In the Season 1966-67 the team gained entry into the Second Division and later, in the Season 1975-76, into the First Division. In the seasons 1985-87 Clydebank FC appeared in the Premier Division. Among the junior teams, Yoker were playing steadily, albeit without recapturing their former 'glory days', celebrating their centenary in 1987. Duntocher Hibs re-formed in 1946, experiencing a 'purple patch' in the Fifties, picking up several titles and trophies, and in 1953 opening a new pavilion. In 1966 financial difficulties caused their demise but, in 1973, they again re-formed only to disband once more in 1980.

Figure 14:28 *Alex Graham, conductor of the Clydebank Lyric Choir from its inception and for many years thereafter.*

Figure 14:29 *TAC trainer Jim Meechan surrounded by his boxers. Jim's career spanned many years. Initially, he was a very promising boxer with the Clydebank & District club and later a wartime charity show promoter. In the 1940s he founded the very successful Clydebank Corinthians before moving on to train the TAC boys.*

Sports such as bowling, cricket and boxing retained their popularity throughout most of the period. In 1949, with the demise of the Corinthians, Jim Meechan formed the TAC Amateur Boxing Club, which performed with great distinction throughout the 1950s. In the Fifties, and later, Scottish titles were won by Robert Cootes, 'Chic' Brogan and Charlie Kane. For many years greyhound racing at Clydeholm Stadium drew large crowds, while clubs such as the Clydesdale Harriers and the Lomond Roads Cycling Club prospered. After the war the Clydesdale Harriers developed in all sections (men, ladies and young athletes) to a peak of success unequalled since the early days. Scottish titles were won once again and runners represented their country. After a relatively quiet spell in the 1960s the club started to pick up again and in the two years since its centenary there has been a further increase in the club's fortunes. Similarly, the immediate post-war years and the 1950s and 1960s were a golden era for Lomond Roads, with riders of the calibre of Alex Linden, Jimmy Nitt, Jock Clark, Jimmy Linden, Norrie Molyneaux, John Clark, Tommy Dougan, Alan McGibbon, Bert McLellan and Aitken Hunter.

A characteristic of sport during this period was the demise of older established activities such as curling and quoiting, and the increasing popularity, or indeed introduction, of others. Although quoiting had quickly fallen away, the Hardgate Quoiting and Social Club stubbornly survived until vandalism, in recent years, spelled its death knell. Earlier, at the unveiling of a memorial plaque to a former Secretary, it was stated that the Hardgate Club was the oldest functioning quoiting club in Scotland.[56] Sports introduced or experiencing revivals included angling, basketball, darts, dominoes, rugby, snooker, hockey and skiing. Since 1976 the activities of all the clubs have been assisted by the Clydebank District Sports Council. Within the arts field, while, paradoxically, many of the older established societies nowadays fight for survival in inadequate accommodation with increased financial commitments met by fewer members, newer clubs, especially within the younger age group, flourish. In 1984 an umbrella organisation, CANDLE, was set up to co-ordinate the activities of the existing societies and to encourage the formation of new societies. Generally, leisure and recreation facilities have responded to and reflected social trends. Rising unemployment and the trend towards earlier retirement have produced clubs such as the UB40 Unemployed Club and the introduction of discounted admission to municipal recreational facilities. Meanwhile early retirement and a more active senior citizen have resulted in greater use of community facilities for senior citizens clubs. Changing employment patterns are likely to influence the form of future leisure pursuits and the local authority will continue to play a key role in the provision of leisure and recreational activities.

Figure 14:30 *Some 'well kent' faces from the Lomond Roads Cycling Club's 'golden era'.*

Part Four

The New Clydebank

CHAPTER FIFTEEN

The New Clydebank

The Response to Crisis

By the summer of 1979 Clydebank faced a mounting crisis as closures threatened to wipe out the town's economic base. The political response to the massive job losses following the closure of the Singer and Goodyear factories was rapid. The Clydebank Campaign on Employment, embracing local clergy, trade unionists, traders, Councillors and the local MP campaigned vigorously in the autumn of 1979 for investment and redevelopment in Clydebank. The Secretary of State's Working Party on Clydebank then recommended a number of immediate priorities for action. The key recommendation was that a 'Task Force' should be set up in Clydebank led by the Scottish Development Agency (SDA). Clydebank was to be given the highest priority by the SDA and the then Scottish Economic Planning Department. It was recommended that Clydebank should become one of the first Enterprise Zones then under consideration by the Government. The SDA was to examine the possibility of establishing an Enterprise Fund to provide risk finance for new, small firms. Provision of industrial sites was to be given highest priority. Clydebank's image was to be improved by means of a strategy of physical and environmental recovery and improvement.

Within a year progress was made on all of these fronts as the challenge of regenerating the battered Clydebank economy was taken up. The first step was the setting up of the Clydebank Task Force in July 1980. The Task Force, set up by the SDA, consisted initially of a small team of six people based in the centre of Clydebank opposite the Singer factory. 'Task Forces' had already been experimented with in Glengarnock following the closure of the steelworks there. The aim of the Task Force was to co-ordinate and focus the resources and powers of the SDA in Clydebank, and to work closely with the District Council and other public agencies and the private sector in their efforts to redevelop the economy of the town. It had an initial budget allocation of £15 million spread over three years.

Earlier in 1980 the Conservative Government had announced its intention to create a number of 'Enterprise Zones'. Considerably watered down from their original free market concept, these Zones were intended to be experiments in encouraging industrial or commercial development in depressed areas by reducing red-tape and providing various financial incentives to business. The main incentives available were a ten year rate-free 'holiday', exemption from

Development Land Tax and 100% Capital Allowance against tax. In addition there was to be a reduction in certain planning controls within the Zones. Although there had been considerable criticism of Enterprise Zones amongst many Labour controlled local authorities over the free market ideas behind the concept, the announcement in July 1980 that Clydebank was to be one of the first of these Zones, and the only one in Scotland, was welcomed by Clydebank's Labour District Council. The then Provost James McKendrick declared, 'We are delighted and geared up to accept the challenge'.[1] Following detailed negotiations between Clydebank District Council and the Scottish Office over the size and area covered by the Zone and details of the planning scheme to be implemented, the Clydebank Enterprise Zone was officially designated in August 1981. It was to last until at least August 1991. The Zone covers 570 acres, about 100 acres of which lie within Glasgow District boundaries in Yoker. A major part of the Enterprise Zone was the 86 acre Singer factory. Most of the industrial areas of Clydebank were also included although the John Brown yard was not.

Figure 15:1 *Alex Fletcher, Minister, Scottish Office, with Provost James McKendrick at the unveiling of the plaque to launch Scotland's first Enterprise Zone.*

In addition to these two initiatives, as suggested, a special fund was set up to assist new business ventures. The Clydebank Enterprise Fund Limited, a joint venture between the Bank of Scotland and the SDA, had half a million pounds available for low interest loans to help new businesses. With the creation of the Clydebank Enterprise Zone, the Clydebank Task Force and the Clydebank Enterprise Fund on top of existing incentives, all the pieces were in place to begin the economic regeneration of the town. Clydebank was in a unique position where the free market forces of an Enterprise Zone were tied in with major injections of public money, largely through the SDA. This combined approach has been stressed by several commentators as vital to the success of Clydebank's recovery with the marketing benefits of Enterprise Zone status adding to the confidence building vote of public investment.[2] The efforts to regenerate the economic life of

Clydebank since 1980 have required a whole range of activities, seeking to establish a fresh image for the town, and improving its environment and facilities as a vital part of the major drive to draw new industry to Clydebank.

The Image of Clydebank

One of the major problems faced in achieving the revival of Clydebank was that its image, rightly or wrongly, was widely perceived as one of declining old industries and decay. One of the first tasks was to try to change this image. The Enterprise Zone monitoring report of 1984 said, 'The change in the (Clydebank) Enterprise Zone since designation has been very considerable . . . existing floorspace has been refurbished (also to very high standards) as well as new floorspace completed. Site reclamation and landscaping projects have also had a very great impact'.[3] Rightly, environmental improvement in its broadest sense has been a priority over the last few years and the SDA and the District Council have worked closely together to this end.

Between 1980 and 1985 the SDA has spent over £5 million on environmental improvements.[4] The banks of the Forth and Clyde Canal, the Clydebank Business Park and Glasgow and Dumbarton Roads have been carefully landscaped. Most of the churches along Glasgow Road and Dumbarton Road were stonecleaned and, in addition, major eyesores along the main roads have been removed such as the Turner's Asbestos Factory and the scrapyards on Dumbarton Road. As part of this concentrated effort at environmental improvement the District Council stonecleaned major public buildings such as the Town Hall and the Central Library. The District Council also declared an Industrial Improvement Area in the town, bringing £600,000 over three years into Clydebank to help older industrial buildings improve their premises. This scheme has recently been extended for a year. Results of its influence can be seen in the stonecleaning of the old Union Church and the painting of cranes in the UIE yard. Without other developments many of these improvements would have been purely cosmetic. One of the problems of the image of Clydebank was the ebbing of activity from the heart of the town. Rejuvenating the town centre was a key objective.

Clydebank Town Centre — Change and Growth

The town centre has been undergoing change for some time. In the late 1970s the new Clyde Regional Shopping Centre was being developed. However, the closure of Singer, empty tenements, very obvious gap sites, closed shops and pubs and a general lack of life indicated a centre in transition or potentially in its death throes. Important steps have been taken over the last few years to bring the centre back to life, leading to major changes in shopping patterns. The old Clydebank Co-Operative Society building remains as a monument to an earlier shopping style. Shopping has been completely altered by the development of the Clyde Regional Shopping Centre. The second phase of the Centre was completed in 1982. The Centre was developed jointly by the Co-operative Insurance Society, Clydebank District Council and the Neale House Group. The Centre and the remnants of the old shopping centre now add up to the seventh largest centre in Strathclyde Region and the biggest single retail development in Scotland.[5] The Centre is quite different from the small shops beneath tenements which characterised the old town centre and which can still be seen in Alexander Street and Kilbowie Road. Its turnover is much higher, it has a much wider catchment area and has a wide range of shops including major multiple chains. Similar but smaller scale centralisation has happened elsewhere in Clydebank, for example, at the Dalmuir Centre. It is clear that this has affected many of the smaller, local groups of shops in Clydebank,

Figure 15:2 *Covered mall, Clyde Shopping Centre.*

again reflecting wider trends in shopping. The development of pubs and offices on several gap sites in the centre such as the self-build offices at Miller Street and the Chandlers pub on Kilbowie Road has furthered improved commercial facilities.

Meanwhile, there have been attempts to bring population back into the town centre. In the early 1980s virtually all of the town centre housing was empty or had been demolished. The remaining tenements were under threat of demolition with funds for rehabilitation being difficult to obtain. Given the difficulties of funding, real advances have only been finally achieved in 1986-7 following a period of frustrating delay. The tenements in Alexander Street and Kilbowie Road were made wind and watertight in 1984-85. In 1985 a new Housing Association, Central and East Clydebank Housing Association, was formed. Its first task was to tackle the rehabilitation of these tenements plus several in Whitecrook Street. Work started in 1986. In the year 1986-87, 46 units were completed with 58 planned for 1987-8.

Private developers were encouraged back into the town centre at Hall Street and Dumbarton Road with the assistance of public money. Perhaps the most innovative project involved Wimpey Homes in the rehabilitation of the key block of tenements fronting onto Glasgow Road and Dumbarton Road. In a joint project between Wimpey, Clydebank District Council and the SDA 70 new houses and five shops and offices were to be provided. The first houses were opened by Michael Ancram on 10 October 1986. Originally scheduled for demolition the total cost of rehabilitation was about two and a half million pounds, £450,000 from Clydebank District Council, £600,000 from the SDA's Leg-up Scheme and the remainder from Wimpey.[6] Further along Dumbarton Road refurbishment of the John Brown tenements by the World of Property Housing Trust was completed in late 1987.

These schemes have been crucial in the aim of bringing people back into the centre of Clydebank. It has not only been in the town centre that housing and housing problems are important. Housing has long been an important issue in

Clydebank and so it has remained in the 1980s as it ties in so closely with the regeneration going on elsewhere in the town.

Housing

In the 1980s Clydebank had faced a number of major challenges in the field of housing: the rehabilitation of sub-tolerable tenements, long waiting lists, defects in housing, cutbacks in Government spending on housing, increasing tenant participation, problems of peripheral estates and increasing private ownership. In all of these areas a large number of bodies has been deeply involved, from Housing Associations and community groups to the District Council. As of March 1986 there were 19,393 houses in the District. Of these 60 per cent were owned by the District Council, 15 per cent by the Scottish Special Housing Association (SSHA), 5 per cent by other Housing Associations and 18 per cent were owner occupied.[7] Clydebank District still has one of the lowest proportions of owner occupied housing of any local authority in the United Kingdom although this picture has been changing. Since the Tenants Rights (Scotland) Act 1980 established the 'right to buy' of council tenants nearly 500 houses have been bought from the District Council. There has been a recent increase in private sector rehabilitation activity in the town.

Much of the housing stock is comparatively modern. Only a quarter of the housing was built before 1945. Of this, a large proportion are the 1,500 older tenement houses in the District. Most of these have been rehabilitated since 1978. The rehabilitation programme through the 1980s has been a major achievement in keeping part of old Clydebank in prolonged use. The programme has been the result of close work between Housing Associations, the District Council and the Housing Corporation, and the involvement of the local community. The heaviest concentration of tenement stock and the most obvious improvements have taken place in Dalmuir, largely through the work of Dalmuir Park Housing Association. Although the Association started in 1977 the first rehabilitation was completed in January 1980. Since then they have modernised about 450 flats. Streets such as Pattison Street, Burns Street and Stewart Street in Dalmuir have been transformed. The World of Property Housing Trust has also rehabilitated about 300 flats mainly in Dalmuir. As well as the modernising of flats and stonecleaning, most of the backcourts have been improved in many backcourt improvement schemes funded by the District Council. The declaration of Housing Action Areas has led to improvements to private tenements such as those in John Knox Street, and Barclay and Stuart Streets in Old Kilpatrick. In these cases the District Council has been able to assist with repair grants in the rehabilitation work. The renovation of tenements here and in the town centre has maintained a part of Clydebank's heritage.

The other major Housing Association operating in Clydebank has been the SSHA with main estates in Faifley and Linnvale. By the late 1970s many of these estates were in need of modernisation. By 1986 the SSHA had comprehensively modernised 256 houses in Linnvale while in the much larger state of Faifley a massive rehabilitation plan to go into 1991 has been established. A Faifley Strategy Team involving residents was set up in 1981 to establish a modernisation plan. Although the project has been delayed by budgeting constraints it is planned to modernise 400 flats by 1987. SSHA have also been involved in new building, for example, in building 53 houses in Shaftesbury Street.

There has been a slight shift in tenure towards the private sector with tenants buying council houses and the rehabilitation of town centre flats. Newly built private housing has been limited to a few small sites mainly in Duntocher and Hardgate. The biggest single change will be the construction of about 700 private houses on the former Ministry of Defence oil tank depot site in Old Kilpatrick.

Figure 15:3 *Modern housing development opened by Provost Grainger in 1986 on Dumbarton Road.*

However, by far the largest proportion of housing in Clydebank is District Council owned. Cutbacks in central government spending on housing has meant that, unlike previous periods, there has been and will continue to be virtually no new council houses built in the 1980s. The main work has been on basic modernisation and repair of existing stock. Major work has still to be done on this. Although 90 per cent of the Council housing has had some form of improvement work done on it, only about one third of the houses have been fully modernised.

It is estimated that 12 per cent of the Council's stock is affected by condensation; the Terraces (441 houses) has been perhaps the most well known example of the severe problems of dampness. The development has gained local notoriety and press comment as various potential solutions to the problem have been tried and tested. The Council does not have the resources to solve the problem and in 1987 was considering selling the properties to a private developer to refurbish. There are also concentrations of particularly severe housing problems in Clydebank. In its Local Plan the Council designated Trafalgar Street, Vanguard Street, Jean Armour Drive, Robert Burns Avenue, Braes Avenue and part of Faifley as 'Priority Treatment Areas'. These areas are among the 10 per cent most deprived in Scotland according to an analysis of the 1981 Census by the Scottish Development Department.[8] Their concentration of social, environmental and physical problems requires much in the way of resources, services and environmental improvement. A pilot scheme of concentrating resources in Second Avenue was carried out in 1984-85 with environmental improvements, employment of wardens etc.

Even with these severe problems and the limited resources of the District Council there is still a lengthy waiting list for the houses. The number of applicants at 31 March 1985 totalled 5,845, an increase of 547 from the previous year.[9] It is estimated that this level of waiting list will continue to grow into the early 1990s, and given the current lack of investment in housing the long waiting lists are likely to remain a problem in the forseeable future. One of the positive trends in housing in Clydebank has been the greater involvement of local people. In June 1984 the

District Council established a Tenant Participation Sub-Committee to increase tenant involvement in housing management matters. The strength of the locally based housing associations in Clydebank is another example of local people getting directly involved in housing matters which affect them. This form of involvement has been seen in Clydebank's approach to tackling some of the social problems which remain in the District.

Social Problems of Change

The decline of the late 1970s and general economic climate of the West of Scotland in the 1980s meant that there have been a variety of social problems to contend with in Clydebank. Homelessness, long housing waiting lists, high unemployment, long term unemployment and a declining population are all signs of continuing problems. An analysis of social deprivation carried out by the Scottish Development Department in 1984 showed Clydebank as having some of the worst concentrations of deprivation in Scotland.[10] A variety of methods have been used to

Table 15:1 *Clydebank's Population, 1980-1985*

1980 — 51,866
1981 — 51,199
1982 — 52,594
1983 — 51,498
1984 — 50,809
1985 — 49,966

Source: General Register Office, Mid-Year Population Estimates.

tackle some of these problems. The Community Programme has become one of the major employers of local people since it was set up in 1983, providing employment and training for the unemployed. The Scottish Development Agency established a Training Employment Grant Scheme in Clydebank in 1985 which has helped 96 companies and 192 local people in finding work and training in new skills. Clydebank has attracted funds from the Government's Urban Programme for a number of projects to assist with social problems; examples include the Antonine Sports Centre and the Fleming Avenue Community Education Centre.

Some of the issues of deprivation were also grasped by Strathclyde Regional Council. In partnership with the District Council two Area Initiatives were established in Clydebank as part of the Regional Council's Social Strategy. The Faifley-Hardgate-Duntocher Area Initiative was the first of these. Between 1978 and 1983 the first Area Co-ordinator, Laurie Russell, helped to establish the area as a priority for the resources of many of the public agencies involved in the area. In 1982 another Area Initiative was established, Clydebank East and Central centred on Linnvale, Drumry and Whitecrook under the Area Co-ordinator, Jim Wilkie (later Stuart Moffat). The aim of this Initiative, as in Faifley, was to establish the area as a priority for attention. In both cases, perhaps the greatest success was in offering a vehicle for the development and growth of the numerous community groups in Clydebank. Partly as a response to its problems Clydebank maintains a very vigorous responsive collection of active community groups. While it is not possible to identify them all here, they include such groups as Faifley Tenants Association, Lennox Drive Action Group, the Community Councils, Clydebank Eastern Tenants Association, Dalmuir Credit Union and UB 40. The strength of these groups has helped alleviate many of the worst aspects of the numerous difficulties faced by the local community and will be an integral part of any other regeneration as it occurs.

Economic Regeneration

The initial efforts of the Task Force, the District Council and the other agencies concentrated on physical redevelopment. According to one commentator 'the objective was to provide the infrastructure for sustained private investment and to make an immediate visible impact on the area'.[11] Even before the Enterprise Zone was established it was clear that there were major physical problems to be overcome if Clydebank was to make any kind of recovery. There was a shortage of good industrial land, few small factories for the new businesses and an image, unfair or otherwise, of dereliction and decay to contend with. The most visible and perhaps the most difficult problem was the old Singer factory. The SDA quickly bought the site for less than one million pounds and work began on clearing it in February 1981. While some of the buildings were refurbished to provide early accomodation for businesses most were demolished.

Figure 15:4 *Aerial view of the former Singer site, now the Clydebank Business Park, showing a mix of new factory development alongside the older remnants of the Singer factory.*

The 86 acre site was to become the Clydebank Business Park and the focus of the efforts to diversify the local economy and bring in new businesses and jobs to the town. By the end of 1980 the SDA had purchased a total of 148 acres of land within the Enterprise Zone to add to the land already in its ownership. As the District Council was the other major landowner there was a high degree of control over the developments taking place.[12] The first part of the regeneration process was to provide the premises to house the new businesses. Initially this was done by the public bodies as it was necessary to re-establish confidence in Clydebank before any substantial private sector investment could be attracted. Between 1980 and 1983, through new construction and rehabilitation, the SDA provided approximately 600,000 square feet of industrial premises mainly in the Clydebank Business Park, Whitecrook Centre and Clydebank Industrial Estate in Dalmuir. Clydebank District Council and Strathclyde Regional Council provided a further 50,000 square feet at Riverside Industrial Estate and at what was Our Holy Redeemer's primary school, respectively. In addition, to help diversify the local economy 60,000 square feet of office space was constructed, primarily at Erskine House in the Business Park. Between 1980 and 1983, 90 per cent of the space was leased and, if private property vacant in 1980 is taken into account, the total amount of space leased and sold exceeded one million square feet.[13]

Table 15:2 *Public and Private Investment, 1980-84*

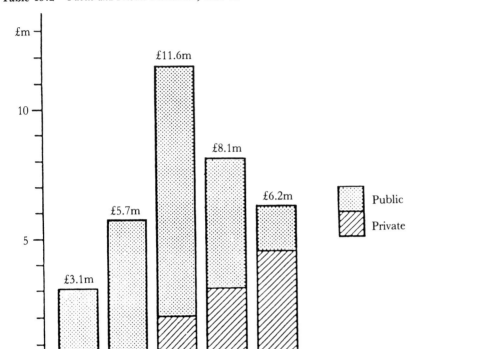

Source: Roger Tym and Partners, *A Review of the Clydebank Task Force 1980-85,* Glasgow, 1986, p.14.

Both the Task Force and the District Council wanted to encourage private sector confidence in Clydebank. The achievements described above meant that by 1983-84 this had begun to take place. Private investment in new industrial or office buildings totalled £9 million over 1980-84 and included the Wykeland units in the Business Park, Erskine House, Radio Clyde, the self-build offices in Dumbarton Road and later the Remploy factory on Glasgow Road.[14] The result of all this development activity was an influx and creation of new firms and jobs. Early Enterprise Zone monitoring reports by the Department of the Environment showed Clydebank as one of the top Zones in terms of job creation (see Table 15.3). A study carried out for the SDA outlines some of the changes taking place.[15] Table 15.4 shows that since the creation of the Enterprise Zone in 1981 the net number of jobs has grown by over 2,000 from 1,942 in 1981 to 3,980 in 1986, an increase of over 100 per cent. However, as the study estimated that about 900 jobs had been lost in some 85 firms which existed prior to 1981 the total number of new jobs was about 3,000 and the number of new firms about 220. Growth in the number of manufacturing and service jobs had been similar at around 1,000 additional jobs

Table 15:3   *Enterprise Zones: incoming firms and jobs June 1981-May 1983*

	Firms	Jobs
Salford	46	322
Trafford	54	730
Swansea	81	1,046
Wakefield	16	156
Clydebank	144	1,637
Dudley	64	523
Hartlepool	34	476
Corby	63	1,591
Newcastle	22	137
Team Valley	27	206
Gateshead	12	103
Speke	31	453
Isle of Dogs	77	353
Belfast (Inner City)	51	240
Belfast (North Foreshore)	3	92
	725	8,065

Source: Roger Tym and Partners, *Monitoring Enterprise Zones, Year Three Report*, DOE, 1984, p.56.

in both. As Table 15.4 shows there has been some diversification in the local economy with new firms in professional services and new high technology companies. New names have appeared in the local Trade directory, such as ET Electrotech, Thor Ceramics, Xynebics Limited and the Image Machine Limited.[16]

Despite this diversification, however, there is still a considerable dependence on John Brown Engineering and UIE. In 1985, when both firms were busy, JBE employed 1,725 and UIE, 1,575. These remain the major concerns and the major employers of Clydebank. In the 1980s both have been suffering from the vagaries of

Figure 15:5 *Councillors and Officers of the Clydebank District Council, 1986.*

Back Row: MR. G. E. WALKER, Councillor J. GILLEECE, Councillor M. CAMPBELL, Councillor G. CAIRNEY, Councillor A. MACDONALD, Councillor F. HEANEY, Councillor A. VEITCH, J.P., Councillor K. SWEENEY, J.P.
Front Row: Councillor E. BROWN, J.P., MR. J. O. SAYERS, J.P., Councillor S. DIVERS, Provost D. S. GRAINGER, J.P., Councillor M. McGARRY, M.A., J.P., MR. J. T. McNALLY, Councillor J. McALLISTER, J.P.

extremely competitive markets. Despite continuing to win large orders in the period both the UIE yard and the JBE factory have laid off large numbers, with UIE on occasion down to a very small core workforce. Both concerns have been under threat of takeover at various points, while JBE was also threatened by a US trade embargo on the Soviet Union, and the UIE by the fall in oil prices in 1986. At the time of writing the UIE yard is under threat of closure following the loss of a major order. It remains important to Clydebank that these two major engineering employers survive and prosper while the new firms grow.

The development of new businesses and the growing confidence in Clydebank

Table 15:4 *Employment Growth in the Enterprise Zone, 1981, 1983 and 1985*

	No. of Employees (1981)	No. of Employees (1983)	No. of Employees (1985)	Increase/ Decrease 1981-1985	% Change 1981-1985
3. Food, Drink and Tobacco	66	155	257	+191	MED.
4. Coal and Petroleum	0	0	7	+7	LOW
5. Chemicals and Allied	29	43	158	+129	MED.
6. Metal manuf.	6	0	258	+252	HIGH
7. Mechanical Eng.	428	553	412^2	−16	NEG.
8. Instrument Eng.	4	22	167	+163	HIGH
9. Electrical Eng.	3	51	137	+134	HIGH
10. Shipbuilding and Marine Eng.	69	39	0^3	−69	NEG.
11. Vehicles	0	0	4	+4	LOW
12. Metal Goods N.E.S.	113	107	85	−28	NEG.
13. Textiles	0	0	54	+54	MED.
14. Leather, Leather Goods and Fur	0	0	6	+6	LOW
15. Clothing and Footwear	126	129	0	−126	NEG.
16. Bricks, Pottery, Glass etc.	33	49	148	+127	MED.
17. Timber, Furniture etc.	45	109	109	+64	MED.
18. Paper, Printing, and Publishing	126	173	283	+157	MED.
19. Other manufacturing industries	56	87	95	+39	LOW
Sub-total	1,104	1,517	2,180	1,076	LOW
20. Construction	295	500	522	+277	LOW
21. Gas, Electricity and Water	0	0	11	+11	LOW
22. Transport and Communication	176	147	142	−34	NEG.
23. Distributive Trades	187	393	403	+216	MED.
24. Insurance, Banking, Finance etc.	37	58	71	+34	LOW
25. Prof. & Sci. Services.	30	182	333	+303	HIGH
26. Misc. Services	113	158	318	+205	MED.
Sub-total	838	1,438	1,800	962	MED.
Total	1,942	2,955	3,980	+2,038	MED.

1. High = Increase of over 10×; Med. = Increase of 2 × 9×; Low = Increase of less than 100%; Neg. = Decrease.
2. Excludes 1275 from JBE.
3. Excludes 1575 from UIE.

Source: Roger Tym and Partners, *A Review of the Clydebank Task Force 1980-85,* Glasgow, 1986, p.24.

meant that from an early stage efforts could be made to strengthen the growing industrial base and its links with Clydebank and to ensure that local people had access to the growing opportunities. One of the first signs of the establishment of the new businesses of the town was the formation in 1985 of the Clydebank Business Club under the chairmanship and inspiration of Alistair Nichol of Scotland Foam which brought together many of the local businesses with the aim of helping them to develop further in Clydebank and with Clydebank. The current emphasis within the Enterprise Zone is likely to concentrate more on business development and training. A Local Collaborative Project was set up in 1985 with Clydebank District Council, Clydebank College, the Clydebank Business Club, MSC and SDA to examine ways of improving training and employment prospects within Clydebank. Despite the improvements made there is still a considerable problem to deal with in Clydebank. With a total of 4,311 people unemployed in February 1987, 3,193 men and 1,118 women, Clydebank had an unemployment rate of 17.6 per cent compared with 19.1 per cent for Strathclyde Region, 16.5 per cent for Scotland and 11.9 per cent for the United Kingdom.[17] It is difficult to compare with earlier periods since there have been 17 changes to the method of calculation of unemployment statistics since 1979. These statistics partly reflect the difficulties of local economic regeneration in the context of high national unemployment; Clydebank could not be isolated from the wider economic effects. It is also the case that modern factories and industrial processes generally provide fewer jobs in the same area than in the past. The Clydebank Local Plan, for example, points out that 'the Singer site (34 hectares), now Clydebank Business Park, employed over 15,000 people. At a quite favourable job density by today's standard of 60 jobs per hectare . . . it could only provide for 2,000'.[18] With the industrial land available in Clydebank, realistically, there is only space for a fraction of these jobs lost. The Enterprise Zone finishes in 1991, having achieved a great deal, but, still with scope for much more to be done towards the economic regeneration of Clydebank. Notwithstanding, Clydebank has bravely entered its second century and looks to the future with renewed hope.

References

Abbreviations
The following is a guide to abbreviations used in the footnotes:

CP   Clydebank Press
CPCM   Clydebank Police Commission Minutes
CTCM   Clydebank Town Council Minutes
DO   Dumbarton Observer
GH   Glasgow Herald
GUA   Glasgow University Archives
GUBA   Glasgow University Business Archives
LH   Lennox Herald
SDA   Scottish Development Agency
SRA   Strathclyde Regional Archives
SRO   Scottish Record Office

Introduction
1. *Directory of the Parish of Old Kilpatrick and the Burgh of Clydebank, 1893-4*, (Clydebank, 1893), p.13
2. Damer, Sean, *Rent Strike! The Clydebank Rent Struggles of the 1920s*, (Clydebank, 1982)
3. McGonigle, Margaret, 'The Hamiltons of Barns and Cochno' In *Clydebank Historical Journal*, vol. 6, Spring 1986
Chapter 1
The Shipbuilders
1. For the early years of J. and G. Thomson see Walker, F. M., *Song of the Clyde*, (Cambridge, 1984). See also, Brown, H. D., *Clydebank Shipyard: A History of the Clydebank Establishment of Messrs John Brown & Co (Clydebank) Ltd., and of their Predecessors, James and George Thomson, 1847-1955*, (1954)
2. Brown, H. D., *op. cit.*
3. *Ibid.*
4. The detail on output, customers, and vessels is drawn from the yard lists and contract records preserved in GUBA. The Clydebank records are in series UCS 1/3.
5. For a brief discussion of technical change in shipbuilding at this time see Slaven, A., *The Development of the West of Scotland, 1706-1960*, (1960), ch.5
6. Warshipbuilding on the Clyde is discussed and illustrated in great detail in Peebles, Hugh B., 'Warshipbuilding on the Clyde, 1889-1939: A Financial Study' *PhD Thesis* (Stirling, 1986)
7. Peebles, Hugh B., *op. cit.*
8. Grant, Sir A., *Steel and Ships: The History of John Brown*, (London, 1950)
9. Peebles, Hugh B., *op. cit.*
10. A biography of Sir Thomas Bell is contained in Slaven, A., and Checkland, S. B. (eds.), *Dictionary of Scottish Business Biography* vol. 1, (Aberdeen, 1986)
11. This section is based on Hume, John R., and Moss, Michael S., *Beardmore : The History of a Scottish Industrial Giant*, (London, 1977), chs. 3 and 4
12. *Ibid.*, p.50
13. *Ibid.*, p.24 and 'Memoir of Mr William Beardmore' In *Transactions of the Institute of Civil Engineers*, 1878, vol. 1, pp.268-70
14. GUA, DC49, papers relating to Robert Napier & Sons.

15. Turton, Alison, and Moss, Michael, *A Tale of Two Sugar Engineers — the History of Fletcher & Stewart; 1838-1988*, (Derby, 1988), ch. 7, and Barnaby, H., *100 Years of Specialised Shipbuilding and Engineering*, (London, 1964), p.45

16. Hume, J. R., and Moss, M. S., *op. cit.*

17. *Ibid.*, pp.69-78 and *Engineering*, 1904, vol. 78, pp.445-58

18. *Engineering*, 1906, vol. 81, p.830

19. GUA, UDG100 (Beardmore collection) 1/8/7 statement of accounts, 1907

20. Hume, J. R., and Moss, M. S., *op. cit.*

21. Admiralty Library, Tweedmouth Papers Box 'A' (1905-1906), Miscellaneous item 399, letter Marquess of Graham to Lord Tweedmouth, 29 November 1906

22. Hume, J. R., and Moss, M. S., *op. cit.* pp.98-99

23. *Ibid.*, pp.99-102

Chapter 2
The Sewing Machine — The Singer Factory
1. The early history of Singer is told in Brandon, Ruth, *Singer and the Sewing Machine* (London, 1978) and Davies, Robert B., 'Peacefully Working to Conquer the World: The Singer Manufacturing Company in Foreign Markets, 1854-1889'. In *Business History Review*, 43, 1969, p.299

2. Davies, Robert B., *op. cit.*, p.316

3. *Ibid.*, p.316; *Report of the Proceedings on the Occasion of Breaking Ground for the Singer Manufacturing Company's New Factory (Report of Proceedings)*, (1882), p.33

4. *Report of Proceedings, op. cit.*, p.33

5. SRA, Glasgow Dean of Guild Court Records, D-OPW23

6. *Report of Proceedings, op. cit.*, p.34; *Evening Times* 13 February 1882, p.4; *Post Office Glasgow Directory*, 1878-79

7. *Report of Proceedings, op. cit.*, p.34; LH, 28 July 1883, p.3

8. *Report of Proceedings, op. cit.* and *Oban Times*, 4 June 1881, p.6

9. *North British Daily Mail*, 19 May 1882

10. *Glasgow News*, 24 July 1883, p.2

11. For the early history of the firm, see Russell, Iain F., *Sir Robert McAlpine & Son Ltd. The Early Years* (forthcoming), Chs. 1 and 2; GUA, Dixon, George, *Monthly Reports on the Location, Listing and Selective Copying of Records Relating to Sir Robert McAlpine & Sons' Early History, 1868-1919*

12. Childers, J. Saxton, *Sir Robert McAlpine: A Biography* (Oxford, 1925), p.42

13. The contract was advertised on 3 June 1882 in the *North British Daily Mail*, p.7 and the GH, p.1

14. *Glasgow News*, 31 May 1883

15. *Report of Proceedings, op. cit.*, p.6 and p.31

16. The factory is described in *North British Daily Mail*, 19 May 1882, p.2 and 10 July 1885, p.3

17. *Edinburgh Gazette*, 23 January 1883, p.59

18. *North British Daily Mail*, 10 July 1885, p.3

19. *Ibid.*

20. LH, 28 July 1883, p.3

21. DO, 24 May 1884, p.3 and 17 January 1885; *Evening Times*, 29 September 1884; Davies Robert B. *op. cit.*, p.36

22. *McAlpine Contracts* (c. 1919)

23. MacLeod, Donald, *The Clyde district of Dunbartonshire* (Dumbarton, 1886), p.185; DO, 22 May 1886, p.3

24. Davies, Robert B., *op. cit.*, p.317; *Evening Times*, 12 November 1881, p.2 and 13 February 1882, p.4

25. Checkland, S. G., *The Upas Tree: Glasgow 1875-1975* (Glasgow, 1976), p.12

26. Murphy, S. J., *op. cit.*, p. 32

27. *Ibid.*, p.32

28. *Ibid.*, p.32

29. 'All sewn up but for Jeans and Socialism', In *Morning Star*, 28 June 1979

30. Wilkins, Mira, *The Emergence of Multi-National Enterprise: American Business Abroad from the Colonial Era to 1914*, (Harvard, Cambridge, Massachussetts and London, 1970), p.216

31. 'How the Directors Kept Singer Stitched Together', In *Fortune*, December 1975

32. See Table 2:1, from Dorman, A., 'A history of the Singer Company (UK) Ltd Clydebank Factory' (unpublished, 1972)

33. Slaven, A., 'A Shipyard in Depression: John Brown's of Clydebank 1919-1938', In *Business History*, XIX, 2, 1977

34. McLean, Iain, *The Legend of Red Clydeside*, (Edinburgh, 1983), pp. 100-2

35. Challoner, Raymond, *The Origins of British Bolshevism*, (London, 1977), p.103

36. Information regarding union recognition provided by Alex Ferry, Factory Convener, 1959-64, in a personal letter to author

37. *The Singer Manufacturing Company*, (Clydebank District Libraries, (n.d.)

Chapter 3
The Town and its Politics

1. *Directory of the Parish of Old Kilpatrick and the Burgh of Clydebank, 1893-4, op. cit.,* p.13
2. Walker, David M., *The Scottish Legal System,* (Edinburgh, 1981), pp.136-37; Pryde, G. S., *Central and Local Government in Scotland since 1707,* (London, 1960), pp.14-15; Pryde, G. S., 'Burghal Administration' In McLarty (ed.) *Source of Administrative Law,* (London, 1956), p.10
3. Muirhead, James, *The Law and Practice relating to Police Government in Burghs in Scotland,* (Glasgow, 1893), p.46
4. SRA, CO4/20/2, 2 March 1886
5. *Ibid.,* 30 March 1886
6. SRO, SC 65/1/32, *Diet Book of the Sheriff Court of Dunbartonshire*
7. CP, 18 January 1904
8. LH, 26 June 1886
9. *Ibid.,* 13 November 1886
10. *Ibid.*
11. GH, 15 November 1886
12. GH, 16 and 18 November 1886; LH, 20 November 1886
13. LH, December 1886
14. DO, 25 December 1886
15. LH, 18 December 1886
16. DO, 25 December 1886
17. LH, 1 January 1887
18. *Ibid.,* 15 January 1887
19. Clydebank Town Council Souvenir Jubilee brochure, 1886-1936, (Clydebank, 1936), pp.80-82
20. CPCM, 13 February 1893
21. Clydebank Town Council, *op. cit.,* p.91 and p.93
22. CP, 30 March 1906, 27 July 1906, and 3 August 1906
23. *Ibid.,* 15 October 1892 and similar comment reported on 31 October 1913
24. *Ibid.,* 8 September 1894
25. Kellas, James G., *Modern Scotland,* (London, 1980), pp.131-33; Smout, T. C., *A History of the Scottish People, 1830-1950,* (London, 1986), pp.240-41, pp.245-47, and p.254
26. *Clydebank Leader,* 9 October 1914 gives Roman Catholic population of Clydebank as 1,500 in 1890, 3,700 in 1901 and 7,000 in 1906
27. Smout, T. C., *op. cit.,* p.258; Kellas, J. G., *op. cit.,* p.140
28. Melling, Joseph, *Rent Strikes : Peoples' Struggle for Housing in the West of Scotland 1890-1916,* (Edinburgh, 1983)
29. Melling, Joseph, *op. cit.,* p.111
30. *Slater's Directory of Scotland,* 1889 and 1900; *Directory of the Parish of Old Kilpatrick and the Burgh of Clydebank, 1893-94, op. cit., Register of Applicants for the Sales of Excisable Liquor,* 1904-14
31. CP, 22 September 1894
32. CP, 27 July 1895
33. Kellas, J. G., *op. cit.,* p.132 and p.136
34. CP, 25 February 1898
35. *Ibid.,* 26 February 1906
36. *Ibid.,* 10 July 1908
37. *Ibid.,* 15 July 1904 and 26 June 1908
38. LH, 17 April 1886 and 8 May 1886

Chapter 4
Social Trends, 1886-1914

1. MacLeod, Donald, *op. cit.,* p.106 and p.117; Hood, John Brown, *Clydebank in Old Picture Postcards* (Zaltbommel, 1985); DO, 20 September 1984, p.2; CP, 22 November 1907, p.2
2. Hood, John Brown, *op. cit.;* SRO, UR96/18, Valuation Rolls, County of Dunbarton 1872-73
3. SRO VR96/32 and 33, 1886-87 and 1887-88. All details of property ownership and tenants' occupations come from this source, unless noted otherwise
4. *Ibid.; North British Daily Mail,* 24 September 1885, p.3; MacLeod, Donald, *op. cit.,* p.118 and p.180
5. DO, 20 September 1884 and 20 November 1886; CP, 27 July 1906, p.3; *Annual Report of the Sanitary Inspector, Burgh of Clydebank,* (Report of Sanitary Inspector), 1914
6. CP, 5 November 1915, p.5; *Report of Sanitary Inspector,* 1922
7. MacLeod, Donald, *op. cit.,* p.118
8. *Ibid.,* p.180; SRO, VR96/32, 1886-87
9. Melling, Joseph, 'Employers, Labour and the Housing Market in Clydebank from 1880 to 1920'. Paper delivered to SSRC/University of Glasgow conference on Social Policy, May 1978; UCS1/23/2 Memo of 26 January 1914
10. MacLeod, Donald, *op. cit.,* p.129; SRO, UR96/32, 1886/87
11. Melling, Joseph, 'Employers, Labour and the Housing Market', *op. cit.*

12. SRO, VR96/60, 1914-15
13. CP, 11 April 1913, p.3
14. *Ibid.*, 27 July 1906, p.3; *Census of Scotland,* 1901
15. *Reports of Sanitary Inspector*
16. CP, 27 July 1906, p.3
17. *Reports of Sanitary Inspector*, 1906 and 1907
18. For the story of McAlpine's operations at Singer and in the Holy City, see Russell, Iain F., *op. cit.*
19. SRO, VR96/52, 1906-7; *The Clydebank Leader*, 3 August 1906., p.5
20. Other reasons are given by Childers, J. Saxton, *op. cit.*, p.95 and by Hardie, Alec M., *'The Story of Robert McAlpine'* (unpublished MS, c1960), p.48
21. CP, 27 July 1906, p.3; *The Clydebank Leader*, 27 July 1906, p.2 and 3 August 1906, p.5
22. SRO, VR/52 and 60, 1906-7 and 1914-15
23. CP, 17 January 1908, p.5, and 25 June 1909, p.5
24. *Census of Scotland.* 1911
25. *Ibid.*
26. Melling, Joseph, 'Clydeside Housing and the Evolution of State Rent Control, 1900-1939' In Melling, J., (ed.), *Housing, Social Policy and the State,* (London, 1980), p.143
27. Russell, Iain F., *op. cit.*; SRO, VR96/60, 1914-15; CP, 15 September 1905, p.5, 19 November 1909, p.4; 19 February 1915, p.3
28. CP, 14 September 1906, p.9; SRO, UR96/52, 1906-7.
29. Melling, Joseph, 'Employers' Labour and the Housing Market, *op. cit.*; SRO, VR96/50 and 60, 1904-5 and 1914-15; CP, 11 January 1907, p.4
30. GUA, Dalmuir and West of Scotland Estate Ltd, Minute Book No.1, 6 November 1914, p.3, and 8 October 1915, p.4
31. *Report of Sanitary Inspector,* 1904
32. *Ibid.*, 1914
33. CP, 3 January 1913, p.3
34. *Ibid.*, 11 and 15 April, p.3; Watson, William C., 'Clydebank in the Inter-War Years: A study in Economics and Social Change', *PhD Thesis* (Glasgow, 1984), p.191; Niven, Douglas, *The Development of Housing in Scotland*, (London, 1979), p.26
35. CP, 27 July 1917, p.4
36. The surviving minutes, covering the period 1868-90, are held in SRA, CO4/20/2, CO4/20/39 and CO4/20/40
37. Medical Directories, *passim*
38. Old Kilpatrick Parish Council minutes, 30 July 1895
39. CTCM, 8 March 1897
40. Medical Directories, *passim* and obituary notice, *Glasgow Medical Journal,* January 1910
41. SRA, CO4/20/1, 13 November 1883
42. SRA, CO4/20/40, 24 June 1884
43. SRA, Old Kilpatrick Parochial Board, Registers of paupers, CO4/20/41 and CO4/20/42
44. Glasgow Western Infirmary annual reports, 1874-1914
45. SRA, CO4/20/39, 10 March 1874; CO4/20/1, 27 July, 30 August, 14 December 1875, 2 May, 6 June 1876
46. SRA, CO4/20/1, 7 June 1881
47. CTCM, 8 and 31 January 1894
48. *Ibid.*, 10 September 1894
49. The first patient was admitted on 18 March 1897; *Ibid.* 1 April 1897. The decision to erect the municipal buildings, fire station etc, was agreed on 12 April 1894
50. *Ibid.*, 26 September 1894
51. GH, 21 January 1907
52. In writing this and the next section on Education, I have been much assisted by the unpublished book by Paterson, A. C., 'The Educational History of Clydebank' (1940), held by Clydebank District Libraries
53. SRA, CO4/6/1/14/1, Old Kilpatrick School Board, MS Minutes (hereafter cited as 'Board Minutes'), 5 July 1873
54. Quoted in Paterson, A. C., *op. cit.*, p.15
55. SRA, CO4/6/1/14/1, Board Minutes, 11 January 1878
56. SRA, CO4/6/1/14/2, Board Minutes, 7 October 1885
57. SRA, CO4/6/1/14/2, Board Minutes, 6 February 1886
58. Quoted in Paterson, A. C., *op. cit.*, p.74
59. SRA, CO4/6/1/14/4, Board Minutes, 3 May 1891
60. Much of the ecclesiastical history of the burgh in this and the later chapters on Religion has been gleaned from the good range of congregational histories. Two important additional sources have been *A Church History of Clydebank* (Clydebank District Libraries (Clydebank, 1983) and Eunson, A. D., *Old Kilpatrick and Christianity: The Parish's Story from Roman Times,* (Dumbarton, 1962)
61. CP, 22 August 1891

62. *Ibid.*, 7 October 1893
63. *Ibid.*, 28 December 1900
64. *Ibid.*, 7 May 1909
65. *Ibid.*, 4 January 1901
66. *Ibid.*, 28 October 1893
67. *Ibid.*, 22 December 1894
68. *Ibid.*, 15 August, 1891
69. *Ibid.*, 21 November 1891, p.2
70. *Ibid.*, 29 September 1905, p.4
71. *Ibid.*, 15 October 1909, p.5
72. *Ibid.*, 7 September 1906, p.8
73. LH, 17 August 1889, p.4
74. CP, 10 August 1889, p.17 and p.4, August 1889
75. *Ibid.*, 5 July 1890, p.2
76. From information supplied by Mark Hope, Knightswood
77. CP, 26 June 1908, p.5
78. *Ibid.*, 12 July 1907, p.8
79. McAusland, Brian, *Clydesdale Harriers 1886-1986,* (forthcoming)
80. Football information from Alan Urquhart

Chapter 5
The Shipyards at War, 1914-1918
1. GUBA, UCS 1/1/1, John Brown & Co Minute Book No.2, 28 July 1915
2. Compiled from appendices in Brown, H. D., *op. cit.* and from yard lists
3. GH, 28 December 1918
4. Peebles, Hugh B., *op cit.*
5. GUBA, UCS 1/1/1, Minute Book No.2, 20 January and 22 February 1915
6. *Ibid.*, 27 May 1915
7. *Ibid.*, 1 June 1916
8. *Board of Trade Committee on Shipping and Shipbuilding*, Minutes of Evidence, 15 December 1916
9. This section is based on Hume, John R., and Moss, Michael S., *Beardmore op. cit.*, ch.5
10. *Ibid.*, pp.105-6 and *History of Munitions* vol. 1, part 1, pp.89-194
11. *Ibid.*, pp.107-8
12. Kirkwood, David, *My Life in Revolt*, (London, 1935), pp.87-117; Middlemas, R., *The Clydesiders: a left-wing struggle for Parliamentary Power*, (London, 1965), pp.54-68 and McLean, Iain, *op. cit.*, ch.7
13. Gillies, J. D., and Wood, J., *Aviation in Scotland*, (Glasgow 1969), pp.40-42 and GUA UGD100/1/12/16, firm's catalogue *Aircraft Department 1914-1919*
14. Highman, Robin, *British Rigid Airships 1908-1931*, (London, 1966), pp.105-32
15. GH, 25 April 1919, p.8
16. Hume, J., and Moss, M., *op. cit.*, pp.132-37
17. *Ibid.*, p.140
18. GUA, UGD100/8/14-19, Beardmore statements of account 1914-1919
19. GH, 25 April 1919, p.8

Chapter 6
Clydebank Politics in War and Peace
1. CP, 4 September 1914 and 8 January 1915
2. *Ibid.*, 21 January 1916
3. *Ibid.*, 22 December 1916
4. *Ibid.*, 18 May 1917
5. *Ibid.*, 22 January 1915
6. *Ibid.*, 5 February 1915 and *Clydebank Leader*, 19 February 1915
7. *Ibid.*, 16 April 1915 and 21 May 1915
8. *Ibid.*, 5 May 1916
9. *Ibid.*, 2 March 1917
10. *Ibid.*, 12 February 1915
11. *Ibid.*, 8 February 1918
12. *Ibid.*, 7 October 1921
13. CTCM, 9 January 1933
14. CP, 18 September 1931 and 16 September 1932
15. *Ibid.*, 16 October 1931
16. *Ibid.*, 30 October 1931
17. *Ibid.*, 20 January 1933
18. *Times*, 16 August 1924
19. Smout, T. C., *op. cit.*, pp.259-71
20. Andrew, Christopher, *Secret Service*, (London, 1986), pp.286-87

21. CP, 2 July 1920
22. *Ibid.*, 5 January 1923
23. *Ibid.*, 20 July 1923
24. *Ibid.*, 17 May 1929
25. *Ibid.*, 16 August 1929
26. Information from author's family
27. CP, 1 November 1935
28. *Ibid.*, 3 November 1933
29. CTCM, 13 October 1931
30. CP, 16 May 1924
31. Constantine, Stephen, *Unemployment in Britain between the Wars*, (London, 1980), p.43
32. See Graves, R., and Hodge, A., *The Long Weekend*, (London, 1971) chs. 16 and 19 and Ceadel, Martin, *Pacificism in Britain, 1914-1945: The Defining of the Faith*, (Oxford, 1980)
33. CTCM, 5 May 1937 and 29 September 1938
34. *Ibid.*, 8 February 1937, 12 April 1937, 13 September 1937 and 15 December 1937
35. McPhail, I. M. M., *The Clydebank Blitz*, (1974), p.3
36. CTCM, 9 March 1936 and 5 May 1937
37. CP, 13 September 1935
38. CTCM, 24 March 1938 and 22 September 1938
39. McPhail, I. M. M., *op. cit.*, p.3
40. CP, 19 April 1935 and 17 May 1935
41. *Ibid.*, 21 May 1937 and CTCM, 29 September 1938
42. *Ibid.*, 11 October 1935
43. *Ibid.*, 21 February 1936
44. *Ibid.*, 28 January 1938
45. *Ibid.*, 4 August 1979
46. CTCM, 14 December 1942 and 21 October 1943
47. *Ibid.*, 7 December 1944
48. CP, 8 September 1939
49. *Ibid.*
50. McPhail, I. M. M., *op. cit.*, pp.56-68
51. CP, 2 March 1945
52. *Ibid.*, 12 September 1941
53. CTCM, 24 June 1943
54. CP, 17 September 1943
55. CTCM, 24 February 1944
56. CP, 12 January 1940 and 2 February 1940
57. *Ibid.*, 4 July 1941
58. *Ibid.*, 31 December 1943

Chapter 7
The Clydebank Rent Strike
1. Englander, David, *Landlord and Tenant in Urban Britain, 1838-1918*, (Oxford, 1983), p.170, pp.179-83
2. *Ibid.*, p.130; CP, 15 September 1905, p.5 and 27 July 1906, p.3
3. Melling, Joseph, *Rent Strikes, op. cit.*
4. *Ibid.*; Damer, Sean, 'State Class and Housing: Glasgow 1885-1919' In Melling, Joseph (ed.) *Housing Social Policy and the State*, (London, 1980); McLean, Iain, *op. cit.*, pp.20-25
5. CP, 5 November 1915, p.5
6. *Minutes of the Evidence to the Committee on the Increase of Rent and Mortgage Interest, War Restriction Act,* Cmd 658, 1920; Melling, J., 'Clydeside Housing' *op. cit.*; McLean Iain, *op. cit.*, p.167
7. McLean, Iain, *op. cit.*, p.168; *Report of the Committee on the Increase of Rent and Mortgage Interest (War Restrictions) Act*, Cmd 9235, 1918
8. CP, 4 June 1920, p.2
9. *Ibid.*, 18 June 1920, p.2
10. *Ibid.*, p.3
11. *Ibid.*, 6 August 1920, p.2
12. *Ibid.*, 27 August 1920, p.2
13. *Ibid.*, 3 September 1920, p.3
14. *Ibid.*, p.8
15. *Ibid.*, 8 October 1920, p.4; 21 June 1921, p.3 and 29 July 1921, p.4
16. Watson, William C., *op. cit.*, p.46
17. CP, 15 April 1921, p.3
18. *Ibid.*, 24 December 1920, p.6, 25 March 1921, p.5
19. Damer, Sean, *Rent Strike!*, *op. cit.*, p.6; Englander, David, *op. cit.*, p.48; Cmd. 658, 1920
20. Damer, Sean, *Rent Strike!*, *op. cit.*, p.5; CP, 24 December 1920, p.6; GH, 15 and 22 September and 26 November 1920

21. CP, 26 November and 24 December 1920, both p.6
22. *Ibid.*, 25 March 1921, p.3, p.4 and p.5 and 29 July, 1921, p.4
23. Damer, Sean, *Rent Strike!, op. cit.*, p.6; GH, 25 March, 17, 19 and 26 June and 13, 25, 26 and 27 July 1920
24. Damer, Sean, *Rent Strike!, op. cit.*, p.6; McLean, Iain, *op. cit.*, p.172; GH, 4 November 1922
25. Moorhouse, Bert, *et al,* 'Rent Strikes — Direct Action and the Working Classes', In *The Socialist Register*, 1972, p.136
26. Clydebank Town Council, *op. cit.*, p.63
27. CP, 19 October 1923, p.3
28. *Ibid.*, 7 December 1923, p.3
29. *Ibid.*, 2 November 1923, p.3
30. *Ibid.*, 8 August 1924, p.4, 2 June 1925, p.3
31. *Ibid.*, 4 December 1925, p.5
32. GUA, Sir Robert McAlpine & Sons: Private Ledger No.4
33. GUA, Letter from Samuel McGavin to Controller Inland Revenue. Edinburgh, 22 June 1927, in Sir Robert McAlpine & Sons: Taxation Letterbook No.1 (McAlpine Taxation Letterbook)
34. GUA, UGD100/2/1/1, Dalmuir and West of Scotland Estates Co Ltd: Minute Book No.1
35. GUA, UCS1/25/5, John Brown & Co: File on Workmen's Houses
36. CP, 8 August 1924, p.4
37. *Ibid.*, 15 August 1924, p.3
38. *Ibid.*, 2 June 1925, p.3
39. Damer/Lambie interview
40. Damer, Sean, *Rent Strike!, op. cit.*, p.10 and p.13
41. *Ibid.*, p.11, Damer/Lambie interview
42. Damer, Sean, *Rent Strike!, op. cit.*, pp.10-15
43. CP, 2 January, p.5, 16 January 1925, p.3, and 10 June 1925, p.5
44. *Ibid.*, 27 February 1925, p.5; GUA, Letter from Samuel McGavin to Secretary of Board of Inland Revenue, 30 April in McAlpine Tax Letterbook
45. CP, 27 February 1925, p.5, 6 March 1925, p. 2 and 13 March 1925, p.8
46. *Ibid.*, 5 June 1925, p.5
47. GUA, McAlpine Tax Letterbook, 10 July 1925, p.8, Letter from Samuel McGavin to Comptroller of Inland Revenue, Edinburgh, 27 August 1925
48. GUA, McAlpine Tax Letterbook, Letter, Samuel McGavin to HM Inspector of Taxes, Glasgow, 1 April 1925, and to Comptroller Inland Revenue, Edinburgh, 1 April 1926
49. GUA, McAlpine Tax Letterbook, Letter, Samuel McGavin to Comptroller Inland Revenue, Edinburgh, 27 August 1952
50. CP, 13 November 1924, p.5
51. *Ibid.*, 4 December 1925, p.5
52. *Ibid.*, 6 March 1926, p.3
53. GUA, McAlpine Tax Letterbook, Samuel McGavin to Comptroller Inland Revenue, Edinburgh, 1 April 1926
54. GUA, UGD100/2/1/1
55. GUA, Sir Robert McAlpine & Sons: Private Ledgers vols 3 and 4
56. Watson, William C., *op. cit.*, p.47
57. CP, 30 April 1926, p.3 and 21 May 1926, p.5
58. *Ibid.*, 19 February 1926, p.5 and 5 March 1926, p.5
59. *Ibid.*, 21 May 1926, p.5; Damer, Sean, *Rent Strike!, op. cit.*, p.21
60. CP, 19 February 1926, p.5
61. *Ibid.*, 5 March 1926, p.3
62. *Ibid.*, 10 July p.3
63. *Ibid.*, 1 January 1926, p.4, 8 January 1926, p.3; Damer, Sean, *Rent Strike!, op. cit.*, p.14
64. CP, 28 May 1926, p.5
65. *Ibid.*, 5 March 1926, p.3, 15 July 1927, p.4; Damer, Sean, *Rent Strike!, op. cit.*, p.21
66. CP, 15 July 1927, p.4, 27 July 1927, p.4 and 12 August 1927, p.5
67. GUA, UGD11/2/1/1, Dalmuir and West of Scotland Estate Ltd, Minute Book No.1
68. GUA, McAlpine Tax Letterbook, Samuel McGavin to Comptroller Inland Revenue, Edinburgh, 12 March 1928

Chapter 8
Social Trends, 1914-1945
1. Watson, William C., *op. cit.*, table 8.6, 8.7 p.207; *Clydebank Town Council, op. cit.*, p.114
8.6, 8.7 p.207; *Burgh of Clydebank Souvenir Jubilee Brochure 1886-1936*, (Clydebank, 1936), p.114
2. *Annual Report of the Sanitary Inspector of the Burgh of Clydebank*, 1919
3. *Census of Scotland, 1921*, part 1, p.662, part 2, pp.xxxix-xli
4. *Annual Report of the Sanitary Inspector of the Burgh of Clydebank*, 1919
5. Inter-war legislation on housing is summarised and explained in Crammond, R. D., *Housing policy in Scotland 1919-1964 : a study in state assistance*, (Glasgow, 1966)

6. Watson, William C., *op cit.*, pp.210-11

7. See for example CTCM, 16/9/1919 for the dispute between the Council and the Local Government Board over the appointment of a consulting architect for housing schemes, or 27/4/1928 and 14/5/1928, when the Scottish Board of Health refused to approve the council's acceptance of tenders from Leslie Kirk Ltd for the entire contract to build 32 houses at Whitecrook

8. CTCM, 1/10/1926, 12/5/1927, 3/1/1928; GH, 18 February 1928, p.8; for Taylor see *Who was who*; GH, 21 September 1936, p.9; CP, 25 September 1936, p.4

9. CTCM, 23/9/1929, 31/10/1929; McAlpine initially applied for subsidies to build 20 houses 'which would be followed by a larger scheme in the same area and for which they would expect same amount of subsidy'

10. GH, 14 January 1920, p.10

11. CTCM, 7/1/1932, 24/3/1932

12. Hansard 264 (1931-32) p.554, 267 (1931-32) p.1174, 269 (1931-32) p.1774

13. CTCM, 12/9/1935, 10/9/1936, 21/9/1936, 10/12/1936, 10/1/1937, 12/8/1937, 24/9/1937, 13/1/1938, 14/4/1938, 17/11/1938; GH, 29 November 1937, p.9

14. *Memorandum by the Local Government Board for Scotland with suggestions in regard to the provision and planning of houses for the working classes* (Edinburgh, 1918) p.7; For early moves to encourage new methods of building see White, R. B., *Prefabrication: a history of its development in Great Britain*, (London, 1965), pp.49-66

15. CTCM, 24/2/1919, 26/4/1920; GH, 21 October 1920 p.11

16. CTCM, 8/4/1925, 9/4/1925, 24/8/1925, 5/1/1926, 26/1/1926, 6/12/1926; for detailed descriptions of the Rae bungalow see GH 19 December 1924, p.12 and 13 February 1925 p.5. For problems in the construction of the bungalows see CTCM 6/8/1926, 15/11/1926

17. CTCM, 24/11/1924; White, R. B., *op. cit.*, p.79. For the Atholl Steel Houses Ltd see Hume, John R., and Moss, Michael S., *Beardmore, op. cit.*, p.192. The Atholl house was perhaps the most successful of the inter-war steel framed houses.

18. CTCM, 21/12/1925, 5/1/1926, 26/1/1926, 6/8/1926, 6/12/1926. The other types were 60 Dennis Wilde houses (steel framed with conventional walls) and 60 Kane Brickwood houses (timber and brick construction). These various methods of construction are explained in *Post-War Building Studies* No.1 (London, 1944)

19. *Hansard* 264 (1931-32) p.554

20. CTCM, 22/6/1920, 8/2/1924, 12/3/1926, 17/11/1938

21. For sample layouts and designs see *Memorandum by the Local Government Board for Scotland with suggestions . . . op. cit., passim*

22. CTCM, 14/11/1932, 17/11/1932, 22/12/1932, 27/11/1934, 3/1/1935, 31/12/1936

23. CTCM, 6/12/1926

24. CTCM, 5/2/1934, where the Parkhall Tenants Association requested a 25 per cent reduction in rents

25. CTCM, 5/10/1925, 1/3/1926

26. CTCM, 4/15/1931

27. Watson, William C., *op. cit.*, table 8.17, p.230

28. Watson, William C., *op. cit.*, table 8.4, p.200 and CTCM, 9/1/1936 for North Kilbowie figures

29. *Clydebank Town Council, op. cit.*, p.114; for the introduction of an electricity supply to the West Kilbowie scheme see CTCM, 6/2/1933, 3/12/1934, 7/12/1936

30. CTCM, 21/6/1927, 6/12/1928, 18/6/1928, 11/3/1929, 10/4/1930, 5/3/1931, 23/6/1932, 14/11/1932

31. *Annual Report of the Sanitary Inspector of the Burgh of Clydebank*, 1940-45

32. *Ibid.*

33. CTCM 12/9/1941; White, R. B., *op. cit.*, p.221

34. Archives, Argyll & Clyde Area Health Board — Renfrew, Vol.1, Minutes of First meeting of Burgh of Clydebank National Health Insurance Committee on 1 August 1912, p.4

35. *Ibid.*, vol. 1, (Choosing general practitioners) Minutes dated 28 March 1913, p.82

36. *Ibid.* (Election of Sub Committees of Insurance Committee) Minutes of 1912 and 1913

37. Annual reports of Medical Officer of Health of Burgh of Clydebank, Tuberculous death rate in five year periods from 1909-1939

38. *Ibid.*, MOH's reports for years 1915-19

39. *Ibid.*, MOH's report for 1921

40. *Ibid.*, MOH's report for 1922

41. *Ibid.*, MOH's reports for 1911-1973

42. *Ibid.* Dr G. A. Allan was on the first list of Clydebank Panel doctors and I knew him when he was senior consultant physician in the Western Infirmary. In 1948 few Clydebank GPs worked in partnership. There was one group of four, two pairs and the other ten were singlehanded. The individual practices were widely scattered and included several on Glasgow Road, Dumbarton Road, Kilbowie Road, Melfort Avenue and in Duntocher, Dalmuir and Old Kilpatrick

43. Dr William Boyd of 'Edradour', Risk Street, Clydebank was a lecturer and subsequently, Reader in Education at Glasgow University who founded the Clydebank Mutual Service Association in April

1932 with financial help from the Pilgrim Trust. In 1973 the Orthopaedic Clinic moved further up Dumbarton Road and into the recently completed Health Clinic. In 1973 it again moved, transferring to the new Clydebank Health Centre

44. *The Leader*, August 23 1907; Minutes of Clydebank Nursing Association Central District Meeting on 2 October 1907

45. *Thirty years of nursing in Clydebank* printed by James Pender in 1938; Miss Bell, Geilston House, Cardross

46. Annual Report of Nursing Association 1922; Miss Bell, Geilston House, Cardross

47. *Ibid.*

48 *Ibid.*; MOH's report for 1920

49. For further discussion of developments in the burgh in the 1920s, see Roberts, Alasdair F. B., 'The operation of the ad hoc Education Authority in Dunbartonshire between 1919 and 1930', In Bone, T. R. *Studies in the History of Scottish Education 1872-1939*, (London, 1967) pp.243-303

50. Paterson, A. C., *op. cit.*, p.138

51. McPhail, I. M. M., *The Clydebank Blitz, op. cit.*, pp.100-06; Hood, John, *Gavinburn Primary School 1887-1987; A Centenary History*, (Clydebank, 1987), pp.18-19; and Begg, T., *Fifty Special Years: A Study in Scottish Housing*, (London, 1987), pp.91-2 and p.99

52. *Reports on the Schemes of the Church of Scotland*, (1919), p.512

53. CP, 30 April 1920

54. *Ibid.*, 5 November 1920

55. The full poem, by 'Auld Monk' is given in CP, 15 November 1929

56. Captain Frederick Miller, quoted in CP, 29 October 1920

57. *Ibid.*, 18 October 1929

58. *Ibid.*, 8 April 1938

59. Singer Manufacturing Company, Programme of Recreational Activities, October 1928

60. CP, 23 May 1925, p.5

61. *Ibid.*, 1 May 1925, p.3

62. *Ibid.*, 30 September 1927, p.5

63. *Ibid.*, 5 June 1928, p.3

64. *Ibid.*, 30 March 1923, p.2

65. *Ibid.*, 28 October 1932, p.9

66. Cameron, John, *A Short History of the Clydebank Male Voice Choir 1900-1980* (unpub mss)

67. Anderson, John, *History of the Clydebank Burgh Band* (unpub mss)

68. CP, 11 November 1927, p.5

69. *Ibid.*, 12 December 1930, p.2

70. *Ibid.*, 18 February 1928, p.5

71. *Ibid.*, 9 October 1942, p.1

72. *Ibid.*, 4 May 1923, p.2

73. *Clydebank Juniors FC, Opening of New Ground (Kilbowie Road) Souvenir Handbook, Season 1939-40*

74. CP, 6 August 1943, p.3

75. McAusland, B., *op. cit.*

76. CP, 11 July 1941, p.3

77. *Sunday Mail*, 6 July 1941, p.14

78. CP, 25 July 1941, p.2

79. *The Boys' Brigade Clydebank and District Battalion War and Peace Report 1940-46*, (1946), p.3

Chapter 9
Shipbuilding in Crisis, 1919-1935
1. For a review of problems arising from the First World War and the aftermath see Board of Trade, 'Committee on Industry and Trade; a Survey of the Metal Industries' 1928, ch.IV, Shipbuilding Industry

2. For a detailed discussion of John Brown in the inter-war years, see Slaven, A., *A Shipyard in Depression, op. cit.*

3. See GUBA, UCS 1/9/5: Scheme for future Syndicate procedure. May 1919

4. Slaven, A., *A Shipyard in Depression, op. cit.*

5. Slaven, A., *A Shipyard in Depression, op. cit.*

6. Slaven, A., *A Shipyard in Depression, op. cit.* See also Peebles, Hugh B., 'Warshipbuilding on the Clyde 1889-1939', *op. cit.*

7. Slaven, A., *A Shipyard in Depression, op. cit.* and GUBA, UCS 1.5.27, Clydebank Committee of the Board Papers, 27 April 1928

8. Peebles, Hugh B., *op. cit.*

9. See Brown, H. D., *op. cit.*

10. Slaven, A., *A Shipyard in Depression, op. cit.*

11. See Peebles, Hugh B., *op. cit.*

12. This section is based on Hume, John R., and Moss, Michael S., *Beardmore, op. cit.*

13. Hume, J., and Moss, M., *Beardmore, op. cit.*, pp.153-8

14. *Ibid.*, pp.157-58 and Appendix 2, p.331, list of locomotives built by William Beardmore & Co., 1920-30
15. Gillies, J. D., and Wood, J. L., *op. cit.*, pp.42-44 and GH, 9 July 1920, p.5
16. Highman, R., *op. cit.*, pp.175-207
17. Hume, J., and Moss, M., *Beardmore, op. cit.*, p.179
18. *Beardmore News*, 1921, vol III, No.11, p.123
19. GUA, UGD100/1/1/2 Beardmore minutes meeting of 29 February 1924
20. National Maritime Museum (NMM), National Shipbuilders Security Ltd (NSS) files, 'Notes re William Beardmore & Co Ltd', 930
21. Hume, J., and Moss, M., *Beardmore, op. cit.*, p.180
22. Cox, E. S., *Locomotive Panorama* (London, 1965), p.97 and *Engineering*, 1928, vol. 126, pp.4997-9
23. Gillies, J. D., and Wood, J. L., *op. cit.*, pp.49-50
24. Hume, J., and Moss, M., *Beardmore, op. cit.*, pp.199-202
25. Bank of England archives, B of EA, SMT2/82, Report to the directors of William Beardmore & Co. Ltd by Lewis Craven Ord, 13 March 1928 and letter of William Paine to Montagu Norman, 28 March 1929
26. *Ibid.*, minutes of meeting of 20 June 1929
27. Hume, J., and Moss, M., *Beardmore, op. cit.*, pp.212-14
28. B of EA, SMT2/280, file on the shipbuilding industry
29. Hume, J., and Moss, M., *Beardmore, op. cit.*, p.216
30. *Glasgow Evening News*, 9 September 1930, front page
31. NMM, NSS files *op. cit.*, Notes re William Beardmore & Co Ltd, 1930
32. B of EA, Secretary's office file No. p.182.10
33. NMM, NSS file 77, minutes of meetings of 5 and 9 February 1934
34. *Glasgow Evening Citizen*, 13 November 1934
35. B of EA, SMT3/143, recommendations for the future development of Beardmore High Speed diesels, 1935
36. GUA, UGD100/1/1/4, meeting on 8 December 1930
37. GUA, UGD100/1/15/1, Beardmore presscutting book 1930-1947

Chapter 10
Shipbuilding; Rearmament and Recovery, 1935-1945
1. For detail on John Brown's provision in these areas see Slaven, A., *A Shipyard in Depression, op. cit.*
2. For a discussion of trends in the market see Slaven, A., *'British Shipbuilders: market trends and order book patterns between the wars'*, and *In Journal of Transport History*, Third Series, 3/2/1982
3. GUBA, UCS 1/5/31 Clydebank Committee of Board Papers, 2 February 1933
4. GUBA, UCS 1/5/31, 1 June 1934
5. GUBA, UCS 1/5/33, Clydebank Committee of Board Papers, 22 February 1935
6. *Ibid.*, 20 September 1935
7. For a discussion of the resurgence of Naval orders see Peebles, Hugh, B., *op. cit.*
8. See Slaven, A., *A Shipyard in Depression, op. cit.*
9. See GUBA, UCS 1/5/34, Clydebank Committee of Board Papers, 26 May 1936
10. GUBA, UCS 1/5/35, 23 June 1937, and UCS 1/5/36, 17 February 1938
11. See GUBA, UCS 1/5/36, 22 December 1938
12. GUBA, UCS 1/5/36, 21 June 1938
13. See Slaven, A., *A Shipyard in Depression, op. cit.*, Peebles, Hugh B., *op. cit.*
14. The Third Statistical Account of Scotland, vol. VI: *The County of Dumbarton* (Glasgow, 1959)
15. GUBA, UCS 1/5/40, October 1939
16. See Clydebank Board Papers 1939-46, *passim*
17. GUBA, UCS 1/5/45, January 1941
18. The Third Statistical Account of Scotland, *op. cit.*
19. GUBA, UCS 1/5/45, March 1941
20. GUBA, UCS 1/5/45, June 1941
21. GUBA, UCS 1/5/47, August and October 1941
22. GUBA, UCS 1/5/51, November 1942
23. GUBA, UCS 1/5/54, October 1943
24. GUBA, UCS 1/5/55, February 1944
25. GUBA, UCS 1/5/62, December 1945
26. Compiled from yard lists; see also Brown, H. D., *op. cit.*

Chapter 11
The Clydebank Blitz
1. *Front Line 1940-41: The Official Story of Civil Defence of Britain*, (London, 1942), p.117
2. Harrisson, T., *Living through the Blitz*, (London/Glasgow, 1976), p.12
3. *Ibid.* p.18

4. This sentiment occurs in several relevant publications. An article entitled *'Clydebank: The Hush-hush Blitz'* In WVS Bulletin, No. 181, June 1963, pp.24-25 suggests that the Clydebank Blitz ranked fourth in the official list of major night attacks.

5. CP, 28 February 1941

6. Harris, P., *Glasgow and the Clyde at War*, (Bowden, 1986), p.7

7. McPhail, I. M. M., *The Clydebank Blitz, op. cit.*

8. CP, 21 March 1941

9. *Report by the Medical Officer of Health for the Burgh of Clydebank*, 1940-1945

10. GH, 18 March 1941

11. CP, 28 March 1941

12. GH, 18 March 1941

13. Singer Manufacturing Co. Ltd., *Singer in World War II, 1939-1945*, (New York, 1946)

14. Evening Times, 15 March 1941

15. *Ibid.*

16. McKendrick, T., *Clydebank Blitz*, (Clydebank, 1986), p.14

Chapter 12
Shipbuilding in Decline

1. Cairncross, A., 'The Economy of Glasgow' *In* Miller, R., and Tivy, J., (eds.) *The Glasgow Region*, (Edinburgh, 1958), pp.219-41

2. Jones, L., *Shipbuilding in Britain*, (Cardiff, 1957), p.205

3. Payne, P. L., 'The Decline of the Scottish Heavy Industries, 1945-83', *In* Saville R. (ed.), *The Economic Development of Modern Scotland*, (Edinburgh, 1985), p.103

4. Robb, A. M., 'Shipbuilding and Marine Engineering', *In* Cunnison, J., and Gilfillan, J. B. S. (eds.), *Glasgow*, (Glasgow, 1958)

5. Jones, L., *op. cit.*, p.210

6. Hogwood, B. W., *Government and Shipbuilding: The Politics of Industrial Change*, (Farnborough, 1979)

7. Moss, M., and Hume, J., *Workshop of the British Empire: Engineering and Shipbuilding in the West of Scotland*, (London, 1977).

8. Johnston, T. L., Buxton, N. K., and Mair, D., *Structure and Growth of the Scottish Economy*, (Glasgow, 1971), p.115

9. Moss, M., and Hume, J., *Workshop of the British Empire, op. cit.*

10. McGill, J., *Crisis on the Clyde*, (London, 1973)

11. McGill, J., *op. cit.*, p.37

12. Broadway, F., *Upper Clyde Shipbuilders: A Study in Government Intervention in Industry*, (London, 1976)

13. Buchan, A., *The Right to Work: The Story of the Upper Clyde Confrontation*, (London, 1972), p.14

14. Murray, A., Secretary of the Scottish Communist Party; speech reported in *Comment*, 11 September 1971, p.238

15. Hogwood, B. W., *op. cit.*, p.156

16. Sykes, A., 'The UCS work-in', *In* Broadway, F., *op. cit.*

17. *Ibid.*

18. Foster, J., and Woolfson, C., *The Politics of the UCS Work-in*, (London, 1986)

19. Hogwood, B. W., *op. cit.*, p.161

20. Foster, J., and Woolfson, C., *op. cit.*, pp350-53

21. Cairncross, A., *op. cit.*

22. Foster, J., and Woolfson, C., *op. cit.*, p.192

23. Hogwood, B. W., *op. cit.*, p.189

24. *Hansard*, 26 May 1976, cols. 445-467

Chapter 13
Singer: Competition and Closure

1. Palmer, 'Singer's Problem Child', *Financial Times*, 31 December 1975

2. Quoted in McDermott, M., 'Singer's Clydebank: Anatomy of Closure', Undergraduate dissertation, (University of Glasgow 1982)

3. *Singer Speaker*, May 1965

4. MacGregor, I., former Company Director, interview with the author

5. Quoted in McDermott, M., *op. cit.*

6. Company statement, 13 December 1978

7. *Ibid.*

8. Shop Stewards' Minute Book, entry for 21 December 1978

9. Shop Stewards' Minute Book, entry for 12 January 1979

10. *Ibid.*

Chapter 14
Social Trends, 1945-1980
1. McKendrick, T., *Clydebank Blitz, op. cit.*, pp.12-14
2. Clydebank Burgh Council Minutes 1942-45
3. Abercrombie, Sir P., and Matthew, R. H., *The Clyde Valley Regional Plan*, (1946), p.320
4. *Ibid.*, p.102 and pp.319-20
5. *Ibid.*, p.323
6. Third Statistical Account of Scotland, *op. cit.*
7. *Clydebank Official handbook*, (Clydebank, 1949), pp.16-17
8. Census of Scotland: Enumeration Abstracts 1951
9. *Ibid.*
10. Gibb, A., *Glasgow: The Making of a City*, (London, 1983), Fig. 7 ii, p.164; Gibb, A., and MacLennan, D., *Policy and Process in Scottish Housing 1950-1980*, Fig. 2, p.278
11. *Clydebank Official Handbooks* 1954 p.14, and 1958, pp.12-13
12. Gibb, A., and MacLennan, D., *op. cit.*, p.280
13. Clydebank Public Library: Local Collection, 613.53L.C., Joint Report by Sanitary Inspector and Burgh Engineer on properties at 494 and 502 Dumbarton Road, 6, 8, 12, 14 Buchanan Street, and 602 Dumbarton Road, Dalmuir, 1956.
14. Third Statistical Account of Scotland, *op. cit.*, p.243
15. Census of Scotland Enumeration Abstracts 1961, 1971; Clydebank Town Council, Department of Architecture and Town Planning 1970. *Quinquennial Review of Development Plan: Survey Report*
16. Gibb, A., *op. cit.*, p.147
17. *Clydebank Official Handbooks*, 1960, 1966, 1967, 1970
18. Clydebank Town Council *Quinquennial Review, op. cit.*
19. Clydebank Town Council, *Kilbowie Comprehensive Development Area: Survey Report*, (1969), p.1
20. Clydebank Town Council, *op. cit.*, p.4
21. Clydebank Town Council, *Kilbowie Comprehensive Development Area*, (1970), pp.4-6
22. Jamieson and MacKay, Consultant Civil and Transportation Engineers, *Eastern Comprehensive Development Plan; Transportation Component*, (1971), pp.2-3
23. Clydebank Town Council, *Kilbowie Comprehensive Development Area, op. cit.*, Sections 13.03-13.07
24. Brotchie, A. W., and Grieves, R. L., *Dumbarton's Trams and Buses*, (Dundee, 1985), p.49
25. Scott, Wilson, Kilpatrick and Co., (Scotland), *Forth and Clyde Canal*, (1975)
26. Jamieson and MacKay, Consultant Civil and Transportation Engineers, *Burgh of Clydebank: recommended road system for 1990*, (1969), pp.4-7
27. Jamieson and MacKay, *Eastern Comprehensive Development Area, op. cit.*, p.4
28. Freeman Fox and Partners, *Erskine Bridge*, (1971) Scottish Development Department, *Erskine Bridge Project*, (1964) GH, 2 July 1971; *Scottish Field*, July 1971
29. Strathclyde Regional Council, *Urban Deprivation*, (1976); GH, pp.105-07
30. Department of Urban and Regional Planning: University of Strathclyde, *Planning for Faifley*, (1978), pp.2-5
31. The Housing Group, Faifley-Duntocher-Hardgate Initiative, *A Discussion Paper on Housing*, (1979).
32. Clydebank District Council Planning Office, *Old Kilpatrick Local Plan: Report of Survey* (1979), *Clydebank Local Plan, Survey and Issues Report*, (1982).
33. Archives of Argyll and Clyde Area Health Board, Renfrew, Minutes of the Clydebank Burgh National Health Insurance Committee, 1912-1948
34. Western Regional Hospital Board (WRHB) *Regional Review* (Winter 1965-6), pp.22-3
35. *Ibid.*
36. WRHB Hospital Services Committee *minutes*, December 1972; Hospital and Health Services Year Books, 1974-7
37. Sister Clark, St Margarets Hospice, Clydebank
38. Minutes of Executive Committee of Clydebank District Nursing Association dated 5 November 1957, Miss E. Bell, Cardross
39. *Clydebank Community Directory*
40. *Ibid.*
41. *Programme and official opening of Centre 5th May 1973, Mr John Dow, MBE*, (Clydebank, 1973)
42. CP, 24 May 1957
43. I am extremely grateful to Father Jimmy McShane and the Rev Stewart Borthwick for giving freely of their recollections, especially in relation to industrial events in the district between 1978 and 1981.
44. Quoted in CP, 10 January 1958.
45. *St Joseph's Church, Faifley: Solemn Opening of the New Church* (1963), p.13
46. Quoted in *In Focus: Duntocher Trinity Parish Church*, summer 1986
47. Father J. McShane, MS copy of speech delivered on 20 February 1981
48. Quoted in *Duntocher Trinity Parish Church Yearbook 1972-73*

49. The Rev David C. Goldie, quoted in *St Columba's Scottish Episcopal Church, Souvenir Brochure, 1896-1966*, (1966)
50. CP, 12 May 1950, p.1
51. *Ibid.*, 24 October 1952, p.2
52. Campbell, J., *Short History of Clydebank Camera Club*
53. CP, 14 February 1969, p.8
54. Education (Scotland) Act, 1945
55. CP, 25 February 1983, p.5
56. *Ibid.*, 26 September 1952, p.3

Chapter 15
The New Clydebank
1. GH, 30 July 1980
2. Botham, R., and Lloyd, G., 'The Political Economy of Enterprise Zones', *National Westminster Bank Review*, May 1983, pp.24-33; Lever, W., and Moire, C., *The City in Transition - in Policies and Agencies for the Economic Regeneration of Clydeside*, (Oxford, 1986), pp.81-83
3. Roger Tym and Partners, *Monitoring Enterprise Zone Year Three Report*, (January, 1984), p.24
4. Roger Tym and Partners, *A Review of the Past Performance of the Clydebank Task Force 1980-1985 and Recommendations for Future Strategy*, (Glasgow, 1986), p.11
5. Clydebank District Council, *Clydebank Local Plan: Consultative Draft*, (1984), p.18
6. Clydebank District Council, *Press Release*, October 1986
7. Clydebank District Council, *Clydebank Local Plan: Consultative Draft*, (1984), p.6
8. *Ibid.*, pp.9-10
9. Clydebank District Council, *Housing Plan 7 1986-91*, (1985), p.22
10. Duguid, G., and Grant, R., *Areas of Social Need in Scotland*, Scottish Office Central Research Unit, October 1984
11. Lever, W., and Moire, C., *op. cit.*, p.82
12. SDA, *Business Opportunities in Clydebank*, (1984), p.2
13. SDA, *op. cit.*
14. Roger Tym and Partners, *A Review of the Past Performance of the Clydebank Task Force 1980-1985, op. cit.*, p.15
15. *Ibid.*
16. Clydebank District Council and Scottish Development Agency, *Clydebank Trade Directory, 1986-87*
17. Clydebank District Council Committee Report, March, 1987
18. Clydebank District Council, *Clydebank Local Plan Consultative Draft*, (1984), p.13
19. *Scotsman*, 12 August 1980

Printed and bound in Great Britain by
Butler & Tanner Ltd, Frome and London

Select Bibliography

Abercrombie, *Sir* P. and Matthew, R. H., *The Clyde Valley regional plan, 1946.* Edinburgh, H.M.S.O., 1949.

Abstracts of the Particular Register of Sasines for Argyll, Bute and Dunbarton otherwise known as the Argyll Sasines. Edinburgh, W. Brown, 1933.

Brandon, R., *Singer and the sewing machine.* London, Barrie & Jenkins, 1978.

Broadway, F., *Upper Clyde Shipbuilders: a study in government intervention in industry.* London, Centre for Policy Studies, 1976.

Brotchie, A. W. and Grieves, R. L., *Dumbarton's trams and buses.* Dundee, N.B. Traction, 1985.

Brown, H. D., *Clydebank shipyard: a history of the Clydebank establishment of Messrs. John Brown & Co. (Clydebank) Ltd., and of their predecessors, James and George Thomson, 1847-1955.* unpub. mss. 1954.

Bruce, J., *History of the Parish of West or Old Kilpatrick.* Glasgow, John Smith, 1863.

Buchan, A., *The right to work: the story of the Upper Clyde confrontation.* London, Calder & Boyars, 1972.

The Canadian Pacific quadruple-screw liner 'Empress of Britain'. Ocean Liners of the Past. London, Patrick Stephens, 1971.

The Clydebank Blitz, March, 1941. A collection of newspaper articles, official papers, etc., relating to the Blitz. Local History Collection, Clydebank District Libraries.

Clydebank District Council and Paton, James Ltd. *Clydebank: 100 years souvenir edition.* Clydebank District Council, 1986.

Clydebank District Libraries, *A church history of Clydebank.* 1983.

Clydebank District Libraries, *Duntocher & Hardgate in pictures.* 1983.

Clydebank District Libraries, *More Duntocher & Hardgate in pictures.* 1985.

Clydebank District Libraries, *Old Kilpatrick in pictures.* 1984.

Clydebank District Scouting Association, *Fifty years of scouting: golden Jubilee.* 1957.

Clydebank Leader, 1905-1915.

Clydebank Post, 1983 — to date. Paisley, James Paton.

The Clydebank Press, *Clydebank fifty eight.* 1957.

Clydebank Press, 1891-1983. Govan, John Cossar.

Clydebank Town Council, *Quinquennial review of development plan. 2 vols.* Clydebank, 1970.

Clydebank Town Council, *Souvenir Jubilee brochure, 1886-1936.* 1936.

Cunard Steam Ship Co. Ltd., *Christmas number, 1931.*

The Cunard turbine-driven quadruple-screw Atlantic liner 'Lusitania'. Reprint from *'Engineering'*, London, 1907.

The Cunard White Star quadruple-screw North Atlantic liner Queen Mary. Ocean Liners of the Past. London, Patrick Stephens, 1972.

Damer, S., *Rent Strike! The Clydebank rent struggles of the 1920s.* Clydebank, 1982.

Dept. of Environment, *Monitoring Enterprise Zones. Year one report: state of the Zones,* London, 1982.

Dept. of Environment, *Monitoring Enterprise Zones. Year two report.* London, 1983.

Dept. of Environment, *Monitoring Enterprise Zones. Year three report.* London, 1984.

Directory of the Parish of Old Kilpatrick and the Burgh of Clydebank, 1893-94. Clydebank, 1893.

Dorman, A., *A history of the Singer Company (UK) Ltd. Clydebank Factory,* unpub. 1972.

Duffy, L., *A history of the Clydebank Bowling Club, 1884-1984.* Clydebank, C.B.C., 1984.

Dunbartonshire constabulary, 1858-1958: a short history of a century's policing of Dunbartonshire with an account of earlier forms of policing employed. Dumbarton, Dunbartonshire Joint Police Committee, 1958.

Duncan, J. B., *The development, construction and characteristics of the sewing machine.* Singer Manuf. Co. Ltd., 1980.

Eunson, A. D., *Old Kilpatrick and Christianity: the Parish's story from Roman times.* Dumbarton, Bennett & Thomson, 1962.

Eunson, A. D., *Old Kilpatrick: its church and its ministers.* Clydebank, John Cossar, 1937.

Foster, J. and Woolfson, C., *The politics of the U.C.S. work-in.* London, Lawrence & Wishart, 1986.

Fraser, W., *The Lennox. 2 vols.* Edinburgh, 1874.

Grant, *Sir* A., *Steel and ships: the history of John Brown.* London, Michael Joseph, 1950.

H.M.S. Vanguard and the Royal visit to South Africa. London, H.M.S.O., 1946.

Halliday, I. S., *A history of Duntocher and the surrounding area.* Undergrad. thesis, Glasgow School of Art, 1982.

Hanson, R. P. C., *St. Patrick: his origins and career.* Oxford, O.U.P., 1968.

Harris, P., *Glasgow and the Clyde at war.* Bowdon, Archive Publications, 1986.

Hood, J. B., *Clydebank in old picture postcards.* Zaltbommel, European Library, 1985.

Hood, J. B., *Duntocher Trinity Parish Church, 1836-1986.* Clydebank District Libraries, 1986.

Hood, J. B., *Gavinburn Primary School, 1887-1987: A centenary history.* Clydebank District Libraries, 1987.

Hood, N. and Young S., *Multinationals in retreat.* Edinburgh, E.U.P., 1982.

Hoyt, E. P., *The life and death of H.M.S. Hood.* London, Barker, 1977.

Hume, J. R. and Moss, M. S., *Clyde Shipbuilding from old photographs.* London, Batsford, 1975.

Hume, J. R. and Moss, M. S., *Beardmore: the history of a Scottish industrial giant.* London, Heinemann, 1977.

Hunter, M., *Musings in prose and verse.* Glasgow, S.C.W.S., (n.d.)

Hunter, M., *Thoughts of a toiler.* Govan, John Cossar, (n.d.)

Irving, J., *The book of Dumbartonshire. 3 vols.* Edinburgh, W. & A. K. Johnston, 1879.

Irving, J., *The history of Dumbartonshire from the earliest period to the present time.* Dumbarton, 1857.

Irving, J., *Place names of Dumbartonshire.* Dumbarton, Bennett & Thomson, 1928.

Johnstone, A., *The wild frontier: exploring the Antonine Wall.* Broxburn, Moubray Press, 1986.

Johnstone, J., *Memoirs of a "Bankie" 1891-1980.* Clydebank District Libraries, 1981.

Jordan, G. and Reilly, G., *Enterprise Zones: non-intervention as a form of intervention: the Clydebank EZ and policy substitution. In Scottish Government Yearbook,* 1982, pp123-148.

Kay, B., *The Clydebank Blitz, In Odyssey: voices from Scotland's recent past; the second collection.* Edinburgh, Polygon Books, 1982.

Keating, M. and others, *Enterprise Zones and area projects: small area initiatives in urban economic renewal in Scotland.* Glasgow, University of Strathclyde, 1983.

Keppie, L. J. F., *Roman inscriptions from Scotland.* Proc. Soc. Antiq. Scot., 113, 1983, pp391-404.

Kirkwood, D., *My life in revolt.* London, Harrap, 1935.

Lacey, R., *The Queens of the North Atlantic.* London, Sidgwick & Jackson, 1973.

Lawson, W. E., *A history of Clydebank Co-operative Society Ltd.* Glasgow, S.C.W.S., 1948.

Lindsay, J., *The canals of Scotland.* Newton Abbot, David & Charles, 1968.

McAusland, B., *Clydesdale Harriers, 1886-1986.* Forthcoming publication.

McDermott, M. C., *Singer's Clydebank: the anatomy of closure.* Undergraduate thesis, Univ. of Glasgow, 1982.

MacDonald, H., *Rambles round Glasgow.* Glasgow, Dunn & Wright, 1878.

McGill, J., *Crisis on the Clyde: the story of Upper Clyde Shipbuilders.* London, Davis-Poynter, 1973.

McInnes, A., *The history of Old Kilpatrick.* 1935.

McKendrick, T., *Clydebank Blitz.* Clydebank District Libraries, 1986.

MacLeod, D., *The Clyde district of Dumbartonshire.* Dumbarton, Bennett & Thomson, 1886.

MacLeod, D., *Past worthies of the Lennox.* Dumbarton, Bennett & Thomson, 1894.

MacNab, Rev. D., *Archaeological dissertation on the birth-place of Saint Patrick.* Dublin, James Duffy, 1866.

McPhail, I. M. M., *The Clydebank Blitz.* Clydebank Town Council, 1974.

McPhail, I. M. M., *Lennox lore.* Dumbarton District Libraries, 1987.

McPhail, I. M. M., *A short history of Dumbartonshire.* Dumbarton, Lennox Herald, 1963.

Mann, L. McL., *The Druid temple explained.* Glasgow, 1939.

Melling, J., *Rent strikes.* Edinburgh, Polygon Books, 1983.

Miller, S. N., *The Roman Fort of Old Kilpatrick.* Glasgow, 1928.

Miller, W. H. and Hutchings, D. F., *Transatlantic liners at war: the story of the Queens.* London, David & Charles, 1985.

Morgan, C. I., and others, *An ecological survey of Clydebank District.* London, Nature Conservancy Council, 1983.

Morris, R. W. B., *The prehistoric rock art of Southern Scotland.* Oxford, B.A.R., 1981.

Mort, F., *Dumbartonshire.* Cambridge, C.U.P., 1920.

Napier, M., *History of the partition of the Lennox.* Edinburgh, Blackwood, 1835.

The New Statistical Account of Scotland, vol. VIII: Dumbarton, Stirling, Clackmannan. Edinburgh, Blackwood, 1865.

Northcott, M., *H.M.S. Hood: design and construction.* London, Bivouac Bks, 1915.

Oakley, C. A., *The last tram.* Glasgow City Corporation, 1962.

Paterson, A. C., *The educational history of Clydebank.* Unpub. mss. 1940.

Paterson, J. R., *Random rhymes.* Clydebank, John Cossar, 1948.

Peebles, H. B., *Warshipbuilding on the Clyde, 1889-1939: a financial study.* Ph.D. thesis, Univ. of Stirling, 1986.

Potter, N. and Frost, J., *The Elizabeth.* London, Harrap, 1965.

Potter, N. and Frost, J., *The Mary: the inevitable ship.* London, Harrap, 1961.

Potter, N. and Frost, J., *Queen Elizabeth 2: the authorised story.* London, Harrap, 1969.

Potter, N. and Frost, J., *The Queen Mary: her inception and history.* London, Harrap, 1961.

The quadruple-screw turbine-driven Cunard liner 'Aquitania'. Reprint from *'Engineering'*, London, 1914

Reid, J., *Reflections of a Clyde-built man.* London, Souvenir Press, 1976.

Rentell, P., *Historic Cunard liners.* Truro, Atlantic Transport, 1986.

Riddell, J. F., *Clyde navigation: a history of the development and deepening of the River Clyde.* Edinburgh, Donald, 1979.

Roberts, F., *The birthplace of St. Patrick*. Dumbarton, Bennett & Thomson, 1940.

Robertson, A. S., *An Antonine Fort: Golden Hill, Duntocher*. Edinburgh, Oliver & Boyd, 1957.

Robertson, A. S., *The Antonine Wall*. Glasgow Archaeological Soc., 1960.

Robertson, D. R., *Drumchapel: being a short historical sketch*. Glasgow, John Wylie, 1939.

Roche, T. W. E. *Samuel Cunard and the North Atlantic*. London, Macdonald, 1971.

The romance of engineering: William Beardmore & Co. Ltd. Glasgow, Albion Publ. Co., (n.d.)

Scottish Economic Planning Department, *Report of Working Party on Employment in the Clydebank area*. (Chairman, Gavin McCrone.) Edinburgh, H.M.S.O., 1980.

Shields, J., *Clyde built: a history of shipbuilding on the River Clyde*. Glasgow, William McLellan, 1949.

Simpson, C., *Lusitania*. London, Longman, 1972.

Sinclair, C., *Radnoristoun chimes*. Glasgow, John Cossar, 1910.

Sinclair, C., *Scotland's winsome charms: a collection of poems and songs*. Glasgow, John Cossar, 1934.

Singer Manufacturing Co. Ltd., *Red "S" Review, 1919-*

Singer Manufacturing Co. Ltd., *Singer in World War II, 1939-45*. New York, 1946.

Singer Manufacturing Co. Ltd., *Singer Speaker, 1963-*. Clydebank.

Skinner, D. M., *The countryside of the Antonine Wall: survey and recommended statement*. Perth, Countryside Commission for Scotland, 1973.

Society of Antiquaries of Scotland, *The archaeological sites and monuments of Dumbarton District, Clydebank District . . .* Edinburgh, Royal Commission on the Ancient and Historical Monuments of Scotland, 1978.

Southampton City Council, *The Queens*. Southampton Corporation, 1968.

Statistical Account of Scotland, vol. V. Edinburgh, William Creech, 1793.

Stevens, L. A., *The Elizabeth: passage of a Queen*. London, Allen & Unwin, 1969.

Strang, T. M., *Round the clock tower*. Clydebank, James Pender, 1926.

Strang, T. M., *Man — the pilgrim*. Clydebank, James Pender, 1921.

Walker, C., *Memory of a Queen: R.M.S. Queen Elizabeth*. Oxford, Oxford Publ. Co., 1972.

The Third Statisical Account of Scotland, vol. VI: the county of Dumbarton. Glasgow, Collins, 1959.

Thomson, G., *Dalnotter Iron Company*. In Scott. Hist. Rev., *XXXV*, 1956, pp 10-20.

Walker, F. M., *Song of the Clyde: a history of Clyde shipbuilding*. Cambridge, Patrick Stephens, 1984.

Watson, W. C., *Clydebank in the inter-war years: a study in economics and social change*. Ph.D. thesis, Univ. of Glasgow, 1984.

Winter, C. W. R., *Queen Mary: her early years recalled*. Wellingborough, Patrick Stephens, 1986.

Yoker Secondary School Pupils, *Both sides of the burn: the story of Yoker*. Glasgow, 1966.

Index

Clydebank Campaign on Employment   197, 205

Clydebank Choral and Operatic Society   104, 107

Clydebank Clergy/Community Liaison Committee   197

Clydebank College   191-3 (illus)

Clydebank Concertina Band   104

Clydebank Co-operative Society   103, 207

Clydebank Co-operative Society Boxing Club   107

Clydebank Corinthians   107, 201, 202

Clydebank Corinthians FC   105

Clydebank Council on Alcoholism   186

Clydebank Cricket Club   57

Clydebank District Nursing Auxilliary   186

Clydebank District Sports Council   202

Clydebank Dramatic Group   105

Clydebank East and Central Initiative   211

Clydebank East Community Centre Camera Class   200
    See Also Clydebank Camera Club

Clydebank Eastern Tenants Association   211

Clydebank Engineering and Shipbuilding Co.   8, 9, 11

Clydebank Enterprise Fund Limited   206

Clydebank Enterprise Zone   165, 197–98, 205, 206, 207, 212, 215

Clydebank Female Voice Choir   104

Clydebank FC   53, 58, 201, 202

Clydebank Foundry   3

Clydebank Health Centre   184, 187–89

Clydebank High School (Janetta St.)   97, 99, 190, 191

Clydebank Higher Grade School   46, 190

Clydebank Housing Association   80, 81, 82, 83, 84, 85, 86

Clydebank Investment Co v Marshall   85

Clydebank Iron Shipyard   3

Clydebank Junior Male Voice Choir   104

Clydebank Junior FC   106, 107, 201

Clydebank Library   53, 200, 207

Clydebank Lyric Choir   201

Clydebank Male Voice Choir   53, 104, 200

Clydebank Masonic Temple   198

Clydebank Medical Society   184, 187

Clydebank Mutual Service Association   76, 94, 103, 104, 200

Clydebank National Health Insurance Committee   92

Clydebank Orthopaedic and Rehabilitation Clinic   94

Clydebank Partick and Yoker Railway Co.   24

Clydebank Peace Council   76

Clydebank Primrose Cricket Club   57

Clydebank Public Library Literary and Philosophical Society   200

Clydebank Recorded Music Society   200
    See Also Gramophone Society

Clydebank Rent Strike   xviii, 52, 71, 72, 73, 75, **79–86**

Clydebank Repertory Theatre   105, 200, 201

Clydebank R.C. Band   54

Clydebank Rovers De'ils Own
    See Clydebank Male Voice Choir

Clydebank School, (First)   43, 45 (illus)

Clydebank School, (Second)   45, 97, 98, 99, 189 (illus), 191, 193, 194 (illus)

Clydebank Select Choir   53

Clydebank Subscription Library   52–53

Clydebank Technical College   190
    See Also Clydebank College

Clydebank Terrace   4, 34, 42 (illus)

Clydebank Trades Council   69

Clydebank Unemployed Workers Committee   72
    See Also NUWM

Clydebank West Free Church   47, 198, 199

Clydebank Football Ground   58

Clydebank Stadium   202

Clydebank Harriers   58, 106, 107, 202

'Clydeside Distress Fund'   107

Clydeside Expressway   180, 198

Clydeview FC   106

Cochno Filters   89

Cochrane, B. A.   25, 26 (illus)

Colquhoun, Sir Iain   134

Communist Party (Clydebank Branch)   72, 73, 77

Comprehensive Development Areas   176–77

Connell, E.   130 (illus)

Constellation (rig)   146

Cootes, Robert   202

Cormack, David B.   80, 81, 82, 83, 86

Cornock, Robert B.   77

Coventry Syndicate   110

'Craigellachie'   186

Cramb, Dr. Ernest H.   92, 94

Cramb, J.   25 (illus), 26

Crawford, Samuel, Provost   5, 24, 25 (illus), 26

Cricket   107

Crombie, Dr. Lawrence   184

Cunard Line   3, 4, 6, 7, 9, 10, 110, 112, 121

Cunningham, William   93

Cunningham, Dr. John T.   184

Curling   57, 202

Curtis, Charles   122

Cuthbertson, Sir John Neilson   189

Dalmuir and Clydebank Burns Club   53

Dalmuir and West of Scotland Estates Company   37, 82, 84, 85

Dalmuir Bowling and Tennis Club   56

Dalmuir Cameron Pipe Band   104

Dalmuir Credit Union   211

Dalmuir Cricket Club   57

Dalmuir Dry Dock Company   12

Dalmuir Former Pupils   104, 200, 201

Dalmuir Former Pupils Choir   201

Dalmuir House   52

Dalmuir Junior Secondary School   190

Dalmuir Masonic Lodge School   45, 194–5

Dalmuir Naval Construction Works   11–14, 37

Dalmuir Parish Church   102

Dalmuir Parish Pipe Band   104 (illus)

Dalmuir Park   52, 199 (illus)

Dalmuir Park Housing Association   209

Dalmuir Quoiting Green   3

Dalmuir Primary School   46, 98, 99

Dalmuir Station   34

Dalmuir Thistle FC   58

Dalmuir YMCA   105